*You have a real talent for promotion and writing advertisements.*

Albert Gore, Former Vice President
United States of America

*There are a lot of great copywriters, but Joe Sugarman is the best. He knows how to build a story and close the sale. Anyone who wants to sell better will enjoy* Advertising Secrets of the Written Word.

Richard Thalheimer, Founder
The Sharper Image

*I have been a fan of Joseph Sugarman's copywriting and marketing ideas for years and have benefited greatly by imitating his long-copy ads. Now he is letting us all in on his secrets in a book that should cost $2,000 because it contains so much detailed information. Thank you, Joe. I really liked the book!*

Jack Canfield, Co-Author
*Chicken Soup for the Soul*

*Every trade has its role models. And for me, there is no better model for ad copywriters or magazine editors than Joe Sugarman.*
Ray Schultz, Editor
*DIRECT* Magazine

*Joseph Sugarman is brimming over with creative ideas. That isn't so unusual; many of us are. But Joe's ideas rocket into our marketing consciousness like shooting stars with one triumphant difference: His ideas invariably work. They motivate. They sell. So this isn't a book for theoreticians. It's aimed like an exquisitely polished arrow into the heart of writing to sell. New to marketing? Read this book. Been in the business for 30 years? Read this book.*
Herschell Gordon Lewis, Chairman
Communicomp

## From Seminar Participants Who Learned What You Are About to Learn

*I enjoyed the seminar, and I learned a lot. I am more determined than ever to start and succeed at running a mail order business.*

> Lee R. Herrington III, President
> Herrington's Catalog

*Your seminar has really opened my eyes to a realization of what makes effective mail order advertising. I am sure that attending the seminar will pay dividends many times over in the years ahead.*

> J. M. Robinson
> Atlantic Richfield Company

*I told you I'd summarize the 6 or 8 major things, new to me, that I got from the seminar. Going over the notes I find it's 36 major things I'll be doing differently.*

> Gordon T. Beaham III, President
> Faultless Starch/Bon Ami Company

*Not only did you teach me some fundamental new concepts in space advertising, but you planted some seeds that may well change our marketing program and perhaps even our way of doing business.*

Frederick J. Simon, President
Omaha Steaks International

*I would recommend your seminars to novices to gain the degree of confidence necessary to write super ads almost instantaneously. Old-timers will also benefit because what they'll learn is that you can help them make their ordinary ads super successful. Although I've been in mail order for more than 15 years I soon found, as a result of your 5-day seminar, that there was more I didn't know than I did know.*

Ed Axel
Energy Group of America, Inc.

*You did two things right. First, you charged $2,000. This clever device guaranteed the quality of the participants and assured you of their rapt and undivided attention. Second, you gave them their money's worth. I did only one thing right. I came.*

Joe Karbo
Huntington Beach, California

*The depth of knowledge and the skill with which you organized and presented it was far above what I anticipated when I signed up for the seminar. But the real payoff was what the course covered that was not in the outline. I feel that the content relating to the philosophy of achieving success in life and the numerous examples you provided to prove this philosophy will have the greatest payoff for us in the long run.*

Ed Scofield
Garden Way Associates

*When you're a farmer you always worry about the crop. It's growing too slow—you worry. It's growing too fast—you really worry. I find it to be about the same when a farmer gets into space advertising. The orders are coming in so good from our space ads, I'm beginning to worry. A high-class worry, I'll admit.*

Frank Schultz
Alamo, Texas

*I most enjoyed your openness in revealing, in depth, how you run your company. Few businessmen have the confidence to give away their "secrets" as you did!*

C. L. Schaldenbrand
Word Processing Exchange

*At times the seminar combined high drama, "made for TV" movie serialization, and mail order technique in an unbeatable blend of education and excitement. It was the best class I have taken since Harvard Business School.*

John E. Groman
Epsilon Data Management

*On my way back, on Friday night I stayed at the Sheraton Centre Hotel in New York. My two bags with my clothes were stolen in the lobby of the hotel. I don't care about the clothes, but I can't tell you how much I regret the loss of the seminar material, which is of inestimable value for me, and which was also in the bags.*

Herman Van Hove
Brussels, Belgium

*It has given me a fresh perspective and the insight I had sought when I first decided to attend your seminar. I now have a much clearer picture of why our successful promotions succeeded and our failures failed.*

Richard J. Guilfoyle
Limited Editions Collectors Society

# The *Adweek* Copywriting Handbook

**Adweek and Brandweek Books** are designed to present interesting, insightful books for the general business reader and for professionals in the worlds of media, marketing, and advertising.

These are innovative, creative books that address the challenges and opportunities of these industries, written by leaders in the business. Some of our writers head their own companies, while others have worked their way up to the top of their field in large multinationals. But they all share a knowledge of their craft and a desire to enlighten others.

We hope readers will find these books as helpful and inspiring as *Adweek*, *Brandweek*, and *Mediaweek* magazines.

**Published**

*Disruption: Overturning Conventions and Shaking Up the Marketplace*, by Jean-Marie Dru

*Under the Radar: Talking to Today's Cynical Consumer*, by Jonathan Bond and Richard Kirshenbaum

*Truth, Lies and Advertising: The Art of Account Planning*, by Jon Steel

*Hey, Whipple, Squeeze This: A Guide to Creating Great Ads*, by Luke Sullivan

*Eating the Big Fish: How Challenger Brands Can Compete against Brand Leaders*, by Adam Morgan

*Warp-Speed Branding: The Impact of Technology on Marketing*, by Agnieszka Winkler

*Creative Company: How St. Luke's Became "the Ad Agency to End All Ad Agencies,"* by Andy Law

*Another One Bites the Grass: Making Sense of International Advertising*, by Simon Anholt

*Attention! How to Interrupt, Yell, Whisper and Touch Consumers*, by Ken Sacharin

*The Peaceable Kingdom: Building a Company without Factionalism, Fiefdoms, Fear, and Other Staples of Modern Business*, by Stan Richards and David Culp

*Getting the Bugs Out: The Rise, Fall, and Comeback of Volkswagen in America*, by David Kiley

*The Do-It-Yourself Lobotomy: Open Your Mind to Greater Creative Thinking*, by Tom Monahan

*Beyond Disruption: Changing the Rules in the Marketplace*, by Jean-Marie Dru

*And Now a Few Laughs from Our Sponsor: The Best of Fifty Years of Radio Commercials*, by Larry Oakner

*Sixty Trends in Sixty Minutes*, by Sam Hill

*Leap: A Revolution in Creative Business Strategy*, by Bob Schmetterer

*Buzz: Harness the Power of Influence and Create Demand*, by Marian Salzman, Ira Matathia, and Ann O'Reilly

*Casting for Big Ideas: A New Manifesto for Agency Managers*, by Andrew Jaffe

*Life after the 30-Second Spot: Energize Your Brand with a Bold Mix of Alternatives to Traditional Advertising*, by Joseph Jaffe

*Pick Me: Breaking into Advertising and Staying There*, by Nancy Vonk and Janet Kestin

# The
# *Adweek*
# Copywriting
# Handbook

*The Ultimate Guide to Writing Powerful
Advertising and Marketing Copy
from One of America's Top Copywriters*

## JOSEPH SUGARMAN

John Wiley & Sons, Inc.

Published by John Wiley & Sons, Inc., Hoboken, New Jersey
Published simultaneously in Canada

For general information on our other products and services or for technical support, please contact our Customer Care Department within the United States at (800) 762-2974, outside the United States at (317) 572-3993 or fax (317) 572-4002.

Wiley also publishes its books in a variety of electronic formats. Some content that appears in print may not be available in electronic books. For more information about Wiley products, visit our web site at www.wiley.com.

ISBN-13: 978-0-470-05124-5
ISBN-10: 0-470-05124-8

Printed in the United States of America

V10015704_111919

*To Mary Stanke, whose support through three-and-a-half decades has been instrumental to my success.*

# Contents

By Ray Schultz, Editor, *DIRECT* Magazine

Every trade has its role models. And for me, there is no better model for ad copywriters or magazine editors than Joe Sugarman.

Bandleader Artie Shaw had a standard question for musicians who wanted to join his band: "Who do you listen to?"

A similar question might be asked of writers applying for work: "Who do you read?"

Sugarman is the guy who sells BluBlocker sunglasses on TV. He also happens to be one of the most amusing and prolific writers in the United States, as I discovered when I started reading his JS&A catalog in 1985.

He was totally out of the box. He cracked me up with the sheer exuberance of his copy approach.

He offered readers $10 for every spelling error they found in his copy. ("Please don't correct my grammar.")

He offered "loaner" watches to customers as part of a service guarantee.

He offered a $6 million home for sale in the airline magazines, accepting American Express, Visa, MasterCard or any negotiable hard currency.

He sold a $240,000 airplane in a single mail order ad.

And he did it all with a very special tone. It's like Nelson Algren said about John Cheever—that he was the one writer you could identify "without turning the pages of *The New Yorker* back to see who wrote it."

Not that Sugarman is the most colorful rogue ever to write great mail order copy. There were others. Louis Victor Eytinge, a convicted murderer who learned how to write in prison. Or Gene

Schwartz, the art collector, who made his living writing stuff like "She Fled the Table When the Doctor Said Cut Her Open."

But Joe surpassed those guys in a few very important ways—the sheer volume of his writing, the trends that he set and my favorite, the personal catalog, one in which the copy and the product reflect the quirks of the owner. And Joe has a lot of imitators who have personalized their catalogs using Joe's catalog as their inspiration.

How did Joe learn his trade? He claims he learned it from his failures and not from the mail order greats who preceded him. Greats like David Margoles, who sold 4 million garlic crushers in the 1950s.

Then there was Max Sackheim, co-founder of the Book-of-the-Month Club and another great pitchman who lived by his wits. As Lester Wunderman in 1996 reflected about Sackheim, "When he talked to clients, he promised a breakthrough—not as we have now, minuscule improvement."

Then there was John Caples, who entered American folklore by writing "They Laughed When I Sat Down at the Piano." The late Larry Chait asked Caples why he stressed the social benefits instead of just selling the virtues of the course.

"You don't understand," Caples answered. "Learning the piano is tough. You can't sell that. But you can sell the idea of social success and overcoming whatever deficiencies you have in order to become popular."

Though he may never have met them, Sugarman knows on a gut level what these guys knew. And that's important, because he's one of the last of a breed.

Now for the good news. He's passed the tradition down in this handbook, the best book ever done on the subject of mail order writing.

Besides the advice on selling, it stresses basic truths about writing, in language anyone can understand. I've even given the manuscript to my new reporters to read.

I'm sad to report that Sugarman doesn't write as much copy as he used to—no more catalogs and very few space ads. He's followed the money into infomercials and home shopping.

Until they reissue old JS&A catalogs (the way they've reissued the 1909 edition of Sears, Roebuck), this book will have to stand as Joe's legacy in print. But it's a fine legacy.

So here it is. Enjoy. As Walter Winchell said when he introduced Damon Runyon, "The next act is better."

*Ray Schultz is one of the top writers and editors in the direct marketing industry and editor of* DIRECT *magazine, a Cowles Business Media publication.*

Many people have contributed to my copywriting skills and to the creation of this book, and to all of them I am very grateful. Mary Stanke, president of JS&A Group, Inc., whose direction, commitment and 35 years of service allowed me the creative freedom to express myself through my writing and who helped me build a substantial business in the process. My ex-wife, Wendy, and our two children, April and Jill, for their understanding and support during the many seminars we held—always behind the scenes, but their presence was very important and always felt. Judy Sugarman, my sister and copyeditor for 25 years—always there to correct my spelling, undangle my modifiers and give me very candid feedback.

I also wish to acknowledge the thousands of customers who gave me a tremendous education and for whom I have an unwavering respect. I wish to acknowledge my many competitors, too. I hated it when they copied me, but in the process of trying to outwit them my copywriting skills grew even stronger. There are hundreds of other people I could mention—too numerous to list here—who have played a vital role in my success and growth.

A special acknowledgment to all my wonderful seminar participants who learned from me and went on to create or build successful businesses—all through the power of their pens. I learned a great deal from them. Finally, I wish to thank, with humility and gratitude, all who have exchanged their hard-earned money for this book. May you, too, learn and prosper.

# The
# *Adweek*
# Copywriting
# Handbook

*The truly creative mind in any field is no more than . . . a cruelly delicate organism with the overpowering necessity to create, create, create—so that without the creating of music or poetry or books or buildings or something of meaning, his very breath is cut off from him. He must create, must pour out creation. By some strange, unknown, inward urgency he is not really alive unless he is creating.*

—Pearl Buck

This is a story about a seminar. It was a copywriting and marketing seminar I presented starting in the 1970s during a time when I was actively involved in both writing copy and marketing a range of products that included everything from electronics to collectibles—from Bone Fones to Picasso tiles.

I was a prolific writer, often writing complete catalogs, print advertisements and direct mailings. And I owned the company, JS&A Group, Inc., that sold these products, so I experienced the direct consequences of my successes and failures.

## Failures Outnumbered Successes

My failures far outnumbered my successes. In fact, I have yet to find anybody who has experienced the number of failures I experienced during the early stages of my career. But it was through these failures that I received a very costly education that to this day has guided me through a successful career in advertising and direct marketing.

To the public, I was a big success. Babe Ruth is remembered for his home run record and not for the fact that he also held the record for the most strikeouts. And so it was with me.

1

Most people just saw my successes, as they were quite visible. And they just saw my successful innovations because they were the ones that worked. So to the general public and to others in direct marketing, it appeared that I had the Midas touch.

I didn't see myself running seminars. I was busy enough running my business. And to share my secrets with the industry was only asking for competition. But it was a series of coincidences that prompted me to offer seminar courses and I'm glad I made the decision to do them. And many of my participants are glad, too—people whose seminar experience made an enormous difference in their lives.

My seminar was different. First, I was an actual practitioner—not an educator or a consultant who never had to make a major marketing gamble or cover a payroll. I was out there on the firing line, making sure each day that the copy I was writing and the marketing decisions I was making were going to be accepted by the marketplace.

Second, it was during a time when my success was reaching a peak. Our mail order ads were appearing everywhere. They appeared in newspapers and magazines and on airplanes and with such regularity and frequency that the format was attracting a great deal of attention and creating an entire flock of imitators.

Finally, I realized what people were willing to pay just to hear me as a speaker or talk to me as a consultant. Bernie Pargh, an entrepreneur and owner of B.A. Pargh, a business equipment sales company, flew from Nashville to Los Angeles one day just to hear me speak to a direct marketing group. "Joe, I've spent over $1,000 just to hear you speak for 45 minutes," he told me.

I would also get calls from people who had marketing problems and would want to fly to visit me in the Chicago suburb of Northbrook, where our company was based, just to sit and talk to me for 15 minutes.

## The Fateful Visit

But the seminar would never have taken place had it not been for a small vacation I took up to northern Wisconsin to visit my sister and her family.

It was during that trip that I discovered the beauty of the

north woods and made the decision, with my family, to find a second home there. The home I eventually found was a 10,000-square-foot, two-story building on a 16-acre site overlooking one of the most beautiful lakes I had ever seen. The property was filled with virgin timber—tall, stately pines and oak trees that had escaped the lumbermen who cleared most of the trees from northern Wisconsin during the 1800s.

But the home was costly and at the time something I couldn't afford. The price in 1977 was $350,000 and I couldn't really justify it until my lawyer and close personal friend, George Gerstman, suggested I could use the facility as a seminar site. "Hold marketing seminars at the place, turn it into a business and you could write off the entire property and even make a profit," he suggested.

The idea really appealed to me. It was a very unique setting. It was isolated and quiet, and the fresh northern Wisconsin air at Minocqua was stimulating and invigorating.

I spent a great deal of the summer going up there with my family and furnishing the facility for a seminar. I cleared away a number of the odd buildings that dated back to the 1800s but were in such disrepair that I had no choice but to remove them. My wife at the time, Wendy, helped pick out the furniture and dishes. She also hired a cook, housekeepers and the support staff needed to run the seminars while Mary Stanke, my operations chief at JS&A, assisted with registering the participants and preparing all the materials for the seminar. And so within a few months the facility was transformed into an enchanting seminar site—a learning center that I called "Nature's Response."

## The Most Expensive Seminar

Back in 1977, I was charging $2,000 for five days—a price that made it, at the time, the most expensive seminar in the direct marketing business. For my seminars 10 years later, I charged $3,000. I announced the seminar in *Advertising Age* and *Direct Marketing* magazines in the format of one of my typical ads. And the response was immediate. If Bernie Pargh was willing to spend $1,000 to fly to Los Angeles to hear me speak for 45 minutes and several people were willing to fly from different parts of the United States to talk to me for just 15 minutes, I had a value that certainly was worth $2,000 for five full days.

Within a few weeks, I had a full class with participants from all over the world. We had somebody from Germany, several from California and quite a few from the East Coast. We had a farmer from Texas and a dentist from Carmel, California. Richard Viguerie, the conservative Washington fund-raiser, enrolled and of course Bernie Pargh attended. I actually had more participants than I wanted so I created a reservation list for my next seminar.

To get to Minocqua, the seminar participants had to fly to Chicago, board a commuter plane there and fly to the town of Rhinelander, Wisconsin, where they then took a bus for the 40-minute ride to their motel. To get to the seminar site, the participants took a pontoon boat from the motel and landed at our boathouse where they walked up a path to the house.

And at the house, they would find several rooms outfitted as classrooms, a large dining room, a kitchen and a very large wooden balcony where they could look out at the lake, relax and enjoy the clean north-woods air.

It was an idyllic setting in a remote part of America—a place where my students would learn a form of copywriting and marketing that they could not learn anyplace else.

## The Book Contains Many Lessons

This book shares many of the lessons and experiences that were taught at these seminars. You'll learn how to mentally prepare yourself to write copy, how to write effective copy, and how to present your product, concept or service in a novel and exciting way. You'll learn what really works and what doesn't and how to avoid many of the pitfalls that marketers fall into— and much more.

I convey my unique approach to copy by demonstrating my thought process on everything from how copy should flow to the elements every ad should have—from the psychology of copy and its motivational triggers to the emotions generated by words. But the seminar was certainly more than learning about copy and marketing.

The seminar turned into a motivational experience for

many who went on to become quite successful. Others, who were already successful, couldn't wait to get back to work and implement their new knowledge. And they too grew in the process.

You too will understand how to relate what you've learned about copywriting to other forms of marketing and you'll see how many of the same principles apply.

## The Goal of Copy

Throughout this book, I talk about the eventual goal of writing effective copy, namely: "To cause a person to exchange his or her hard-earned money for a product or service." It's really as simple as that.

Direct marketing is truly the tool of this century. Using it, you can move millions of people to reach into their pockets for millions of dollars—all from the power of your pen or the message you convey in print, on TV, on radio or on a computer screen.

For most of what I teach in this book I use a print ad as a reference point. Print ads are among the most difficult of all forms of direct marketing. On a single page, in two dimensions, located in a medium with hundreds of competing messages and without sound or motion, you've got to entice a person to start reading your ad, convey the complete story of your product or service and then convince the person to reach for the phone and order. To understand this process and to effectively implement it requires a lot of experience and skill. But once you have mastered the skills, you will have the ability to build a business from just the power of your pen and with very little capital.

When Mike Valentine attended my seminar, he was operating his radar detector company out of his garage. Later, using many of the skills I taught him, he grew his company, Cincinnati Microwave (developer of the Escort Radar Detector), to a $140 million public company. Jimmy Calano was a young 20-something entrepreneur who had been giving small management seminars when he attended my course. He eventually became a major force in the seminar business with CareerTrack—a multi-million-dollar company. Victoria's Secret sent two of their top marketing people when the company consisted of just two stores and a catalog. They eventually were acquired by The Limited and became a powerful retail chain throughout the country.

From a UPS driver who had a fascination with direct marketing and came to the seminar with his last $2,000 to Joe Karbo, author of *The Lazy Man's Way to Riches*, who already was a very successful mail order entrepreneur—they all came with great anticipation and they all left with valuable knowledge that helped them continue to grow and prosper.

## 17 Seminars Given

I had 312 students attending 17 seminars—from the first one in the summer of 1977 to the last one given in Maui, Hawaii, in the spring of 2000. The rest of my writing and marketing insights come from several years of experience since then in the visual medium of TV—infomercials, TV spots and home shopping.

Regardless of your current educational level or knowledge of marketing, this book will give you fresh insights into the world of copywriting, marketing, human behavior, the Internet, public relations and other lessons taught at my seminar.

Even if you are not interested in writing copy, you'll have a better appreciation and understanding of the copywriting process—so much so that you will be confident that you too can write good copy or, at a minimum, critique copy.

So pull up an easy chair, prop your feet up and sink into one of the most comprehensive contemporary books on the subject of copywriting, marketing and creative expression—a treasure chest of insights that will entertain as it teaches.

# Section One

This handbook is based on a book I wrote in 1998 called *Advertising Secrets of the Written Word*. The book consisted of the lessons I had taught at exclusive seminars I conducted beginning in 1977.

My challenge was to take the first book, revise it to make it current and add many of the copywriting techniques to be considered when you write for the Internet, direct mail, public relations releases and other copywriting tasks. In the revision process I had to reread my book chapter by chapter and revise it where necessary. What I discovered in this process was that all the principles remained the same regardless of changes in the way we communicate that have occurred since I wrote it.

The modifications were primarily to update certain facts and figures that had changed over time or to cite a few examples that were more contemporary. Regardless of the media, however, one fact emerged. You should always first express whatever product or service you are selling in a print direct response ad. It is in this format that you can develop the real essence of your product or service.

That's exactly what I do. If I have to sell something on the Internet, in a catalog, or on TV, I first produce a print ad. And from the print ad, if I do my job correctly, I will find the clues and the concepts that best reflect the strong selling points that I can use in any other media.

With a print ad, you won't have the interactive nature of the Internet or the motion of TV images. You'll need to sell your product or service on a flat piece of paper with no sound, no motion—just your words.

In the first section of this handbook, I take you through the step-by-step creative process of writing that print direct response ad. I think you will be surprised at how easy it will seem once you read the simple steps involved and learn about the thinking process you have to develop.

I take the mystery out of the process and at the same time show you how you can create great copy even if you've never written any direct response copy before.

In fact, the most often heard comment I've gotten from those who read my book is simply "I now realize how easy it is to write great copy."

I have built several businesses from the power of my pen. Being able to write copy for your own business is a powerful tool that will serve you for the rest of your life. And to learn how, let me guide you through the steps you will follow as you quickly master this skill.

The preparation to become a copywriter involves knowledge. There are two types. The first is a very broad or general knowledge and the second is a very specific or targeted knowledge. Let me explain.

The best copywriters in the world are those who are curious about life, read a great deal, have many hobbies, like to travel, have a variety of interests, often master many skills, get bored and then look for other skills to master. They hunger for experience and knowledge and find other people interesting. They are very good listeners.

Look at my background. I'm an instrument-rated multi-engine commercial pilot, an amateur radio operator, and a professional photographer; I love computers, music, reading, movies, travel, art and design. I've done the complete catalog for my company including everything from setting the type to doing the layout. I've done all the photography and even some of the modeling. (My hand became quite famous, but more on that later.) I've tried many sports—golf, tennis, football, baseball, basketball, scuba diving, skiing, and snowmobiling. I've traveled to every continent on the globe with the exception of the Antarctic and I know I'll eventually get there. I've mastered a second language—German—during the three years I spent with the military in Germany. I've had hundreds of failures and many successes, with each representing a learning experience.

*The best copywriters have a variety of interests and master many skills.*

The thirst for knowledge, a tremendous curiosity about life, a wealth of experiences and not being afraid to work are the top credentials for being a good copywriter.

If you examine the lives of some of our greatest writers, you will see that they experienced a great deal and wrote about their experiences. Hemingway, Steinbeck—both lived and then wrote about their adventures. The more we experience and the more knowledge we have, the easier it is to come up with that big copy idea or marketing concept.

But more significantly, it is important to experience as much in life as possible and not to fear failure. It's not whether you win or lose in life that's important but whether you play the game. Lose enough and eventually you will win—it's only a matter of time. Edwin Land, the inventor of the Polaroid camera, said it best when he described his definition of a mistake: "A mistake is a future benefit, the full value of which is yet to be realized."

I can remember when I was very young and would fail at something I had tried very hard to accomplish. I'd often say to myself, "No big loss—it's in my back pocket. One of these days I'll use what I've just experienced simply by reaching into my back pocket, and presto, I will have the answer just when I need it."

## Experiences Create Ideas

Our minds are like giant computers. Every experience that goes into your brain—both good and bad—becomes more program material and data to recall and assemble in new ways in the future. Remember when the first Apple computers came out with their big 64K memories? You might also remember the slow speed and the poor graphics compared to the high-powered personal computers we have today. Today's computers are faster, are more efficient, can accomplish more and can interrelate information faster and more easily. So it stands to reason, the more we've experienced, the more we can draw upon when it comes time to relate those experiences to new problems or opportunities.

There is nothing really new in life. It's simply a matter of taking previous pieces of knowledge and putting them together in a unique and different format. Matter is not created and destroyed. Everything on earth that was here a billion years ago is pretty much here now. The only difference is that it has taken new forms.

The more you have stored in your brain from experiences and knowledge and the more you are able to interrelate that knowledge and come up with new combinations of old material, the greater an idea person you will be and the more powerful your capabilities as a copywriter will be.

There is a saying that goes, "If all you have is a hammer, you look at every problem as a nail." The more tools you have to work on a problem in the form of experiences or knowledge, the more new ways you can figure out how to solve it.

## Lateral Thinking for Ideas

Edward de Bono, one of the great creative thinkers of our time, coined the term *lateral thinking* to describe the process of coming up with ideas by not focusing or thinking of just the problem. Often, by relating the problem to something that has nothing to do with the problem, a new idea emerges.

De Bono created a product that he called his "Think Tank," which encouraged people to think more laterally and consequently more creatively. It was an eight-inch sphere mounted on a platform. Through a small window you could see a selection of 14,000 words printed on small plastic pieces. You shook the Think Tank and then looked into it and wrote down the first three words you saw.

You then tried to relate the three words to your marketing problem, to come up with a fresh perspective toward solving the problem. For example, let us say I wanted to sell my airplane. Typically, I would run an ad and focus on just the airplane, its features and equipment. But in using the Think Tank for lateral thinking, I might draw three totally unrelated words, *farm*, *salesman* and *compassion* and have to create an ad incorporating those three words. This process would cause me to search my brain, my data bank, and all my past experiences for some way to relate the three words while keeping in mind that I had to sell the airplane.

## The Dictionary as a Tool

Lateral thinking is simply a tool. So is your dictionary. And so is your mind. Probably one of the most important keys in copywriting and conceptualizing is the ability to relate totally divergent concepts to create a new concept. Once again, the more data you have to work with from your life experiences and the more your mind can relate this data to a problem, the better you are going to be at coming up with that really great idea.

## Running Your Own Company

Another factor that makes a great copywriter is the experience of running your own company and being responsible for every word you write. The really great direct marketing copywriters often don't work for advertising agencies, but rather run their own companies and experience their own successes and failures. Ben Suarez, Gary Halbert, the late Gene Schwartz and dozens of others recognized as top copywriters have owned their own companies and learned over years of trial and error—years of both big mistakes and great success. You can't beat that type of experience.

In my case, I have been presented with thousands of products, have written ads for hundreds of them and have had to come up with that big idea hundreds of times a year. Even as I look back at my advertising, I see a learning curve that would not have been possible had it not been for that immense wealth of broad experience. You're going to read about many of those experiences throughout this book. You'll be able to avoid many of the pitfalls and mistakes I made climbing my way up the ladder and you'll understand why these mistakes were indeed learning experiences.

The preparation for becoming a great copywriter is a lifestyle. It's a hunger for knowledge, a curiosity and a desire to participate in life that is broad-based and passionate. If you have this personality, you are already well on your way. If you don't, simply being aware of it is often enough to start a mental process and movement that will take you to where you would like to be. But being a great copywriter is more than just having a lot of experience in life. What you will learn in the next chapter is just as important.

I was sitting in the laboratory of the Sensor Watch Company in Dallas, Texas, looking through a microscope and learning everything I could about how a new digital watch was designed, produced and assembled.

I was becoming an expert on digital watch technology, on integrated circuits, quartz crystals and oscillator circuits. "Why are all the contacts gold-plated?" I asked the engineer. "They're gold-plated in every integrated circuit. It's part of the technology," was the reply.

The conversation continued. It had been two days and I was still delving into every aspect of this new digital watch I was planning to introduce. I still hadn't reached the point where I could write an ad on the advantages of the new product. At the time, most digital watches had liquid crystal displays, and in order to see the time, you had to press a button to illuminate the display. On the new Sensor watch, the display glowed constantly, thanks to an inert but radioactive substance that was placed in a small flat capsule behind the display.

## New Technology Required Powerful Presentation

This new technology meant that you could glance down at your watch and, in an instant, tell the time—even at night—without pressing any buttons. But I felt that there had to be a powerful way of presenting the product and I still wasn't comfortable with what I had.

The Sensor 770 was very expensive to make and sell. So I knew that I needed something that made the watch I was selling really different and special.

"Why didn't somebody think of this radioactive material for watches before?" was my next question.

The engineer looked at me, paused for a second and then said, "We haven't had the technology to seal the radioactive material in a transparent capsule without it leaking out until somebody developed a technique with a laser. The laser is what seals the capsule. Without the laser, there is no way you could completely seal the capsule."

That was all I needed. The concept was clear. And the ad headline that I wrote for the new Sensor digital watch was, "Laser Beam Digital Watch."

The story told of how the watch was made possible thanks to a laser beam and how its new technology benefited the consumer. That single concept resulted in millions of dollars in profitable sales for the digital watch.

When I had reached the point about the laser beam sealing the capsule, I knew I had found that unique headline concept that made the watch stand out from the competition. But it took a few days of very intensive learning and study before the concept emerged. Sometimes this can happen in a few minutes, sometimes it can happen in a few hours and sometimes it may take weeks. This time it took a few days of patience along with specific knowledge.

## You Must Become an Expert

You need to become an expert on a product, service or anything you write about to really be effective. Becoming an expert means learning enough about a product to obtain enough specific knowledge so you can communicate the real nature of what you are trying to sell. Say to yourself, "I am an expert or have learned enough to be able to effectively communicate this product to the consumer." That's what we mean by "specific knowledge."

This doesn't mean that you have to learn everything there is to know about a subject every time. There have been times when I simply looked at a product or service and came up with the big idea from my own past experience or specific knowledge in a particular category. Remember, I'm a pilot, ham radio operator and photographer. I already had not only vast knowledge of the gadgets I would sell in my business, but knowledge of my customer, as well. I myself was my typical customer. I was the type of individual I had to sell products to because I was as gadget-oriented as the person I was trying to appeal to.

## You Must Know Your Customer, Too

And that's another point. In addition to knowing your product or service, you've really got to know your customer. You've got to be an expert on who your customer is by gathering specific information on whom you are selling to. You may already be an expert by virtue of being a typical customer. You know your likes and dislikes, what excites you and what you yourself would expect from a company selling you a product. But if it is your assignment to write copy for a product or service that you really don't have a feel for, then you have a great deal of studying to do to make sure you understand who your customer is and what motivates him or her.

## You Must Understand a Product's Nature

And even if you understand your customer and understand your product, you must realize one more thing. There is a specific way that each product should be presented to your customer. In short, the product has a nature of its own and it's up to you to discover what the nature of that product is in the mind of the consumer.

Let me cite a good example. Back when I first started JS&A in the basement of my home, I met Howard Franklin. Howard was an insurance salesman from Chicago who bought his first calculator from me from an ad I ran in the *Wall Street Journal*. He loved his calculator and stopped by one day to buy a few more of them. After that, Howard would stop by every once in a while and buy more calculators as gifts for his better clients.

One day, Howard stopped by and said that since JS&A was a growing concern, I should buy insurance. "You want to protect your family because if anything ever happened to you, there may be quite an estate and lots of taxes to pay before your family would realize anything."

"Thank you, Howard. I appreciate the offer, but I don't really believe in insurance," was my standard reply.

But Howard was a good salesman. Every once in a while Howard would clip out an article on calculators from a local paper or an article from some magazine on some new gadget and send it to me with his card. And every once in a while, Howard stopped by and picked up a calculator and again dropped the comment, "Joe, you should really have insurance."

"Thanks, Howard. I appreciate the advice," was my typical comment.

Then one day I heard a siren in front of my next-door neighbor's house. I looked out the window and within a few minutes, my neighbor was being carried out of his home on a stretcher with a white sheet over him. He had died that morning from a massive heart attack. He was only in his 40s. I was 36 at the time.

The next day I called Howard on the phone. "Howard, remember our many discussions on insurance and protecting your family and stuff? Well, I think that we should sit down and work out some sort of program for an insurance plan for my family and me."

I had finally made the plunge. Was it Howard's salesmanship? Was it his persistence? Maybe. But I realized from that

*It took an event close to home to make me take action.*

experience a really effective way to sell a whole series of products. Howard succeeded because he had planted enough seeds in my mind for me to realize what insurance was for, who should sell it to me and who was a good friend and customer. When it came time to buy, only I, Joseph Sugarman, would know. And only when there was an immediate experience that hit close to home would I see the value of insurance. I went through the experience and I responded.

Some of the implications from this example will be referred to later in this book, but the point concerns the nature of a product. Every product has a nature to it that you must understand to be successful when creating a marketing concept behind that product. For example, from the insurance experience, I soon realized how to sell burglar alarms and became one of the largest burglar alarm sales companies in the country, protecting more homes than any other company.

The alarm was called the Midex and my thoughts went back to Howard as I created the ad. I knew that to scare people into buying a burglar alarm was like Howard coming into my basement and saying, "Joe, when you die, are you going to leave your wife and kids in financial disaster?" That would never sell me insurance. Nor would a similar technique of quoting crime statistics work to sell burglar alarms.

I realized that if I were to buy a burglar alarm, I would first have to recognize a need for one: perhaps if my neighbor was robbed or crime in my community was on the rise or I had recently purchased something expensive.

Once I had a need for a burglar alarm, I would look for one that really made sense for my situation. The first thing I would insist on is that it worked. After all, the first time I really need my alarm to work may be the only time it would be called upon to work, and I'd want to make sure it worked flawlessly.

The second thing that would be important to me is the ease of installation. It would have to be so easy to install that it wouldn't require any outside person stringing wires all over my house. So when I wrote the ad on the Midex burglar alarm, I made sure that I spent several paragraphs on the reliability of the product and the testing each unit went through before it was shipped. And I used astronaut Wally Schirra as my spokesperson for the alarm. He was quoted as saying, "I'm very pleased with my unit."

## Scare Tactics Don't Usually Work

Never did I try to scare the prospective customer with crime statistics. It would look as ridiculous as Howard screaming or warning me in my basement to get insurance because I may die. All I did was realize the nature of the product I was selling, bring out the points in the product that were important to the consumer and then wait until the consumer saw the ad enough times or was threatened close enough to home before he or she bought.

We received many orders from people who had cut out the ad and put it in a file. When indeed they were threatened, they then called and placed their orders. Fortunately, there were enough people who wanted a unit when they saw the ad to earn us a nice profit, but we also received orders months after we stopped running our ads. And despite the fact that many of the electronic products of the time were obsolete just a few months after they were introduced, we managed to run our ad for over three years before sales slowed down.

I have one other example on the importance of becoming an

expert on the product you sell by gaining specific knowledge in order to write outstanding copy on a subject. It happened in 1975, right at the start of the citizens band (CB) radio boom in the United States. Back then, the U.S. government had imposed a reduced nationwide speed limit of 55 miles per hour to conserve fuel. The lower speed limits really affected those 18-wheel long-haul truck drivers. Truck drivers responded by buying CBs to communicate with each other.

The truck drivers would travel in caravans and truckers ahead of the caravan would signal if there was a "Smokey" (police officer) in the area. Soon CBs became so popular that the average motorist started buying them and a whole new fad emerged in the United States—a fad so big that songs, movies and a variety of products were created to capitalize on it. The CB units themselves were in such demand that you couldn't even get one without a wait, and thieves were stealing them out of cars and turning a very hefty profit reselling them.

As a ham radio operator, I knew of the fun in radio communications and the advantages of having a unit in my car. This was my general knowledge. So I wanted to experience the fad and I decided to get a CB radio. I then became somewhat of an expert on it. There was a lot less to master with CB than there was with ham radio, where I had to learn the Morse code at 13 words per minute and a great deal of technical information before passing my operator's test.

During the early stages of the fad, I was attending the Consumer Electronics Show in Chicago when I bumped into Mike Weschler, a salesman, who showed me a new product. "Joe, here is a miniature walkie-talkie."

## The Product Was Not Unusual

I looked at the small sliver of a product he handed me and realized that a small walkie-talkie was no big deal. You could get them at any RadioShack store. But Mike then pointed out that the unit had an integrated circuit—it was one of the few units using this new type of technology and it indeed was smaller than any of the other products on the market.

The product seemed a little more interesting after Mike

explained its features. It was so small that it could easily slip into a shirt pocket. "What frequencies can you broadcast on and what is the power?" I asked, calling on my knowledge of ham radio.

"The unit has two frequencies. One takes a crystal for any of a number of frequencies and the other would be permanently set to a frequency around 27 megahertz."

I looked up at Mike as he was demonstrating the unit and asked him, "Mike, isn't 27 megahertz near one of the CB frequencies?"

"Right. It's channel 12 but don't worry, there is not that much radio traffic on channel 12. It's normally reserved for walkie-talkies," Mike assured me rather sheepishly as if I had discovered a fault with the unit.

"No, Mike, I think that will turn out to be an advantage." And indeed it was. I took the unit, called it a Pocket CB and sold over 250,000 of them at $39.95. It was a huge success and fully attributable to my general knowledge combined with the specific knowledge of the unit and the discovery of that unique feature that might have been overlooked by somebody else.

Realize how important it is to know your product and know your customer. It is this specific knowledge that will make a dramatic difference in your ability to communicate your thoughts in copy.

**O**ne of the first things I would ask my seminar students to think about was the definition of good copywriting. Is it the skill of being able to accurately put words on paper? Can it be taught? What sort of background do you need to be a good copywriter?

We would then talk about both general knowledge and specific knowledge. But I explained that there was more to the art of copywriting.

Copywriting is simply a written form of communicating facts and emotions. It is a mental process. Some copywriters will tell you that many of their greatest works were well thought out in their minds even before they put them on paper.

Joe Karbo wrote one of the most successful income opportunity ads ever written for his book, *The Lazy Man's Way to Riches,* in one draft and without corrections. It just poured out of his mind onto a sheet of paper. And it was one of the few ads he ever wrote.

Some copywriters will tell you that they just sit down and start writing. Some find that sitting in front of a computer does the trick and others need something like a pen and a pad of paper.

My greatest ads were written during a variety of circumstances. Many were well thought out before I put the first word to paper and they flowed out with hardly a correction. Other times they would flow but you wouldn't recognize the first draft from the last because of the number of corrections I made. Sometimes I would sit in an airplane and just write from takeoff to landing and come up with great copy. And other times, I used my computer with great success.

## It's All a Mental Process

The bottom line for all these approaches is that copywriting is primarily the mental process of first getting your thoughts organized in your mind and then eventually transferring them onto paper. There is no best method—just what works for you.

But the best place to start, without question, is to start. That's right. Pick up a piece of paper and a pen, and start. Do enough of it over a long enough period of time and I guarantee you, you'll improve each year. Write articles for a local newspaper. I started writing for my high school paper. It gave me experience and confidence. Write letters, write postcards—just plain write every opportunity you can.

I look over my very first JS&A direct response ads and can't believe I wrote them. They were horrible. But I matured and I learned with each ad I wrote. In my first ads, I used clichés—"It's the product the world has been waiting for." And my sentences weren't flowing as they do now. Sheer volume and experience will do wonders. As they say to anybody wanting to make it to Carnegie Hall, "Practice, practice, practice."

### Don't Worry about the First Draft

Another fact to realize about writing copy is that the first draft of an ad is often terrible and the real skill in copywriting is taking that rough draft and polishing it. You might add words, delete entire sentences, change the order of sentences or even paragraphs. It's all part of the copywriting process. I often pointed out to my students that if everybody in the class were given the assignment of writing a draft of an ad for a product, the first draft of my ad would quite likely be terrible compared to everybody else's. It is what I do with the copy after my first draft that really makes the difference.

In that first draft the goal is to put something—anything—on paper, the emotional outpouring of everything you are trying to convey about your product or service. Don't worry about how it reads. Just get it down onto something you can work with like a computer screen or a piece of paper and then go from there.

To define exactly what copywriting is, I often presented the following axiom:

**Axiom 1**    *Copywriting is a mental process the successful execution of which reflects the sum total of all your experiences, your specific knowledge and your ability to mentally process that information and transfer it onto a sheet of paper for the purpose of selling a product or service.*

And in this book you will learn some of the valuable techniques to use to expand your knowledge of the copywriting process so you can write copy that motivates people to take an action—specifically to take their hard-earned money and exchange it for your product or service.

Copywriting is the key to any successful direct marketing venture. You can have the world's best product or service, but if you can't communicate your ideas, you have nothing. I will give you the skills and insights you need to successfully write copy. I've already personally taken the most expensive course ever. If you would add up my failures and their cost to me, add the insights I received mostly from my failures, and then add the experiences I've had in copywriting and marketing, you would see that it has indeed been an expensive education. And you're about to share in it.

You are now ready to start to learn the techniques I use to write copy. You already understand the importance of having a broad general knowledge. This takes time and is a lifelong quest. And you understand the importance of obtaining specific knowledge on a project you are working on. This I hope is quite clear from Chapter 2.

But what you are about to learn in this chapter and the chapters that follow is the specific knowledge you will need to understand my copywriting approach and to become a top copywriter.

In these chapters, I present several axioms. Each one is in bold type and each one is critical to your understanding of my philosophy. The axiom presented in this chapter is very important and very difficult to believe at first. Understand this concept, believe in it and it will give you a good foundation for your future writing skills. Don't believe in it and you'll fall into the trap that many copywriters typically fall into.

To introduce the concept, let's look at the CB radio ad on the next page, which ran from 1975 through 1977. The ad has all the elements you would expect any space ad to have. And to understand this first axiom, I would ask my students to define the purpose of each of the 10 elements in an advertisement. The following is what we finally decided:

1. **Headline:** To get your attention and draw you to the subheadline.
2. **Subheadline:** To give you more information and further explain the attention-getting headline.
3. **Photo or Drawing:** To get your attention and to illustrate the product more fully.
4. **Caption:** To describe the photo or drawing. This is an important element and one that is often read.

*Headline*

*Subheadline*

*Paragraph Heading*

*Photos & Drawings*

*Captions*

*Copy*

*Price*

*Logo*

*Response Device*

# Pocket CB

*New integrated circuit technology and a major electronic breakthrough brings you the world's smallest citizens band transceiver.*

*The PocketCom measures approximately ¾" × 1½" × 5½" and easily fits into your shirt pocket. The unit can be used as a personal communications link for business or pleasure.*

**SMALL ENOUGH FOR YOUR POCKET**

Scientists have produced a personal communications system so small that it can easily fit in your pocket. It's called the PocketCom and it replaces larger units that cost considerably more.

**MANY PERSONAL USES**

An executive can now talk anywhere with anybody in his office, his factory or job site. The housewife can find her children at a busy shopping center. The motorist can signal for help in an emergency. The salesman, the construction foreman, the traveler, the sportsman, the hobbyist—everybody can use the PocketCom—as a pager, an intercom, a telephone or even a security device.

**LONG RANGE COMMUNICATIONS**

The PocketCom's range is limited only by its 100 milliwatt power and the number of metal objects between units or from a few blocks in the city to several miles on a lake. Its receiver is so sensitive, that signals several miles away can be picked up from stronger citizens band base or mobile stations.

**VERY SIMPLE OPERATION**

To use the PocketCom simply turn it on, extend the antenna, press a button to transmit, and release it to listen. And no FCC license is required to operate it. The Pocket-Com has two Channels—channel 14 and an optional second channel. To use the second channel, plug in one of the 22 other citizens band crystals and slide the channel selector to the second position. Crystals for the second channel cost $7.95 and can only be ordered after receipt of your unit.

*The PocketCom components are equivalent to 112 transistors whereas most comparable units contain only twelve.*

**A MAJOR BREAKTHROUGH**

The PocketCom's small size results from a breakthrough in the solid state device that made the pocket calculator a reality. Mega scientists took 112 transistors, integrated them on a micro silicon wafer and produced the world's first transceiver linear integrated circuit. This major breakthrough not only reduced the size of radio components but improved their dependability and performance. A large and expensive walkie talkie costing several hundred dollars might have only 12 transistors compared to 112 in the Mega PocketCom.

**BEEP-TONE PAGING SYSTEM**

You can page another PocketCom user, within close range, by simply pressing the PocketCom's call button which produces a beep tone on the other unit if it has been left in the standby mode. In the standby mode the unit is silent and can be kept on for weeks without draining the batteries.

**SUPERIOR FEATURES**

Just check the advanced PocketCom features now possible through this new circuit breakthrough: 1) Incoming signals are amplified several million times compared to only 100,000 times on comparable conventional systems. 2) Even with a 60 decibel difference in signal strength, the unit's automatic gain control will bring up each incoming signal to a maximum uniform level. 3) A high squelch sensitivity (0.7 microvolts) permits noiseless operation without squelching weak signals. 4) Harmonic distortion is so low that it far exceeds EIA (Electronic Industries Association) standards whereas most comparable systems don't even meet EIA specification. 5) The receiver has better than one microvolt sensitivity.

**EXTRA LONG BATTERY LIFE**

The PocketCom has a light-emitting diode low-battery indicator that tells you when your 'N' cell batteries require replacement. The integrated circuit requires such low power that the two batteries, with average use, will last weeks without running down.

EXECUTIVES · POLICE · MOTORISTS

SHOPPERS · HIKERS · FOREMEN

*The PocketCom can be used as a pager, an intercom, a telephone or even a security device.*

**MULTIPLEX INTERCOM**

Many businesses can use the PocketCom as a multiplex intercom. Each employee carries a unit tuned to a different channel. A stronger citizens band base station with 23 channels is used to page each PocketCom. The results: an inexpensive and flexible multiplex intercom system for large construction sites, factories, offices, or farms.

**NATIONAL SERVICE**

The PocketCom is manufactured exclusively for JS&A by Mega Corporation. JS&A is America's largest supplier of space-age products and Mega Corporation is a leading manufacturer of innovative personal communication systems—further assurance that your modest investment is well protected. The

PocketCom should give you years of trouble-free service, however, should service ever be required, simply slip your 5 ounce Pocket-Com into its handy mailer and send it to Mega's prompt national service-by-mail center. It is just that easy.

**GIVE IT A REAL WORKOUT**

Remember the first time you saw a pocket calculator? It probably seemed unbelieveable. The PocketCom may also seem unbelieveable so we give you the opportunity to personally examine one without obligation. Order only two units on a trial basis. Then really test them. Test the range, the sensitivity, the convenience. Test them under your everyday conditions and compare the PocketCom with larger units that sell for several hundred dollars.

After you are absolutely convinced that the PocketCom is indeed that advanced product breakthrough, order your additional units, crystals or accessories on a priority basis as one of our established customers. If, however, the PocketCom does not suit your particular requirements perfectly, then return your units within ten days after receipt for a prompt and courteous refund. You cannot lose. Here is your opportunity to test an advanced space-age product at absolutely no risk.

**A COMPLETE PACKAGE**

Each PocketCom comes complete with mercury batteries, high performance Channel 14 crystals for one channel, complete instructions, and a 90 day parts and labor warranty. To order by mail, simply mail your check for $39.95 per unit (or $79.90 for two) plus $2.50 per order for postage, insurance and handling to the address shown below. (Illinois residents add 5% sales tax). But don't delay.

Personal communications is the future of communications. Join the revolution. Order your PocketComs at no obligation today.

**$39⁹⁵** NATIONAL INTRODUCTORY PRICE

**JS&A** NATIONAL SALES GROUP

DEPT. PS     JS&A Plaza
Northbrook, Illinois 60062
CALL TOLL-FREE . . 800 325-6400
In Missouri call . . . . 800 323-6400
©JS&A Group, Inc. 1975

September, 1975

5. **Copy:** To convey the main selling message for your product or service.

6. **Paragraph Headings:** To break up the copy into chunks, thereby making the copy look less imposing.

7. **Logo:** To display the name of the company selling the product.

8. **Price:** To let the reader know what the product or service costs. The price could be in large type or could be buried in the copy.

9. **Response Device:** To give the reader a way to respond to the ad, by using the coupon, toll-free number or ordering information, usually near the end of the ad.

10. **Overall Layout:** To provide the overall appearance for the ad, by using effective graphic design for the other elements.

After they clearly understood each of the elements that comprise a direct response ad, I then told the class that there is a singular purpose for all the elements in an ad—a purpose so important that it constitutes one of the essential concepts in my approach to copy.

When you were first attracted to the ad you might have looked at the photo at the top of the page or the other photos. You might have then read the headline, read the subheadline and then glanced down to the name of the company selling the product. You may have read the captions to both the pictures and the sketches and you may have noticed the toll-free number indicating that you could order the product on the phone.

When you looked at the ad overall, you may have noticed the layout, the paragraph headings scattered about the layout and the attractive graphic and typographic presentation.

There are plenty of elements that can draw your attention before you start reading the copy. But one of the most important axioms you will learn for becoming a great copywriter is my second axiom. Here it is:

*All the elements in an advertisement are primarily designed to do one thing and one thing only: get you to read the first sentence of the copy.*

**Axiom 2**

*Each element should lead you to the first sentence.*

At this point, there was usually a confused look on the faces of my students. They thought that each of these elements had its own reason for existence. But I was saying, "No, they are there strictly for the sole purpose of getting you to read the first sentence."

I know what you're thinking. "What about the headline? Isn't it supposed to have a benefit, be 16 words long and what about . . ." Stop. Just accept my word at this point that each element has a single purpose and that is to get you to read the first sentence. Don't question me. Don't jump to any conclusions. Just remember this axiom.

This means if somebody asks you, "With the Sugarman approach to copywriting, what is the purpose of the subheadline in the ad?" don't answer, "A subheadline is designed to give you more information and to further explain the attention-getting headline."

Neither of the above reasons is as important as the fact that the subheadline is designed to get the reader to read the copy.

If somebody asked you for the main purpose of the logo in an advertisement, you could answer, "To establish the corporate identity of the company selling the product," or you could answer, "To provide a degree of continuity." But the real answer is to get you to read the copy. Really.

If you don't believe it, have patience and I will prove it to you. But if you'll open your mind and just accept what I tell you, you will eventually realize that what I am saying is correct. Most importantly, though, when you realize this and start writing with this in the back of your mind, you'll be amazed at the change in your results—whether your copy is in a print ad or on a web site. But like I said, just take my word for it now and let me prove it to you later in this book.

If the purpose of all the elements in an ad is therefore to get you to read the copy, then what we are really talking about is reading the first sentence, aren't we? What does this tell you about the first sentence? Pretty important, isn't it? And if the first sentence is pretty important, what do you hope the person who looks at your ad does? Read it, of course. If the reader doesn't read your very first sentence, chances are that he or she won't read your second sentence.

Now if the first sentence is so important, what can you do to make it so compelling to read, so simple, and so interesting that your readers—every one of them—will read it in its entirety? The answer: Make it short.

If you look at many typical JS&A ads, you'll notice that all of my first sentences are so short they almost aren't sentences. Some typical ones might be:

> Losing weight is not easy.
> It's you against a computer.
> It's easy.
> It had to happen.
> Hats off to IBM.

Each sentence is so short and easy to read that your reader starts to read your copy almost as if being sucked into it. Think about the analogy of a locomotive. When the locomotive starts to chug from a standing start, it really works hard. The amount of commitment and energy that the train must exert is monumental. But once the train starts to move, the next few feet become easier and the next few even easier. So it is with copy.

## Magazines Use This Technique

Many magazines use a variation of this technique in their articles. They start an article not with a very short sentence but maybe with very large type. Once they have you sucked into reading the copy and you turn the page to read the rest of the article, you notice that the typeface has gotten smaller. But that's okay. The purpose of the large type was to get you into the article and it worked. Now it's up to the author to keep you reading and turning the pages.

In an advertisement, you've got a lot going against you unless the readers are genuinely interested in your product. And if they are, then you've got to really grab and keep them. So your first sentence should be very compelling by virtue of its short length and ease of reading. No long multisyllabic words. Keep it short, sweet and almost incomplete so that the reader has to read the next sentence.

If all the elements are designed to get you to read the first sentence in an ad, then what is the purpose of the first sentence? If you guessed that it is to "convey a benefit or explain a feature," that would be impossible. How could a short first sentence do anything more than get you to read it? The correct answer is, of course, "The purpose of the first sentence is to get you to read the second sentence." Nothing more, nothing less. You probably figured this one out already anyway.

## The Purpose of the Next Sentence

Now if you're starting to get a feel for my approach to copywriting and I asked you what the purpose of the second sentence is and you answered, "To get you to read the third sentence," you would be absolutely correct. And for those of you who missed that last answer and I asked you what the purpose of the third sentence was and you answered, "To get you to read the fourth sentence," congratulations. I think you've got it.

Was there any mention of benefits? Or product description? Or unique features? Of course not. The only purpose of those first few sentences in an advertisement is to get you to read the following sentences. True, you may at one point have to start talking about product features or benefits, but if you lose sight of the fact that your sole purpose at the beginning of an ad is to hold that reader's attention at almost any cost, then you may lose your reader for lack of interest. Therefore we have the third axiom:

***The sole purpose of the first sentence in an advertisement is to get you to read the second sentence.***

**Axiom 3**

Just compare the situation in our ad example with a salesperson selling somebody face-to-face. If the first few minutes of the sales presentation put the prospective customer to sleep or if the customer stops hearing the presentation and walks away, that salesperson has lost everything. So in copywriting as in selling, if your reader is not riveted to every word you write in the first few sentences, then your chances of having that reader get to the real sales pitch are very remote.

My most successful ads have followed this format, with very few exceptions. What about making the sales pitch at the beginning of an ad? This is certainly possible, of course, but then it is often not very effective. I've tried putting the sales message at the beginning of an ad. I've tried using every trick in the book to prove my theory wrong and have failed at each attempt. Just remember that the sole purpose of all the elements of an ad is to get you to read the first sentence. Make that first sentence so easy to read that your reader is almost compelled to read it. If you grasp this, you've got an awfully good start and a great understanding of copywriting and the persuasive process.

**B**esides holding the reader's attention, there is another important function we are trying to accomplish in the first paragraphs of an advertisement and that is to create a buying environment. Let me cite an example.

Picture this. You're a salesperson and you need to sell a prospect. You've been given a choice of five environments in which to meet the prospect, and you must pick one.

The product you are selling is very expensive and you'll need at least one hour to explain and properly sell the product. The choices you have are:

**1.** At noon at a very fancy restaurant near the prospect's office.

**2.** After lunch in the boardroom at the offices of the prospect.

**3.** After work at the prospect's health club while working out with him.

**4.** In the evening with the prospect at his home while the prospect babysits his three children.

**5.** Any of the four above might be an acceptable choice.

The correct answer is 5. Why? Because the correct answer to the question "Which is the best location?" is simply "in the best selling environment for what you have to sell."

If the product is a piece of exercise equipment, the health club might be perfect. If the product has something to do with parents and children, at home with the prospect and his children in the evening might be the perfect environment.

Now if the correct answer for the salesperson is "in the environment best suited for the selling activity," is it true in print advertising, too? Yes, but let me cite another example before we discuss print advertising environments.

## The Honolulu Experience

I was in Honolulu after a trip to the Far East. I usually stop at Honolulu to recover after traveling so long and so far and over so many time zones. As I was walking down one of the main streets in Waikiki, I stopped to look into an art gallery and saw a painting of scenes from outer space.

Since JS&A was known for selling space-age products, I thought that the painting would fit very nicely in my office. I walked into the gallery noticing how very elegant it looked and saw the paintings neatly displayed on the wall. The gallery looked like it sold expensive paintings. In short, I expected the prices to be high.

It didn't take too long before a well-dressed saleswoman noticed me, walked over and asked if I needed assistance. "Beautiful painting, isn't it?" she asked.

"Very nice," I nodded. "It really looks great."

At that point the lady said, "Please follow me," as she lifted the painting off the wall and walked toward the back of the large gallery. I followed.

We entered a large room, carpeted from floor to ceiling. In the middle of the room were three very comfortable easy chairs all facing the front of the room where the saleslady mounted the painting on the wall. She then went back to the entrance of the room, turned up the classical music being piped in through loudspeakers and dimmed the lights, leaving two spotlights focused on the painting.

## Painting Looked Incredible

I must admit that the painting looked incredible. The vibrant colors, the quality of the art, and the nice feeling I experienced from hearing the classical music put me in such a buying mood that I was ready to reach into my pocket and pull out my credit card and buy the $2,000 painting.

That lady and that gallery had put me in such a focused buying mood by creating the perfect environment for selling me that painting that I almost bought it right then and there. By the way, I eventually sponsored the artist, Mark Rickerson, and sold his paintings and prints through JS&A. I personally ended up with 50 of his paintings.

Once you realize the importance of setting up a buying environment, you'll know that it must be done in the early stages of an advertisement. When you establish the reading momentum at the start of an ad, you also want to start establishing the buying environment as well. The saleslady first had to get me into the store and then slowly get me in that room to put me in the ideal buying mood. If this all sounds hard to do in print, it really isn't. You'll see examples later of how to establish the buying environment as you establish the momentum.

*Your copy has to put the prospect into a relaxed buying environment.*

Since you are creating your own environment in a print ad, you have total control over its appearance. Common sense will dictate the rest.

For example, if I was selling products at a discount, I would use big type for my prices and lots of busy graphic elements. In short, I would make the ad look like a typical discount ad. And conversely, if I was selling something expensive, I would present myself in an environment that showed class and refinement—that exuded confidence and trust.

Unlike the salesperson who may or may not be able to create the ideal selling environment, you can create your own. And unlike the salesperson who sometimes can't control the environment, you can.

So for selling products through Battram Galleries, the collectibles company I formed, my graphic and copy approach was upscale and conservative—just what you'd expect from an expensive gallery. However, when I presented my Consumers Hero concept, a club that sold refurbished bargains, it had a totally different environment—one that was clearly bargain-oriented.

The JS&A ads all had a uniform, well-organized format that seemed to be the perfect environment for all my space-age electronic products. I rarely deviated from it, but when I did, it was to create a better environment for a specific product I was selling.

You wouldn't expect to buy an expensive painting from an Army surplus store and you wouldn't expect to find much of a bargain at Tiffany's.

## You Control the Environment

As a writer of direct marketing, you have control over the environment. The environment you choose is created in both the graphic elements and the copy, but especially the copy—by the way you phrase your words, the choice of words and the level of integrity you convey.

Unlike a store where you spend thousands of dollars to create an environment, you can do it all simply in the copy of your ad or the look of your web site.

The environment is critical in getting a prospective customer into the buying mood. And to create that environment, you attract the customer's attention (the headline, photos, logo, etc.) and then you've got to get the person to read the first sentence by making it so simple and so compelling that the reader cannot help but read it. And the next sentence and then the next.

And while the reader is reading, you are creating an environment just as surely as that art gallery was drawing me into that back room. So now we are ready for the fourth axiom.

| | |
|---|---|
| **Axiom 4** | *Your ad layout and the first few paragraphs of your ad must create the buying environment most conducive to the sale of your product or service.* |

Creating the ideal buying environment comes from experience and the specific knowledge you get from studying your product and potential customer. It comes from understanding the nature of your product or service. Greater understanding will come as you read this book. But for now, realize how important creating the buying environment is to eventually selling your product.

To understand how we get the reader not only to read, but to feel comfortable and be in a buying mood in that environment, let's take time out for a little lesson on personal sales ability in general, in the next chapter.

When I was only 20 years old, my father sent me to New York City to run the branch office of his printing equipment company, Consolidated International. He was having financial difficulties and I was happy to help him out after my first two years in college. I dropped out of college, and while in New York I took an interest in salesmanship. I knew that he expected me to eventually help him sell his equipment, so I set out to prepare myself.

I went to bookstores and bought everything I could on selling. I read every book available at the public library—all to become an expert in salesmanship. And during that year in New York I would stroll down Broadway and visit small auction shops located right on Times Square.

## Wonderful Sales Technique

These small auction shops would prey on unsuspecting observers by appealing to their greed. The shop's proprietor would auction off what appeared to be terrific bargains, hook one of the prospective bidders in the audience and create a buying frenzy that plenty of the onlookers would get sucked into. The bidders ended up buying junk that wasn't much of a bargain. The sales techniques were wonderful to watch and I spent hours just observing them and human nature.

Then I would go back to my small apartment and read more books on selling. It wasn't easy for a young, inexperienced 20-year-old to sell expensive and complicated printing equipment. I thought that if I could become an expert on selling in general and printing equipment in particular and then, through experience, pick up specific knowledge about selling the equipment, I could be an effective salesman for my dad.

Selling was something I was suited for. In the preference tests I took in high school, my highest score was in a category called "persuasion" and another high score was in "literary." My career in advertising could have been predicted even back in high school, for when you think about it, print advertising is nothing more than "literary persuasion."

Some of the significant lessons I learned in New York were the steps in selling a prospect, which also apply to selling in print advertising. Let me review the procedure.

The first thing you do in selling is to set up the selling environment. Whether it be a private room in a gallery or a car dealer's showroom, you configure the physical environment to be your selling environment.

Next, you have to get the attention of the prospect. That certainly makes sense and is related to the headline of a print ad.

Once you have the prospect's attention, the next step is to introduce yourself and say something that will keep the attention of the prospect. This is similar to the subheadline and the photos and captions. Then comes the sales pitch or the copy in a print ad.

During this activity, the seller has two thoughts in mind. The first is that the buyer must like and develop confidence in the seller. The buyer must believe that the seller knows the product. Second, the seller must somehow relate the product to the buyer and the buyer's needs. That's clear. But the buyer and the seller must vibrate together. There must be a harmony struck between the buyer and seller, or the persuasive sales message won't come through.

*Get the customer to nod in the affirmative and agree with you.*

There are many methods for creating this harmony and two of the most important apply very directly to space advertising. First, you've got to get the prospective reader to start saying yes. Second, you've got to make statements that are both honest and believable. Let's cite an example. A car salesman says, "Nice day, Mr. Jones." Mr. Jones then answers, "Yes." (It is a nice day, the statement is truthful and the customer answers in the affirmative.)

"I see, Mr. Jones, that you keep your car very clean." "Yes, I do." (At this point, the salesman has Mr. Jones saying yes and nodding his head.) "I see, Mr. Jones, that since you now own a

Buick and we sell Buicks, you probably could use a new one?" "Yes." (The salesman asks a rather obvious question and Mr. Jones, nodding, replies in the affirmative.)

"May I show you one of our latest models with improvements over the model you currently own?" "Yes." (The salesman once again says the obvious to get a yes answer, and the harmony continues.)

*Get your reader to say "Yes."*

In short, you try to get the customer to nod his or her head in the affirmative and agree with you, or at least you make truthful statements that the prospect knows are correct and would concur with. Make sure that the prospect does not disagree with something you're saying. If for example the salesman said, "Could you use a new Buick?" and the customer said "No," the sale would have taken a bad turn right there and the harmony would have been lost. In a print ad, the reader would have stopped reading and turned the page.

## Harmony Is the Key

The moment you get the reader to say "No" or even "I really don't believe what he is saying" or "I don't think that relates to me," you've lost the reader. But as long as the reader keeps saying yes or believes what you are saying is correct and continues to stay interested, you are going to be harmonizing with the reader and you and the reader will be walking down that path toward that beautiful room in the art gallery.

To show you a specific approach to this method, let's take an example from an ad I wrote for one of my seminar participants. Entitled "Food Crunch," it offered dehydrated survival food. On occasion, when one of my students wrote a good ad that did not succeed, I would help him or her by either suggesting minor copy changes or sometimes rewriting the entire ad myself if I felt I had a better overall concept. The first ad, by John Sauer, was written right after our major fuel crunch in 1973, when there were lines of cars at gas pumps that had little or no fuel to pump. The ad is shown on the next page with my ad above it. John chose the concept of insurance as the best approach in his ad. I felt that insurance put people to sleep.

*Which ad would
you read first
right after the
fuel crunch?*

See if you agree with the copy statements in my ad as I tie in the then-current feelings of helplessness during the fuel shortage with John's product.

We all take our food supply for granted. And for good reason. Americans have always had plenty. But we may be heading for one of the most serious periods in our history. Let me explain.

The ad then goes on to explain the writer's first-hand experience of arriving at a supermarket right after the news of the Kennedy assassination only to discover that the shelves were bare and that people in time of distress or calamity think first of their own survival.

Notice that the reader's attention was riveted. The headline, "Food Crunch," and subheadline, "We've all experienced the fuel shortage and most of us were unprepared. Will you be prepared for the food crunch?" caused us to read the first sentence. The first sentence was short and the typical American who could afford this offer would nod his or her head in the affirmative. The sentences were both interesting and true and caused the reader to start nodding his or her head.

So now we have three things we are trying to do at the beginning of an ad. First we want the reader to read the copy. Remember, that's the objective of all copy. Without the prospect reading the ad, you have nothing.

Then we create the type of environment through copy that causes the prospect to feel comfortable in exchanging his or her hard-earned money for your product or service. And finally, we want the prospect to harmonize with us—to agree with us—by feeling that indeed we are saying something that is truthful, interesting and informative and that the prospect can agree with. In short, we want agreement. We want that head to nod in the affirmative. We want harmony.

Look what *Cycle* magazine did to create the perfect harmony with me when they tried to get me to buy media in their magazine. They created a knockoff of my ad format and sent it to me with a copy style that resembled mine. Of course it could have backfired if I was upset that they were copying me, but they also knew that I would quickly recognize the format and the effort they were making to land me as a customer and that I would respect their creativity. Indeed I harmonized with their effort and bought some space in their magazine.

Another illustration of this concept is in the ad I wrote trying to appeal to bargain hunters for a company called Consumers Hero. After a few sentences the copy read as follows:

> Consumers are being robbed. Inflation is stealing our purchasing power. Our dollars are shrinking in value. The poor average consumer is plundered, robbed and stepped on.

If you were a consumer looking for bargains when inflation was skyrocketing during the years when I wrote this, you would very likely be in harmony after that brief paragraph. I used words that the consumer could relate to. I spoke in the consumer's language.

A top-producing salesman once said to me, "Joe, I really admire you. I can sell anybody on a one-to-one basis. Put me up against the toughest customers and I'll melt them down and sell them. But you have the ability to do that on a scale that dwarfs mine. When you sell, you manage to duplicate yourself and sell millions of people all at the same time."

And that's what is so incredible about selling in print. You can duplicate yourself on billions of pages. You've got to be able to reproduce a selling job in print that will harmonize with the consumer, and then you've got the essence of a powerful tool that will bring you rewards for the rest of your life in all forms of communication whether they be in print or on TV or in any of the new electronic media of the future.

*This is the ad that* **Cycle** *magazine created as a sales tool to harmonize with JS&A and convince us to buy.*

So our fifth axiom is simply:

## Axiom 5

*Get the reader to say yes and harmonize with your accurate and truthful statements while reading your copy.*

Now you have the basis for another very important principle in writing effective copy.

**B**y now you have learned several very important points about copywriting. First, you learned that you have, in your life, experienced general knowledge through your actions, circumstances and personality. You have also been given the tools to obtain specific knowledge, such as the ability to inquire, read and research. Then you learned that practice is a great teacher—that the more you write, the better you get. And finally you learned that copywriting is the mental process of transferring what is in your head onto a sheet of paper.

Then we got into the pure Sugarman stuff. We learned what most people think elements like the headline and captions do for a typical ad. And then we learned what I believe their primary purpose is: to get the reader to read the first sentence.

And if you remember, we said that the sole purpose of the first sentence is to get prospects to read the second sentence and that the sole purpose of the second sentence is to get them to read the third and then the fourth—all while you are building a selling environment for the sale of your product.

*Every element must be so compelling that you find yourself falling down a slippery slide unable to stop until you reach the end.*

We also compared the selling process in print to what a live and in-person salesperson does. You learned that ideally, as your reader starts reading your copy, you get the reader to start nodding in agreement with everything you say.

So now the reader is reading your first few sentences, is feeling comfortable in the environment you have created and is nodding in agreement. Now comes the critical part called the "slippery slide."

Picture a steep slide at a playground. Now picture somebody putting baby oil or grease along the entire length of the slide including the side rails. Picture yourself now climbing up the ladder, sitting at the top of the slide and then letting gravity force you down the slide.

As you start to slide down and build momentum, you try holding on to the sides to stop, but you can't stop. You continue to slide down the slide despite all your efforts to prevent your descent. This is the way your copy must flow.

Every element in an advertisement must cause that slippery slide effect. The headline must be so powerful and compelling that you must read the subheadline, and the subheadline must be so powerful that you are compelled to read the first sentence, and the first sentence must be so easy to read and so compelling that you must read the next sentence and so on, straight through the entire copy to the end.

## The Force of "Reading Gravity"

I once received a letter from a reader of *Scientific American* magazine in response to one of our ads on thermostats. The lady who sent me the typewritten letter told me that she had no need for a thermostat, was not interested in the subject, rarely reads advertisements and when she does, she just scans through them. But, she went on, "I am a busy scientist. When I started reading your ad, I wasted five minutes of my valuable time reading the entire thing and I was so upset at the complete waste of my time, that I wanted to write you and complain." As a copywriter, I couldn't have gotten a more complimentary complaint letter.

If you can get the majority of the people who scan a magazine to read your ad, maybe you won't sell every one of them but you will sell a good percentage. Creating the slippery slide will cause people to "traffic" your ad—to go through the entire text of your ad and then decide if they want to buy.

*Traffic* is a good word in retail selling. Any shopping center that can draw increased traffic will have increased sales for its stores. But the traffic generated by these stores can only be compared to the people who actually read your copy. That's why some of the greatest magazines with the largest circulations do not guarantee the success of your advertisement. Traffic is strictly the number of people who get into your copy. When I say "get into," I mean falling down the slippery slide all the way through to the end of your copy.

Creating the slippery slide effect is not that difficult once the reader is well into your copy. In fact, it's been proven that if a reader reads more than 25 percent of your ad, there is a great probability that he or she will read the entire ad. So once you've grabbed your reader at the start of your ad with your perfect environment and once they're reading your compelling first sentence, you've got them started down the slippery slide.

## Slippery Slide Examples

Let's look at a few examples of the use of the slippery slide in some of the advertising I've written through the years. I referred to the thermostat ad earlier, so let's start with that. The copy starts out with the following headline, subheadline and first two paragraphs:

> **Headline:** Magic Baloney
>
> **Subheadline:** You'll love the way we hated the Magic Stat thermostat until an amazing thing happened.
>
> **Picture Caption:** It had no digital readout, an ugly case and a stupid name. It almost made us sick.
>
> **Copy:** You're probably expecting our typical sales pitch, but get ready for a shock. For instead of trying to tell you what a great product the Magic Stat thermostat is, we're going to tear it apart. Unmercifully.
>
> When we first saw the Magic Stat, we took one look at the name and went, "Yuck." We took one look at the plastic case and said, "How cheap looking." And when we looked for the digital readout, it had none. So before the salesman even showed us how it worked, we were totally turned off.

Now if you're reading the above ad, you're starting down the slippery slide unable to stop. You might find yourself reading the copy even though you have no intention of buying a thermostat by mail. You're curious. What's the gimmick?

The environment was set by the very clean layout. The tone of the ad was one of a flip, sarcastic and skeptical company exploring the possibility of selling a product that we were not very impressed with.

Of course the rest of the ad told of how we discovered a few nice points and then a few more and then some really great features and finally decided that this was one great product. At the end of the ad, we finished with:

> Beauty is only skin deep and a name doesn't really mean that much. But we sure wish those guys at Magic Stat would have named their unit something more impressive. Maybe something like Twinkle Temp.

That single ad ran more than three years and not only generated large volume for us but propelled the Magic Stat people to become one of the major thermostat contenders nationwide.

Another example of the slippery slide theory is in my ad for a company I started that sold bargains, called Consumers Hero.

Picture yourself scanning through a magazine and coming across the following copy:

> **Headline:** HOT
>
> **Subheadline:** A new consumer concept lets you buy stolen merchandise if you're willing to take a risk.
>
> **Highlighted Copy Block:** Impossible-to-trace Guarantee—We guarantee that our stolen products will look like brand-new merchandise without any trace of previous brand identification or ownership.

Well, if you're like most readers, you had to start reading the copy. How could you help but read it?

> **Copy:** We developed an exciting new consumer marketing concept. It's called "stealing." That's right, stealing!
>
> Now if that sounds bad, look at the facts. Consumers are being robbed. Inflation is stealing our purchasing power. Our dollars are shrinking in value. The poor average consumer is plundered, robbed and stepped on.
>
> So the poor consumer tries to strike back. First, he forms consumer groups. He lobbies in Washington. He fights price increases. He looks for value.
>
> So we developed our new concept around value. Our idea was to steal from the rich companies and give to the poor consumer, save our environment and maybe, if we're lucky, make a buck.

I then went into the concept, which was our plan to take defective merchandise, repair it and then make it available to the consumers through a club that cost $5 to join. Newsletters were sent to members offering the products. One of the paragraphs near the end of the ad summed it up beautifully:

> So that's our concept. We recycle "lousy rotten" garbage into super new products with five-year warranties. We steal from the rich manufacturers and give to the poor consumer. We work hard and make a glorious profit.

The Magic Stat and Consumers Hero ad examples are but two of the many I've written through the years that illustrate the slippery slide theory. Once you start reading the headline, which forces you eventually down to the first sentence, you are in my slide. And then I take you all the way to the bottom of that slide so before you know it you've read the entire ad. You've been in my store; you entered and didn't get out until you fully examined the merchandise I offered you. I took you into my private room and gave you a demonstration of my product in an environment that was so compelling, you couldn't help but buy. And I did it with integrity and honesty while getting you to nod your head as I sold you.

That's what the slippery slide is all about: getting your reader to read all of the copy. So a major axiom of mine is simply:

*Your readers should be so compelled to read your copy that they cannot stop reading until they read all of it as if sliding down a slippery slide.*

**Axiom 6**

As we explained earlier, one of the most important elements in creating the slippery slide is the start of your ad copy. I often will start my copy with a story or even pick up a piece of news from a magazine that I feel would be of interest to my readers. The story is often offbeat, always interesting and a great short story.

A good example of this technique is the story about a trusted accountant who was caught embezzling money from his company. Here's the copy I wrote based on that article and the very unusual connection I made to the product I was selling:

**Headline:** Last Wish

**Subheadline:** He was a prisoner confined to a cell block. "Give him one last wish," pleaded his wife.

**Copy:** George Johnson is in a state penitentiary for a white-collar crime. His seven-year sentence gives him plenty of time to exercise.

Johnson, 36 years old, always took care of himself. He exercised regularly, ate good food and took vitamins. But he got greedy. As a company accountant he kept issuing bogus checks to "Cashin Electric Company" for electrical contracting work.

One day his boss noticed the large payments being made to the Cashin Electric Company and discovered that the outfit didn't exist. Johnson was actually typing out checks to "Cash," cashing them himself and then after the checks cleared the bank and were returned to his company, he carefully typed on the checks "in Electric Company" after the word "Cash." Since he was a trusted accountant, who would suspect?

### WIFE MORE SYMPATHETIC

His wife was more sympathetic than was the judge. She wanted to help her husband and suggested he pick an exercise product for his cell—something that was easy to store and could give him a complete workout. And the prison agreed. Johnson chose a Precor precision rower. Here's why.

I then described the Precor rower and how beneficial it was for your entire body, how it stored easily out of the way and why George selected the product for his primary exercise device.

Later in the ad I admitted the liberty I had taken with the story out of frustration. The copy ended with the following:

Before I tell you which rower Johnson selected, I have a confession to make. I love the Precor line of rowers so much that I probably committed a crime too. The story about Cashin Electric Company is true. Some trusted accountant was sent to prison. But his name wasn't Johnson and his wife never called JS&A to order a thing, let alone a rower.

But one night, while I was trying my hardest to figure out a new way to share my enthusiasm for the Precor rowers, I started getting a little silly and concocted this dumb story about Johnson and his interest in the rower. Copywriting is not easy and sometimes you go a little bonkers.

I then finished the ad with a selection of rowers and my usual close. In this case the offbeat article about Cashin Electric Company had nothing to do with the product I was offering but it created a very strong beginning for my slippery slide.

The news item could have nothing to do with your product or it could tie in perfectly. For example, I was reading *Forbes* magazine, and in the "Informer" section there was an article entitled "Growth Market." The copy read as follows:

> It looks like U.S. underwear manufacturers have overlooked a potential growth market. According to a survey of 1,000 adult Brits conducted by London-based Survey Research Associates, one in ten British men wears the same underpants two or three days running. One in a hundred wears the same pair all week. Half the women polled said they kept wearing underwear after it went gray with age.

I would cut out articles just like this one and keep a collection of them. And then when appropriate, I would use one of them to begin an ad that somewhat related to the news item.

For example, I was in England appearing on QVC, the TV home shopping network. QVC has a branch office in England and I often appeared on TV selling my products there. While in the lounge waiting to go on the air, I met a man who showed me a new product he was presenting called Scrub Balls. They were simply nine golfball-sized spheres that you put in your washing machine with your laundry. They sloshed around scrubbing the clothes to bring out more dirt and make the clothes cleaner and whiter. They also saved on detergent and made your clothes cleaner while using less water. If I were marketing that product in print, I might pull out that *Forbes* article and start my ad with something like the following:

**Headline:** British Men Have Underwear Problem

**Subheadline:** New survey shows that many British men do not change their underwear for up to three days, and some even as long as a week.

**Copy:** Holy Odor Eaters! Has Britain got a problem. It seems that the men in Britain don't change their underwear often and the survey mentioned above shows that many men change their underwear just once a week. But there's an important question I'd like to ask you.

How often do you change yours? If you're like most Americans, you change it every day. And as an American, you probably use more detergent than most Britons. But there is one more surprise that you may not realize, either. Americans have a serious waste problem. Let me explain.

I would then go on to explain how we waste our resources by not efficiently washing our clothes and that there was this product I discovered in England called Scrub Balls and how efficiently it cleaned your clothes with less water and laundry detergent.

I could also use the same article to sell an electronic product simply by saying:

Now you probably wonder what dirty British underwear has to do with this new pocket-sized computer. I'm glad you asked. It has nothing to do with it except for one important fact that I will reveal shortly. But first let me explain an unimportant fact.

I would then go into the computer features, playing off British men, and I would use odor or smell to relate to some of the computer features. I would then come up with a computer feature at the end of the ad that would tie into the story.

## Save Those Articles

I realize that it may seem a little far-fetched to sell a rower tied into an embezzlement story or a computer using that *Forbes* article on British underwear habits. But the point I am making is simply this: The use of an interesting article or bit of information, when tied into your product or service, often makes for a good start to the slippery slide. And when blended nicely with your product, it can work to cause a reader to read every bit of your copy. So save those offbeat articles you come across that tweak your interest and might interest your readers—regardless of how ridiculous or offbeat they may be.

Some magazines create the slippery slide by simply starting out their stories with larger type to get you into the copy. Larger type is easier to read and so you tend to start reading the copy,

**Quest/80** *magazine started their feature story on the cover to hook the readers and get them interested.*

which may seem less imposing. *Quest/80* magazine (no longer around) started the copy of an article on the front cover and then continued it inside the magazine to get you into their slippery slide. Many articles written for magazines use similar graphic elements to get you into their stories. Of course, the key is to make the copy so compelling that once you start reading it, you can't put it down. And there are even more techniques to create the slippery slide that I will cover later in this book.

You're now in store for some fun. For in the next few chapters, I'm going to stretch your imagination and then continue to build the foundation we've been building in Section One of this book. So stay with me as we cover the timely topic of assumed constraints.

**H**ave you ever looked at a circus elephant anchored to the ground? If you have, you might notice that the elephant has a metal collar around its leg to which is attached a small chain. And the chain is attached to a wooden peg driven into the ground. Pretty good protection?

Pretty lousy, if you ask me. That 12,000-pound elephant could very easily pick up its foot and with one fell swoop yank the peg out of the ground and walk away. But the elephant doesn't. Why? I'll explain.

When that elephant was still a baby, that same collar and chain and peg were used to hold the elephant in place. The restraint was sufficient to hold the baby elephant in place even if it wanted to break away. And break away is indeed what the baby elephant tried to do.

So every day while the baby was chained up, it would pull at the chain and pull and pull until finally a cut appeared on its leg exposing the sore sensitive layers of deep skin tissue. It hurt to pull like that and soon the baby elephant, realizing the effort was both futile and painful, stopped trying to escape.

## Elephants Never Forget

As the baby elephant grew older, it never forgot that bad experience with the chain and the peg. And so whenever it was anchored down in a spot, it would think, "Hey, it's impossible to break away and besides, it hurts."

The adult elephant had what I call an "assumed constraint." And all of us have the same problem to one degree or another. We all have the power to be great copywriters. But at one point in our lives, we may have written something and gotten a bad grade in English. Or we may have attempted to communicate something in writing to somebody else and had a bad experience as a result. As we've grown older, those hurt feelings, the feelings of inadequacy and the wrong guidance we may have received from teachers or friends are still in our subconscious, and whether we want to admit it or not, they really do affect us.

If you understand the hurt and you understand some of the constraints we put upon ourselves, then you are better able to cope with breaking out of those assumed constraints and becoming anything you want to be and accomplishing anything you want to accomplish. Let me cite some examples.

One of the best is the following nine-point puzzle. I gave this puzzle to my students as an example of an assumed constraint. The rules to solve this puzzle are very simple. You must draw four straight lines and connect all the points without taking your pen off the page. In short, all the lines have to be connected. Please do the puzzle before reading on.

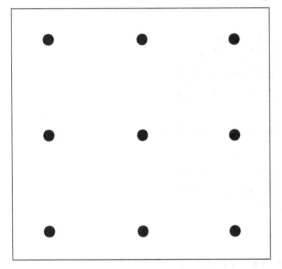

*See if you can connect the dots in this puzzle with four straight lines without taking your pen off the paper.*

Most people who try to solve the puzzle make one fatal error and it is simply that they don't realize the constraint they subconsciously put upon themselves. The solution is in Appendix A on page 317. Turn to it now for the answer.

As you can see, you were constrained by the box surrounding the points and did not go out of the box in order to find the solution. Often, to solve that very important problem, you've got to go out of the problem area itself to find the answer.

A good example of assumed constraints was my choice of mailing lists for my first direct mailing when I sold the first pocket calculator by mail. I had to select 10 mailing lists for my 50,000-piece mailing and I picked eight good lists that made a lot of sense to me.

I selected engineers, accountants and surveyors, for example. I selected wealthy people at their home addresses. I chose the mail order buyers from a certain catalog that sold similar products. But when it came to the last two lists, my list broker suggested the presidents of corporations with $20 million in sales or more.

I thought the idea really didn't make sense. I thought that the presidents of these companies would be so busy that more than likely they wouldn't even open their own mail and that some secretary would throw my mailing in the garbage. But I went along with the list broker and to my surprise, those lists he suggested turned out to be the best ones, while the others really pulled poorly.

I can point to hundreds of assumed constraint examples that I personally experienced. Here are five of them:

1. "You can't sell your airplane for over $190,000." I sold it for $240,000 in 10 days.
2. "You can't sell a $600 pinball game through the mail." We sold more than 3,000 of them.
3. "Consumers will rip you off if you let them buy using their credit cards over a toll-free line without having them sign anything." We launched toll-free order taking in the United States and were very successful with very few problems before everybody else caught on.
4. "This calculator isn't selling at all at retail. It's the biggest bomb in calculator history. How are you going to sell it via mail order?" We sold over 30,000 of them at $59.95.
5. "Who would buy sunglasses through the mail? People need to try them on first, and besides, people buy different styles." We sold more than 10 million pairs of the same style.

Or how about the following three business examples of other historical assumed constraints:

1. "There is no reason anyone would want a computer in their home." This was said by Ken Olsen, president, chairman and founder of Digital Equipment Corporation, in 1977.
2. "Computers in the future may weigh no more than 1.5 tons." This was quoted by *Popular Mechanics* magazine forecasting the relentless march of science in 1949.
3. "The concept is interesting and well-formed, but in order to earn better than a 'C,' the idea must be feasible." This was said by a Yale University management professor in response to Fred Smith's paper proposing reliable overnight delivery service. Smith then went on to found FedEx.

If you'd like to read more examples of assumed constraints, look in Appendix A, which lists other historical quotes.

## You Never Really Know

I can give you dozens of examples from history and from our company or from friends, but my point is simple. You never really know what will work or what won't. If you believe in your idea, do it. Step out of those assumed constraints.

This concept also applies to coming up with marketing solutions. When thinking about a problem or looking for a solution, don't rule anything out. Sometimes that big idea will come to you if you step out of the traps that we very often fall into. Remember Edward de Bono's concept of lateral thinking, which is somewhat the opposite of assumed constraints. Step away from the problem, think of some possible situations that have nothing to do with the problem and guess what? You'll be amazed at how often you find a solution.

As you proceed in this book, remember the baby elephant and the nine-point puzzle and break out of those assumed constraints.

**Axiom 7**    *When trying to solve problems, don't assume constraints that aren't really there.*

**W**e have already learned that *traffic* is a key word to any retailer. A shopping center that increases traffic will generally see an increase in sales for its stores. And since the traffic generated by these stores can only be compared to getting a prospect into your copy, you increase traffic by increasing readership.

One way to increase readership is by applying a theory I call "seeds of curiosity." It goes like this. At the end of a paragraph, I will often put a very short sentence that offers some reason for the reader to read the next paragraph. I use sentences such as:

> But there's more.
> So read on.
> But I didn't stop there.
> Let me explain.
> Now here comes the good part.

These seeds of curiosity cause you to subconsciously continue reading even though you might be at a point in the copy where the copy slows down. This concept is used a lot on TV before the show host goes to a commercial. She may say, "When we come back, we'll see something that you've never seen on TV before. Stay tuned." Well, it should be done in print, too. And here's why. (Notice how I just used it.)

In print, the ideal situation is to create such interesting and compelling copy that you don't need the seeds of curiosity, but often that is very difficult. And using these seeds of curiosity enhances most copy. But like every good thing, don't overdo it. Later in this book I will be showing examples of seeds of curiosity at work in many of my ads. Use them; they are very effective. But there's another example.

Seeds of curiosity can be used at the beginning of an ad where you mention some benefit or payoff that you are going to reveal somewhere in your copy. In short, the reader has to read the entire ad to find it. A good example of this technique was in our Consumers Hero ad mentioned in Chapter 8 and reproduced in Chapter 34. In that ad, you had to read the entire copy before you got to the punch line.

A great example of both seeds of curiosity and traffic is what happened to me at my office. It's something that I've quite frankly never experienced again but it is very relevant to this subject.

## A Very Unusual Call

I received a call one day from a very sensuous-sounding young woman who called herself Ginger. She started the conversation with: "Mr. Sugarman, I love you."

I was a little taken aback and at first thought that this was a practical joke. "Thank you," I responded. "I love you, too."

"No, I'm serious," continued the woman. "I've been reading your advertisements for the past five years and I love your mind, I love your thought process and I love your creative personality. I really believe that I can tell a great deal about you from what you write and I really believe in you and truly love you."

I was surprised and then flattered. Even before I received her call, I had gotten comments from people who claimed that my personality really came through in my copy. And I believed it.

If you are dishonest, it is sensed by the reader. If you are hiding something about a product you are describing, it comes through. If you're very creative, it, too, is picked up. And it is the combination of all of these impressions that creates the buying environment that we referred to in Chapter 6.

If you study the copy of others, you can sense what they are like from their copy. You'll be amazed at how the copy reflects the personality of the person writing it. Any copywriter working for a CEO of a company will try to reflect the personality of the CEO and not him- or herself. Since I'm the guy who writes all the copy, you can pretty well tell a lot about my personality. But back to Ginger.

## An Invitation I Couldn't Refuse

Was Ginger just flattering me or did she have an emotional attachment to me personally without having met me—strictly from reading my copy? She continued.

"Mr. Sugarman, you are the only one who could help me. I

need your help. Please, may I have an appointment to see you, privately? I promise you that you'll be very glad to see me."

When she arrived at my office I could see what she meant when she said that I'd be glad to see her. She was a beautiful blonde with long legs and a miniskirt so short I was embarrassed to have her sit down. "Mr. Sugarman, may I call you Joe?"

"Sure," I replied, looking away as she adjusted her skirt.

"Joe, I want to be very frank with you. I have admired your copywriting for years. I'm not even into electronics and gadgets but I enjoy so much what you do in print that quite frankly I have a real emotional attachment to you. I know this sounds silly but when I got in trouble, I couldn't think of anybody else who could help me but you. I really need you."

She paused for a moment as if to hold back tears. She then continued.

"I run a beauty shop in a shopping center. I know that when the shopping center is full, I get a percentage of that traffic and they buy my cosmetics. I also know that when the shopping center is empty, I get a smaller number of people who come to my store. It's almost directly proportional to the traffic in the shopping center.

"So Joe, when I decided to offer my cosmetics in a direct mailing, I thought that if I sent out 50,000 mailing pieces, I would get a certain percentage of response and I would make a profit. All I needed was half a percent return rate to make a nice profit.

"I then invested all the money I had to get this 50,000-piece mailing out. I borrowed from my friends. When I launched the mailing, the results were so bad I couldn't believe it. I ended up with one-tenth of what I needed to break even. I need you to look over my mailing piece and just tell me what went wrong with it. And Joe, if you could help me get it to work, I'd be extremely grateful."

## What Was Her Angle?

Was I being propositioned in return for my help? Was this all a ploy or a guilt trip to get me to write her next mailing piece? I was a happily married man with two children and quite busy running my own business. And quite frankly, I didn't like the idea of somebody trying to use guilt or sex or anything else to entice me to write copy or do a mailing piece. Still somewhat reserved, I said, "Show me the mailing piece."

Ginger reached for her purse, which was on the floor, and as she reached, she exposed even more of her legs. I was convinced she was in my office to seduce me. No question about it now. I was convinced that she was determined to entice me into writing copy for her. But I wondered how far she would go. I was soon to find out.

She pulled out her mailing piece and handed it to me. I examined it for a few minutes, read the copy and studied the entire package. I also asked her which mailing list she used. "From the entire local area served by the beauty shop," she said.

I looked at the mailing again and saw many problems. She was using a mail-in offer yet her mailing list was not oriented toward mail order buyers—just the retail community—so it was no wonder her mailing didn't work. Even the copy in the letter was very poorly written. It was a horrible presentation. It wasn't that it looked bad, but it violated many of the principles I discuss in this book and some that apply to direct mail. I told her the presentation was not very good and that I wasn't surprised that the piece did so badly.

You already know the principles on traffic. You already know from previous examples that unless the recipients read all of her copy, the mailing most likely won't work. Of course, she also used the wrong mailing list and that didn't help, either.

## I Explained the Problems

After I explained to Ginger the problems with her mailing piece and mailing list, I brought out another very important fact about direct response advertising. "You can't spend that kind of money without testing. That's one of your problems, too. You just mailed to too big a list. You could have picked just 5,000 names and not 50,000 names for your mailing. And then you would have known if the mailing was successful without risking too much money."

I finished talking and there was a short pause. As she looked straight into my eyes, she said, "Can you help me? I mean really help me? Like write the copy for the mailing piece, help me pick the proper list and guide me as my mentor?"

Since I was a little turned off by Ginger's use of sex and guilt to get me to do her piece, I responded, "Ginger, I really don't have the time. Plus, I have established a seminar in the north woods of Wisconsin where I take 20 people and teach them as a group. I just don't have the time to help you on an individual basis."

## A Shock I Never Expected

What Ginger whispered to me next took me totally by surprise. In fact, there have been very few times in my life when I have been at a complete loss for words. But wait. This is a book on copywriting and not about the secret goings-on behind the doors of successful direct marketing executives who are perceived by beautiful cosmetic executives as the answer to their dreams. "Aw shucks," you're probably saying. "Why doesn't he finish the damn story and tell us what happened?"

Okay, I will. But not here. I want you to continue uninterrupted with my thought process on copywriting, so I have devoted Appendix B on page 319 to the rest of the story—an episode that actually took place in my office and that could be part of a very steamy novel.

Once you understand the concept of traffic in retailing and how it relates to direct marketing, then you should realize how important the slippery slide concept is in getting the reader to read the entire text of your ad. And one of the most powerful techniques to keep your slippery slide greased is the use of seeds of curiosity. Your readers must get into your copy. They must read your headline and be so compelled to read further that they read your subheadline. Then they must be so moved that they read your first sentence. And the rest of the copy must be so compelling that by the time your prospects read 50 percent of your ad, they are helplessly caught in a slippery slide and can't escape.

Once you understand the slippery slide and the seeds of curiosity, you will have two of the most powerful copywriting tools you can use.

---

*Keep the copy interesting and the reader interested through the power of curiosity.*

**Axiom 8**

Up to now we have covered some general principles of copywriting. You learned that all the elements of an advertisement are designed to get prospects to read the first sentence, and we showed you how to get them to start reading your copy by creating a very simple first sentence. And then we told you how important it is to get the second sentence read and the third and so forth. We mentioned nothing about benefits or features of a product because the sole purpose of the copy was to first get people to read the copy. The benefits come later.

And then we covered the environment you create at the beginning of your copy. We explained the importance of resonating with your reader by getting the reader to say yes, believe you or agree with your assumptions.

We expressed the importance of the reader slipping through your copy as if on a slippery slide—reading the copy so they can traffic your ad—and we gave the example of Ginger and her failed mailing. And we just showed you how seeds of curiosity work to keep the slippery slide fully greased.

## You've Learned Most of My Concept

Armed with the above principles, you have a major portion of the overall philosophy of my copywriting concept. There are only a few more points to learn to have the complete foundation upon which you can build your skills and write great copy.

I can still remember the first seminar when I taught these same philosophies. At the end of the course, a Texas farmer named Frank Schultz, inspired by the seminar, shut himself in a room at the nearby Holiday Inn motel and wrote his first ad for the grapefruit he wanted to sell nationally in a print campaign in major magazines.

His very first space ad was so powerful that it sold more fruit than he could pick and ship. He received letters from other prominent copywriters congratulating him on his simple yet beautiful ad. We'll study that ad in Chapter 24, but if knowledge of the principles I teach can make a Texas farmer a great copywriter, it can do the same for you.

## Emotion in Advertising

This chapter is about emotion in advertising. And there are just three points to remember about the subject.

> **Emotion Principle 1: Every word has an emotion associated with it and tells a story.**

> **Emotion Principle 2: Every good ad is an emotional outpouring of words, feelings and impressions.**

> **Emotion Principle 3: You sell on emotion, but you justify a purchase with logic.**

Let's take the last point first. Why do you think people buy the Mercedes-Benz automobile in the United States? Is it because of the rack and pinion steering or the antilock braking system or the safety features? Other cars have the same features, so why spend a fortune to buy one when, for a fraction of the cost of a Mercedes, you can get an American or Japanese car or even a Volvo that has many of the exact same features?

The answer: We buy on emotion and justify with logic. I know that when I first bought a Mercedes and my friends saw it, I told them that the reason I bought it was because of a series of technical features that I found very impressive. The real reason I bought the car was not for the technical features at all. I wanted to own a prestigious car and belong to the crowd that drove a Mercedes. But when I had to explain the reason for my purchase, I ended up using logic—something that I really believed was correct when I used it.

## Mercedes Advertising

Look at a Mercedes ad. Since the Mercedes advertising agency knows the real motivation behind the purchase of their cars, they focus on the reasons people use to justify their purchase. All their ads talk about the terrific drive you get or the technical features that make the car a breed apart. In reality, feature by feature, there is nothing so revolutionary that it can't be duplicated in a less expensive car. The car is sold by virtue of its emotional appeal and then justified in its advertising by an appeal to logic.

Look at the emotion of a message conveyed in the form of a song. The music is like the vibration or that special harmony that you work at creating in an advertising message. If the music appeals to the audience and their soul, they are really set up to receive the sales message—or in the case of a song, the words, which incidentally also have an attached emotion. A song is similar to an advertisement.

Take a song and say the words without the music and it may sound rather funny. Steve Allen back in the 1950s on *The Tonight Show* would recite the words of a number one hit song and get lots of laughs reciting, "Ooh pappa doo pappa doo pappa woo. I love you. Ooh pappa doo da ditty." Without the music, the words sounded absolutely ridiculous.

## Logic Often Doesn't Work

In writing copy for an advertisement, often you get your reader in an emotional frame of mind as a result of the environment you have created, and logic becomes less important. For example, I've always used the phrase near the end of my ads, "If you aren't absolutely satisfied, return your product within 30 days *for a prompt and courteous refund.*" Who ever heard of a refund being courteous? It doesn't matter. The emotion or the feel of that phrase really says that we are a very respectful and understanding company that will return your money very promptly. With very few words, I conveyed the feeling of being a concerned company that acts promptly. And even though the phrase makes no logical sense, it has been picked up by several direct marketers and used in their catalogs and print ads.

Often, a phrase or sentence or even a premise does not have to be correct logically. As long as it conveys the message emotionally, it not only does the job, but does it more effectively than the logical message.

A good example of this was an ad I wrote for a device that had a breakthrough digital calculator display. The new display showed both alphabetical and numeric characters. And because it had such a large memory, you could use it to hold the phone numbers of your friends along with their names.

At the time I had two competitors who got hold of the product first and came out with advertisements—both of which failed. There were several reasons they failed, but one of the main reasons was the way they pitched the product—on a logical level. They tried to explain what the term *alphanumeric* meant in a display and how much memory the unit had. The ad was filled with facts and logic, and because it was such a new breakthrough product you would think it would sell just based on logic. It didn't.

On a lark, I decided to sell a similar product myself in my catalog. Canon Corporation had approached me and told me that if I took their product, they would give me an exclusive for several months as long as I advertised it nationally.

I first tested the ad in my catalog and came up with the headline "Pocket Yellow Pages" with the subheadline being "Let your fingers do the data entry with America's first computerized pocket telephone directory." Now listen to the emotional version of the copy.

> You're stuck. You're at a phone booth trying to find a phone number, and people are waiting. You feel the pressure.
>
> To the startled eyes of those around you, you pull out your calculator, press a few buttons, and presto—the phone number appears on the display of your calculator. A dream? Absolutely not.

## The Emotional Approach

The ad was a terrific success. We eventually placed the ad in dozens of magazines and while the other competitors dropped out, we succeeded handsomely. But look at the emotional approach I used. There is nothing about the product's technical advantages, nothing about the powerful memory of the unit. I just knew the nature of the product and the person buying this product. Each product has an inherent nature, and understanding that inherent nature will help you sell it. (I explained this partially when I talked about the Midex burglar alarm and the insurance salesman in Chapter 2, "Specific Knowledge," and will explain it in more detail later.) I realized that the product would appeal to the gadget-motivated person who would want to show it off to his or her friends. The ad copy reflects this specific knowledge.

Later on in the ad I justified the purchase with the facts and the technology but not too deeply. The real motivation for people to buy this product was the emotional appeal of the sales message.

I was invited once to speak at New York University to a class on direct marketing. As I addressed all the students on copywriting, I told them that if I was handed a product, showed it to the class and told the class to write an ad on the product, I would venture to say that everyone in the class would write a better ad than I would. I said, "Your grammar would be correct, your spelling would be perfect and mine would be just horrible."

## What Comes after the First Draft Is What Counts

But it is what I do after that first draft that makes my copy successful compared to the rest of the class. I then went on to explain the editing process and its importance. But the reason, I explained, for my ad appearing so poorly written in my first draft is because it is simply an emotional outpouring of my thoughts on the product and how I feel it should be sold. It is a free release of my emotions.

And as you write copy, keep this in mind. It makes absolutely no difference what your first draft looks like. If you can get all your feelings and emotions about the subject out on paper and work from there, you will have mastered a very important technique.

The final point on the emotion of copy relates to words themselves. If you realize that each word has an emotion attached to it—almost like a short story unto itself—then you will also have a very good understanding of what emotion means in the copywriting process.

Look at a dictionary not as a collection of words but as a collection of short stories. Webster once was quoted as saying that if you took every one of his possessions away and left him with just his words, he'd get all his possessions back. The power of words is enormous.

## Words Have Strong Emotions Attached

What emotions do you feel when I mention the following words: Cleveland, rip-off, consumer, farmer, lawyer, Soviet? Cleveland may have evoked a little laughter as a place you might not consider moving to unless you live in Cleveland, and if you do live there, please accept my apologies. Cleveland is a very nice city. But every country has a famous city that everybody makes fun of. The Russian comedian Yakov Smirnoff once said that in Russia they also have one city that the Russian comedians make fun of. He says it too is Cleveland.

And then what do words like *consumer* and *rip-off* make you feel? The word *farmer* may not only remind you of what a farmer does for a living but also bring to mind words like *honesty, integrity, earthy, hardworking*. Think of all the feelings the word *farmer* conjures up, not only from your experience but from what you feel emotionally. The word *Soviet* sounds more sinister to me than *Russian*. What thoughts come to mind with the word *lawyer*?

When you analyze these words and see how you can use them to create a message that has emotional impact, then you have mastered an important lesson in writing copy.

Here's some copy I wrote that points out the emotional differences in copy. Which sounds better?

> **Example 1:** The old woman in the motel.
> **Example 2:** The little old lady in the cottage.

I was writing an ad on some rubbing oil I had discovered in Hawaii and describing how I had discovered it. Example 1 was in my first draft but example 2 sounded much better.

I'm not suggesting that you materially change the facts of a situation to suit an emotional feeling. In this case, the motel office was in a small cottage, and the word *cottage* gave the copy a better emotional feel. What do you think? Do you "feel" the difference?

Sometimes changing a single word will increase response in an ad. John Caples, the legendary direct marketer, changed the word *repair* to the word *fix* and saw a 20 percent increase in response.

Don't feel that you have to have a total command of the emotional impact of words to be a great copywriter. It takes testing and common sense more than anything else. And knowing the emotional feel of words is like your general knowledge—it comes with time. It is enough for now that you realize the importance of the emotional values in every word. As time goes on, you will feel this influence play a bigger and bigger role in your successful copywriting.

Let's discuss one of the most important and basic copywriting principles I teach. In fact, if you can understand and learn this single point, you will have mastered a major lesson in writing good advertising copy.

*Never sell a product or service. Always sell a concept.*    **Axiom 9**

What do I mean by "concept"? There are many words that mean the same thing. One day, for example, the hot buzzword in advertising might be *positioning*. A product is positioned or placed in such a way as to appeal to the consumer.

Other terms commonly used are *Big Idea*, or *USP* (unique selling proposition), maybe even *gimmick*. Whatever it's called, it means basically the same thing. You sell the sizzle and not the steak—the concept and not the product.

The only exception to this rule is when the product is so unique or new that the product itself becomes the concept. Take the digital watch for example. When the watches first came out, I could hardly keep them in stock. When I first announced them, my main thrust was to explain the various features, which were all new, and then just take orders.

But as the digital watches became plentiful and everybody understood what they did and how they worked, each ad had to differentiate the features of the watch through a unique concept. For example, the world's thinnest digital watch or one with a built-in alarm or one with the most expensive band, or the one with the finest quality, or even one that required a laser beam in its manufacturing process—all were different concepts. Concepts started selling watches; the product was no longer the concept.

Another example is the Pocket CB. It had its concept right there in the headline. There were walkie-talkies and there were mobile CB units, but we had the first Pocket CB. And it was the name itself that expressed the concept.

Or take the example of the Pocket Yellow Pages I referred to in the previous chapter. Doesn't that name express everything you really need to know about the product in a simple concept? In that ad I didn't sell the product, but rather the concept of standing in a phone booth and pulling out an electronic directory to the surprise and delight of those around you.

Another example was a smoke detector I was selling. Instead of selling it as a smoke detector, the headline screamed, "Nose"—a product that just sat on your ceiling and sniffed the air. It sold quite well.

## Combining Products into Concepts

Sometimes the concept naturally comes from the product and other times the concept can be created. I remember once running several products in my catalog without much copy and discovering two that sold quite well. Rather than run them as separate products in full-page ads, I decided to run them together in one full-page ad as a concept.

The two products were a miniature travel alarm and a chess computer. But rather than develop a concept for each, I wrote the headline "Winners" and told how both products were the top-selling products in our recent catalog. The headline put both products under a single concept and made them both winners while drawing attention to our catalog.

Sales continued briskly with the chess computer in 1978 when I received a call from the company in Hong Kong from whom we were importing the product. "Joe," said my friend Peter Auge, the man in Hong Kong supplying me with the computer, "I think I can get Anatoli Karpov, the Soviet chess champion, to endorse our chess computer. I'm friends with him through a contact in Russia and it might make the chess computer sell better."

Indeed it would, I thought, but let's come up with a concept using Karpov—not as a person who will endorse the product but as somebody whom we can challenge to play our unit. And indeed, that's what we did. Our first major ad with Karpov's name appeared with the headline "Soviet Challenge."

> **Subheadline:** Can an American chess computer beat the Soviet chess champion? A confrontation between American space-age technology and a Soviet psychological weapon.
>
> **Copy:** The Soviet Union regards chess as a psychological weapon, not just a game. It is a symbol of Communism's cultural struggle with the West.
>
> So when Russian Anatoli Karpov competed against the Russian defector Victor Korchnoi, he had the entire Soviet Union's resources at his disposal, including a hypnotist and neuropsychologist.
>
> Karpov won. And with it the world's undisputed chess championship. Karpov, however, has never confronted American space-age technology and in particular JS&A's new chess computer.

Of course the copy continued to talk about the challenge we were making against Karpov. That was the concept. We weren't selling chess computers. We were selling the challenge against the Russian champion and as a consequence selling chess computers. It was taking a very staid product and giving the entire promotion a more emotional appeal.

Then the ad went on to explain how the unit worked, its features and ended with the challenge to Karpov.

The ad had some pretty effective copy. And I've reproduced it in Appendix E at the end of the book. Read it. It's a lot of fun.

## Soviet Intrigue

I was sitting in my office as the ad was breaking throughout the United States when I received an urgent telegram from overseas. Opening it up, I saw right away it was from Karpov. "I am going to sue you for using me in your advertising without permission." Signed: Anatoli Karpov.

I was told that I had permission to use his name by my friend Peter, who said, in fact, that he would be sending me the endorsement contract and that I should go ahead and run the ad. So I did, thinking all was okay.

What to do? Simple. I could just see my next headline: "Soviet Union Sues JS&A" or maybe "Little JS&A Attacked by Soviets." What a great concept. But before I could sit down and write it, my friend Peter called and advised me that he had gotten a copy of the telegram, too, and that everything had been worked out with Karpov's agent and there was nothing to worry about. Karpov would endorse the chess computer and I could continue my ad campaign.

I then sat down and wrote the third ad in the series, entitled "Karpov Accepts," which talked about the challenge made to Karpov and how he then decided that for whatever reason, he didn't want to play the chess computer as part of the challenge. Instead he could just endorse it and hope that many Americans would learn to improve their chess game on it.

## Concept Selling Does Well

All three ads did very well and more than 20,000 chess computers were sold. And all three had different concepts associated with them. Meanwhile, my competition was out there in force trying to sell their chess computers but not succeeding because they were selling chess computers and not Soviet Challenges and Karpov Accepts—concept advertising.

If your advertising just sells the product, be careful. You need a concept. If you've come up with a unique concept, fantastic. You'll do much better.

## Price Can Also Affect Concept

Sometimes simply changing the price of a product can dramatically alter its concept. For example, when we were offering our Pocket CB at $39.95 it came across as a serious electronic product similar to a full-sized CB radio. When we dropped the price to $29.95 it became more of a sophisticated walkie-talkie. And finally when we dropped the price to $19.95, the product was perceived as a toy—all this despite the fact that the copy in the ad was pretty much the same.

Finding the concept is often not easy. It takes all the skills of a conceptual thinker to come up with the right idea and the right position. One of my favorite advertisements that really captured the essence of this chapter was an ad I once read from the Leo Burnett ad agency. It was a full-page ad that appeared in *Advertising Age* magazine and is reproduced on the next page.

---

> # Tcudorp
>
> The first job of an ad agency is to look at your product in every imaginable way: frontwards, backwards, sideways, upside down, inside out. Because somewhere, right there in the product itself, lies the drama that will sell it to people who want it.
>
> There may be 10,000 ways to bring that inherent drama to the stage. And given a world in which "me-too" products multiply like mayflies, the drama may seem that much harder to find.
>
> It is.
>
> But every good product has it.
>
> And every good agency finds it.
>
> (Please note: The "t" in tcudorp is silent.)

It's so true. Every product has that unique selling proposition that makes it stand out from the rest. And it is indeed up to you, the copywriter, to realize this fact and discover each product's uniqueness. If you do, the simple positioning of a product and the developing of a concept can be so powerful that it can make the difference between a huge success and a loser.

In the next chapter, you'll discover how to come up with that great idea as we study the incubation process.

It's fine to read about the real secrets of copywriting, but let's get serious. One of these days you're going to have to implement what you've learned and start writing copy. What are some of the mental steps required to write copy in general and how do you go about writing effective copy?

Let's establish a few things that you have learned already in this book and then take everything a step further. As you recall, I referred to general knowledge—the knowledge you have picked up simply by living—and specific knowledge—the knowledge you acquired while studying the specific product you want to write copy about.

Assume you are now an expert on a particular product and you are ready to start writing. The first thing I would do is go over all the material you have on your subject and give a great deal of thought to what you have just read and studied. Do plenty of thinking about what you want to write. You may jot down some headlines and some of the copy points you would like to bring out. You might list those points that best describe the nature of the product you are selling and you might like to list some of the strong reasons that your product would appeal to your customers. Put all your thoughts down on paper. But keep in mind, you have not yet started to write the copy. This is just preparation.

I'M SORRY, MR. SUGARMAN CANNOT BE DISTURBED - HE'S INCUBATING RIGHT NOW.

*Take a break from your work and do something pleasurable while your brain incubates.*

Or don't put a thing on paper and just think through everything you know about the challenge you have to solve through copy.

You might even visualize the end result of your work. Maybe it's imagining that a stack of mail has arrived showing what a great response you received. Maybe it's your boss coming up to you and patting you on the back for a job well done.

Once you've done all that, do something that may seem strange to you at first. Stop.

That's right, stop. Do something else. Forget about the project. Do something pleasurable—a stroll in the park, a walk down the street or lunch with a good friend. Whatever you do, let it be a total diversion from what you are currently working on, and please don't even think of the copy project.

Whether you realize it or not, you are actually working on the ad constantly even though you've put it out of your mind. Your subconscious mind is actually processing everything you've learned—all of that data that you have accumulated in general and all of the information in particular. And your mind is then taking all of that data and running it through everything you know about copywriting and communications, mentally preparing the first version of your ad copy.

It is taking this information and working through the millions of permutations possible to come up with the best solution to your marketing problem. And you're doing absolutely nothing about it. You're just out having a good time while your brain is working like crazy. And ironically, if you start thinking about your project again, you interrupt this process and the results won't be as good. This entire subconscious activity is called the incubation process, and the time you are giving to it is called the incubation period.

Your subconscious is processing millions of bits of data like a computer in your brain running a very important program in the background. Then, while you're taking a walk or standing in a shower or even daydreaming, suddenly that big idea will flash across your mind. Eureka! Then go to your desk and start writing down some of that good stuff your subconscious mind has created and organized for you.

### Your Mind Is Always Working

Sure, you might think you can eliminate the incubation period. You never do. Even when the pressure of deadlines prevents me from taking the luxury of time to incubate, I'm still incubating but at a much more rapid speed. The results may not be as good, however. The time pressure only increases the incubation process and speeds up the assimilation of data in your brain. If you have the luxury, your copywriting and what you produce will improve if you balance the pressure of deadlines with time away from the project. This could also mean working on one project, then going to another and subsequently coming back to the first one. This is another way of allowing you the luxury of having your subconscious mind work on a project while you do something else.

The incubation process actually works best with pressure of some kind. If you have no pressure, your brain will not work as fast or as efficiently. So it is a balance of various pressures that produces the optimum results.

What causes pressure? We already know that time causes pressure but there are other factors as well. Ego for example. If you have a big ego, it creates a certain amount of pressure. This pressure can be very positive in the incubation process. For example, your boss expects you to produce some knockout copy and your ego won't let you disappoint her. You've added to the incubation pressure. Your creative orientation plays a role, too. For example, if you are naturally creative, you have a big advantage over someone who is not. And finally, the environment plays a role. If you are in a creative environment that encourages those incubation activities required in the creative process, it will help the incubation process along.

## Just Allow It to Happen

Now don't show this chapter to your boss and say, "See, Joe Sugarman tells me to take a pleasurable walk in the park on company time and enjoy myself while my brain incubates." That's nonsense and not the purpose of this chapter. In this chapter, I just want you to realize that there is a constant process going on in the background of your brain. And with the proper balance, you can create blockbuster copy by allowing the incubation process to function.

The biggest mistake a manager can make in a mail order company is to have the creative department in the same building as any other department in the company. Imagine the operations people walking in to see the creative people incubating—staring into space or taking a long break with one of their peers. "Those privileged bastards in creative really get away with murder" would be a typical comment. But the creative department needs that atmosphere in order to function to its optimum.

If management imposed the same rules on the creative department as on the rest of the staff who have to function on a conscious level during their jobs, the end result would be a sure drop in good creative work. It's important to keep the creative staff separate from the rest of a company because the copywriter needs a little more freedom to incubate and create.

When it comes time to sit down and knock out that copy, discipline comes into play. You've got to let that copy come pouring out of your brain, forgetting about spelling and grammar. Remember, your mind takes the data you've accumulated and runs it through everything you know about copywriting, communications and life in general. Well, hold back the stuff on spelling and grammar just long enough to let the copy flow out freely.

## Left Brain versus Right Brain

If you're knowledgeable about writing and creative thinking, you know that there has been much said about the different hemispheres of our brains controlling different types of thinking. The right brain does the intuitive or emotional thinking and the left brain does the logical. Which side of the brain should write the copy? The right brain of course. Let the copy flow out of that right brain and let it pour out unencumbered by any left-brain restraints.

The pouring out of that copy or idea is the culmination of the incubation process. It is the end result of all the mental activity that has been running in the background. And so, the axiom that I suggest you remember is:

**Axiom 10**    *The incubation process is the power of your subconscious mind to use all your knowledge and experiences to solve a specific problem, and its efficiency is dictated by time, creative orientation, environment and ego.*

If you've gone through the incubation process and then put your thoughts on paper, you've accomplished half the challenge of writing good copy. (Next comes the fun part—the editing process. We'll have to wait for that process in later chapters of this book.) Now that you are mentally prepared to tackle the copywriting process, it's time to decide how much copy you should actually write.

**I**ncubate, slippery slide, seeds of curiosity—all may be neat concepts, but often at my seminars the question would come up: Do people read all the copy in your ads? Students of direct marketing learn that there is no such thing as copy that is too long. And there is some truth to this.

The key is simply this: Copy is never too long if the reader takes the action you request. Therefore, it can't be dull, it must be compelling, it must relate to the reader and, finally, it's got to be about something the reader is interested in.

What we're talking about here is the slippery slide concept. The copy must be so compelling that it will be read from the beginning to the end. Everything else is secondary. If you don't write compelling copy, you'll never get the reader to read the part of the copy that sells your product.

Will people read long copy? Let me answer the question in a different way by having you go through a little experiment. On the following lines I want you to fill in the blanks for an article as I direct you.

**Headline:** _____ (Your Last Name) Family Chosen as Heirs of Multimillion-Dollar Fortune
**Subheadline:** Family who lives on _____ (Your Street) in _____ (Your City) was willed millions of dollars by an anonymous person.

If you saw that headline and subheadline in your local newspaper, would you read the first sentence? Of course you would. Let's say the copy read as follows:

Wow, what a score! How would you like to inherit millions of dollars from somebody you don't even know?

Well, that's what happened to _____ (Your Full Name), who has yet to be found but who might have fallen into one of the greatest fortunes ever received from somebody who remains unknown.

Of course you would read the entire 3,000-word article. After all, the article is talking about you. You are involved, you relate to what is being written in a very intense way and it's both informative and interesting, to you in particular.

And that's my point about long copy. If the copy does all the things I've just described, the reader will be intensely interested in it and will read it all—maybe not with the intensity of somebody who just won millions of dollars, but with an intensity that could come very close if your copy is effective.

## Intense Interest

I'm writing this book on a Macintosh computer. A short time ago while I was mastering my word processing program and had an intense interest in this computer, I would read anything on the Macintosh. And I would read an entire article or advertisement if it was on the subject I was interested in. Later, after I mastered what I had to learn, the information was not as interesting to me and I did not seek it out with the same intensity.

BE WITH YOU IN A MINUTE, HONEY, I'M ALMOST FINISHED READING THIS JS&A AD IN MY MAGAZINE.

*If the copy is interesting, the reader will read it all.*

This is also true about products. When digital watches first appeared, my customers were very intense about buying them. And they bought them in droves. They read every word of my copy. It was informative and helpful, it involved them and they read the ads with interest. When the market for digital watches deteriorated and the fad was over, my customers were not as intense about the product category and went on to other things. Therefore readership dropped.

Copy will be read if it is interesting to the reader. I can remember when I would visit the car showrooms in the 1950s looking at new cars with their huge tail fins and sleek new designs. Ads would talk about rack and pinion steering and I often wondered what that meant. All that the copy would do is go into the feel of driving the car, which is good emotional copy but didn't really tell me enough. And when something doesn't tell you enough, it will cause you to go to the showroom and ask questions, which is maybe what the car companies want you to do.

But often the salesmen didn't know much, either. Rack and pinion steering was foreign even to them.

I learned a lesson from those visits to car showrooms. You can't tell the prospect enough about a subject he or she is truly interested in. And so it is with copywriting. People will read with a high degree of intensity if you are talking about something they are genuinely or passionately interested in.

## Long Enough but Short Enough

Back in the days when copywriters were mostly men, there was an old adage about copy length: "Copy is like a woman's skirt. It should be long enough to cover the essentials but short enough to make it interesting."

Let's use the same example of the salesperson visiting a prospect that we used earlier in this book on page 35. But this time, the salesperson appears for the appointment and the prospect explains that he can't meet for 45 minutes because he is in the middle of a budget session. Could the salesperson make the presentation in 15 minutes? What would you do?

A good salesperson would make a new appointment. If the sales presentation takes an hour, then it should be an hour long—not more and not 15 minutes. And so it is with copy. Depending on how long your sales pitch is, the copy should cover the amount of time you need to create the selling environment, develop interest in the product, relate to the prospect's needs and make the sale.

The copy has to be long enough to tell the entire story or make the entire sales pitch—no longer and no shorter. Of course there are certain practical limits, but even these can be broken. When Gary Halbert, one of the great mail order copywriters, was looking for a girlfriend, he ran a full-page 3,000-word personal ad in a local Los Angeles newspaper. He was deluged with potential dates.

And when Richard DelGaudio wanted a personal assistant to help him run his fund-raising company, he ran a 4,000-word want ad that pulled in more qualified respondents than he was able to interview.

## The Long-Copy Approach

There really is no limit to how long copy should be if you get results. For example, if a good salesperson made his or her pitch in

10 minutes and sold a prospect on purchasing a $19.95 household gadget and another salesperson selling a million-dollar high-speed printing press took several months to consummate a sale, then who would be the better salesperson? There is, of course, no answer. Both could be great or both could be lousy. Why then should there be such controversy over copy length? If, as I hope you believe by now, selling in print is very similar to selling in person, then shouldn't the same rules apply?

So let's take a moment and look at two factors that increase the need for a lot of copy.

**Price Point:** The higher the price point, the more copy required to justify the price or create the need. This is a general rule unless the price point is perceived to be a tremendous value (then less copy may be required) or the lower price point appears to lack credibility (then more copy is required). More copy will allow you to increase the value of a product and add many more dollars to your retail price. In short, by educating the consumer you can demand more money for your product.

**Unusual Item:** The more unusual the product, the more you need to relate that product to the user and the more you've got to focus on creating the buying environment and explaining the product's new features. At retail, generally, this type of item will not sell. Mail order is the perfect method to use when you have the right amount of copy.

In conclusion, there are two basic reasons for using the long-copy approach. The first is to allow you to create an environment that will place your prospect in the proper buying mood, and the second is to give you the time necessary to tell the full story of your product.

## Short Copy Works, Too

Robert Scott of Scottcade Ltd., an English mail order company, came to my seminar and told me that his approach broke all of my rules. His catalog copy was very short, yet he still sold a lot of merchandise.

But his catalog really appeared to follow my rules. First, he created his environment through photography. The products were placed in elegant settings using fine photography. Second, his prices were very low compared to those of other companies or retailers. Since he was offering his products at such low prices and since his environment was so effective in placing the customer in a buying mood, a lot of what normally would have been done in copy was being done visually and through the price points of his products. Then too, his medium was a catalog, and in catalogs long copy is often not required. The catalog creates the environment, thus saving you the time of creating it with copy.

I am not trying to sell you on using long copy. I use short copy at times and sometimes very short copy indeed. But the short copy I use is usually all that is required and the price points are low enough that the short copy does the job. In fact, I am not for long or short. I'm for causing the prospect to exchange his or her hard-earned money for your product or service, and quite frankly, copy length has always been just one of several considerations in producing an advertisement.

So the axiom to remember from this chapter is simply:

---

*Copy should be long enough to cause the reader to take the action you request.*

**Axiom 11**

---

Do people read all that copy? Some do. And there are enough of them who do to have earned me and several other copywriters a nice living.

If you have read the chapters of this book in sequence, you are building a good foundation to understand and learn copywriting.

This chapter builds upon the knowledge that took me several years of copywriting to really understand and learn. Learning it wasn't difficult, but understanding why it was so important took a little longer.

One of the things that ads should do is harmonize with the reader or viewer. Advertising is the ultimate form of communication in that its purpose is to cause an action to be taken by consumers—usually to exchange their hard-earned money for a product or service. But for some reason, many advertisers are missing an important key in this form of communication— namely, it should be personal.

As a good example of personal communications, let's first cover direct mail. In direct mail, personal communication is easy to understand. After all, you are writing a letter to a single individual.

*Every advertisement should be a personal message from the advertiser to the prospect.*

But in creating the letter that goes with a mailing, too many copywriters write their letters as if they were hiding behind a podium, speaking through a microphone and addressing a large audience. For example:

> We at ABC Company wish to invite all of you to visit our exhibit again at the upcoming trade show. Our staff will be there to meet you and demonstrate our new and novel button machine.

The personal way of saying it might be:

> Hi. You might remember me from the last trade show. Well, I'd like to invite you to the next one where I will be looking forward to meeting you again to demonstrate our new and novel button machine.

You see the difference? The second version is more personal and direct. It is me talking to you—not me talking to a large crowd. It is as if I, as an individual, were writing that letter to another individual.

Now, in direct mail this makes sense. Why not make your letters more personal and direct—more like one person talking to another in a direct and eyeball-to-eyeball sort of folksy way? Of course, folksy might not be the best way in certain circumstances. That's okay. As long as you use words like *I*, *you* and *me*, you create the feel of a personal form of communication.

## Emotional Process in Communication

Remember I said earlier that copywriting is an emotional outpouring of an idea onto paper. And I said that copywriting is very much an emotional process. Look at the following two letters from the same company and see how much more emotional one sounds than the other.

> Dear Customer: We here at Consolidated International would like to thank you for your recent order. We realize that you could have given your business to many of the other companies in our industry, but the fact that you chose Consolidated International is really appreciated by our entire staff. Thank you very much. Sincerely, Mr. John Smith.

Now compare it to the following:

> Dear Mr. Jones: I just wanted to thank you personally for your recent order, which I've just received. I took your order and even showed it to the president of our company. I realize that you had a number of other choices, but I really appreciate the fact that you chose my company. Sincerely, John Lee.

Both letters would have served the same purpose. But the second letter was warmer, more personal and you felt that Mr. Lee was talking to you directly. Indeed, he was happy to get your order—so happy that he went to his president and showed it to him. It was a genuine expression of thanks and a direct message—all with genuine emotion.

On the other hand, the letter from Mr. Smith could have been a form letter that the company sends to all its customers, thereby losing the personal feeling that Mr. Lee's letter had. It lacked the warmth and personal touch. The difference should be obvious. Read both letters again, and this time feel the difference. Put yourself in the place of Mr. Jones and imagine how he would have felt if he had received both letters.

## Letters Should Be Personal

Good examples of a personal letter were the letters I used to send out to a membership program in my Consumers Hero club. They may have been totally off the wall, but they served my purposes well.

The membership program was created in response to our advertisement for our discount club in which we refurbished new but defective products and then sold them, at discount prices, through a club we established.

Part of the club program was our regular monthly bulletin. It listed all the buys for that month, and along with it came a very folksy letter talking about the club.

The image I conveyed was not that of a very large, impersonal corporation filling the needs of its membership but that of a bunch of hardworking people, of all ethnic backgrounds, working together in harmony to make the company a success.

The company had to be portrayed as being small. That was essential for the concept. After all, that was part of the image—a little consumer-oriented company fighting the big U.S. corporations and the effects of inflation.

And one of the techniques we used to keep the image of a small company was to use old envelopes from companies that had gone out of business. We simply explained that the envelopes were no longer good and it was our way of saving money as well as the environment and passing the savings on to the consumer.

So in one month, members might get an envelope from Ski Lift International, a defunct company, and the next month they might get a letter from CMT Machine Tool Company, another defunct company, but the contents of the envelope were always from Consumers Hero.

As membership cards, we sent out Batman credit cards. (There is a whole story on that card, but that's for some other book I plan to write.) And one of the qualities we tried to convey was absolute total honesty. We were so honest that the reader would actually be embarrassed for us. The typical letter is on the following page.

Three JS&A Plaza, Northbrook, Ill. 60062  (312) 564-9000

Dear Member:

Enclosed are the latest bulletins on our Consumers Hero program.

Two new companies now join our group. The first is Panasonic and the second is McGraw Edison--both highly respected and well established companies.

We want to thank many of you for the very nice letters we receive about our efforts. We appreciate receiving those very much.

The other day, we received the following letter from a Mr. R. F. in Glastonburg, Ct. It read, "I am thoroughly disenchanted in your Consumers Hero gimmick. I sent in $5 in the hope that your offer would be worthwhile. To date I have received only one bulletin which offered rebuilt items for more than I would pay at most discount stores. If any item was less it was just plain junk. You did not live up to your promises. Therefore I am returning your silly Batman card and please return my $5."

I'm truly sorry that Mr. R. F. feels this way about our company. We are growing and we will be offering many more products from many more different companies but in the meantime we must work very hard to attract all these new offers that are finally starting to come our way. Please bear with us as we are trying our best. We try to insist that these manufacturers keep their prices as low as possible and we will continue to put pressure on them to make sure the bargains are truly great bargains. We think most of them are and although we disagree with Mr. R. F. we respect his opinion.

We are pleased to announce the addition of Dennis Delaney who joins our staff to assist us in stuffing envelopes. Dennis is a student at our local high school and is on the football team and has worked on the school paper. His hobbies are skin diving, waterskiing and photography.

It's rather difficult keeping our staff together. Betty Jane Williams has decided to move to Los Angeles with her boyfriend. She will be missed as she always added a bit of sunshine whenever she showed up for work.

In the next mailing we hope to add a few more bulletins from some new companies so thank you all very much for your patience and understanding. We even appreciate Mr. R. F.'s letter even if his letter was not very complimentary. We promise to continue to do our best.

Sincerely,

CONSUMERS HERO

*Your Heros*

Your Heros

Your Heros:

| | | | |
|---|---|---|---|
| Cindy Donner | John Handmeister | Dennis Merrins | Burt Mertz |
| Allan Milnik | Doug Ramis | Toni Venturini | Dorothy Vinkowski |
| Dennis Delaney | | | |

*The very down-to-earth and personal letter sent to Consumers Hero members.*

Even though the letters were from the staff as opposed to an individual, they still conveyed a personal feel to the reader. And weren't they fun to read? We often got comments that the letters alone were worth the price of the membership.

In print ads, the need to be personal becomes less apparent. After all, you are talking to the masses, aren't you? But the fact remains that you are indeed talking to a single individual—that person reading your ad. And he or she is listening to a single individual—the person who wrote the ad. So it is essential that you write your copy as if you are writing to that single individual. Your copy should be very personal. From me to you. Period.

## Use of a Byline

An effective way to do this in print is to use a byline. Use your name or the name of somebody in your organization such as the president—like the news organizations do in a magazine or newspaper article. This allows you to use words like *I* and *me* and *we* and *you*. Let's look at the example of the ad I first ran for BluBlocker sunglasses that launched a multimillion-dollar company.

> **Headline:** Vision Breakthrough
>
> **Subheadline:** When I put on the pair of glasses what I saw I could not believe. Nor will you.
>
> **Byline:** By Joseph Sugarman
>
> **Copy:** I am about to tell you a true story. If you believe me, you will be well rewarded. If you don't believe me, I will make it worth your while to change your mind. Let me explain.

Read that personal copy. It's as if I were talking to that person directly. I used the words *I* and *you* and *me*—all very personal words used in a one-to-one conversation. Let's examine the first paragraph of copy from a few other ads that were written in this personal tone.

> This may surprise you. In fact, if my hunches are correct simply reading this article may change your idea of aging for the rest of your life. Here's why.

Or how about the following:

> If I were to buy a ticket in the Illinois State Lottery, my chances of winning would be a million to one. But if I were to bet that you, as a reader of this publication, have high blood pressure and don't even know it, my chances of being correct would be eight to one.

The above paragraphs show how very personal you can get in copy and still convey a very powerful thought or develop the environment and slippery slide you need to cause your reader to continue reading and then respond.

When I started writing, I kept a low profile and never used my name in any advertising communications. But as I became more proficient and saw the effect a personal message could create in direct mail, I started using my byline in print on a regular basis. In my catalog, I could speak in the first person about all the products because on the first page of the catalog I introduced myself in a letter to my customers.

## Even Magazines Have Personalities

I remember reading a story about the image conveyed by the magazine itself. *Forbes* magazine has a strong personality. Steve Forbes now runs the publication and his editorials appear in every issue. A reader feels more personally involved with the publication. In contrast, *BusinessWeek* appears more like a corporate publication even though it has many bylines. A business-woman once commented that she could put her arms around *Forbes* and hug the magazine but would only feel comfortable shaking *BusinessWeek*'s hand. So it is with copywriting.

You want to create a very personal image so that people will emotionally respond to you, feel close and feel very comfortable parting with their hard-earned money and buying your product or service.

| | |
|---|---|
| **Axiom 12** | *Every communication should be a personal one, from the writer to the recipient, regardless of the medium used.* |

So as you start to write copy to reach and motivate an individual, think in terms of writing in the first person with a personal message.

You are now ready to write that first ad. Everything you've read has prepared you for this moment, and everything that you are going to learn later in this book will only polish what you already know. True, you're also going to get a whole bunch of new insights, too. But right now you're ready for the big plunge. In the next chapter, we discuss writing your first ad using my techniques and thought processes.

You are now really ready to write that first successful ad. You already know how important it is to know your subject. You already know the purpose of all the elements in an advertisement—to get the prospect to read the first sentence. And you know all the axioms to get the reader to read beyond the first sentence and all the way to your last word.

Copy must also flow. And its flow must make sense. It must be in an understandable order where each thought flows logically to the next.

Many people have told me that when a question comes into their minds as they read my ads, I answer it in the next sentence. They often claim that it's almost uncanny. But that's the skill that makes the good direct response copywriter the envy of any one-on-one salesperson.

## Leading the Reader

Since we copywriters do not have the benefit of having the prospect in front of us to ask the questions, we must craft our ads in such a manner that they literally lead our prospect (by the flow of the copy) to ask the question we want to answer. Sounds hard, doesn't it? It really isn't.

Start by writing the headline. Will it grab the reader? Then write the subheadline. Will it compel the reader to read further? Then write the caption to go under an imaginary picture. Is all this strong enough to get people to read the first sentence? And then write the first sentence.

Once you start using my thought process, you'll find a discipline and a direction that you might not have experienced in writing copy before.

You might even write a paragraph in the copy to stand out in boldface type similar to the Consumers Hero ad that reads:

**IMPOSSIBLE-TO-TRACE GUARANTEE**

**We guarantee that our stolen products will look like brand new merchandise without any trace of previous brand identification or ownership.**

At my seminar, I would call on various students and ask them to read their headlines. The class would then critique each headline to determine if it would get us all to read the subheadline. It was a good process with 20 students from all walks of life coming up with some of the most creative approaches on a variety of subjects.

One day, my eight-year-old daughter April was sitting in one of the chairs in the class. She was taking notes, listening intently and, in short, acting exactly like one of the students. I would always allow my children free access to the entire seminar process and they had never been a nuisance. In fact, the students liked this family touch.

## April Becomes a Real Nuisance

After I had assigned an ad-writing exercise and asked for volunteers to read their ads, April started waving her hand wildly. I called on a man from New Zealand—Archie Mason—who was in the wool business. Later, when I asked for another volunteer, April once again waved her hand wildly but I called on another student—Fred Simon, president of Omaha Steaks. Finally, April came up to me in front of the class and whispered, "Dad, let me read my ad. It's a good one. It follows your principles."

I was annoyed. "Later, April. Can't you see I'm trying to teach the class?"

Finally, at break time, April came up to me and handed me her ad. I read it. It indeed was a good example of anticipating what a consumer would ask and then answering it. It was very simple—after all, an eight-year-old had written it—but it contained a question-and-answer format that was very logical and covered a topic of interest that her eight-year-old peers would enjoy reading. Her product was a guinea pig. The ad read:

**Headline:** The Best Pet
**Subheadline:** Do you want a pet that doesn't shed?
**Copy:** Think about it. You can get a pet that doesn't shed, doesn't run around the house, and is easy to take care of.

You have probably guessed it's a rabbit, bird, fish or a turtle. Well, you're wrong. It's a guinea pig.

You probably want to know how do you take care of the guinea pig? Where should I keep it? What does it eat?

It's all simple. If you don't have a guinea pig cage, then get a box high enough so it won't get out and large enough so it can run around.

Feed it guinea pig pellets and feed it a couple fresh greens. Put plastic at the bottom and newspaper on top then at least an inch high of shavings. Put a bowl in for food and a water bottle for water.

That's all you need to know. To order, call [phone number] and order today.

April's ad made an important point, which I have reminded each class of since. Good copy can be written at any age and by anybody. Simply understanding the principles and applying them to something you intuitively know is all it takes.

## Logical Progression of Flowchart

In class I would ask my students to write a headline and a sub-headline. I would then ask for the first sentence, then the next sentence and then the next until each student had composed a complete ad.

The ads had to flow on paper and then, once they were on paper, the editing process was of paramount importance. One of the tips I gave during this process was to create a block diagram of a logical way the copy should flow and the questions that might logically be asked.

In order to develop a sense for this, you break your ad into small abbreviated copy blocks similar to those in a corporate flowchart. But this flowchart goes in one direction only—down.

I made a block diagram of the ad I did for an electronic pin-ball game from Bally manufacturing. I showed that at the start of the ad, I wanted to get my reader into the copy and then I wanted to set the environment for the product. So, I started the ad with the fun times that this product represented. The ad started like this:

It's you against a computer. And the action and excitement from Fireball, your own computerized pinball machine, is nothing short of spectacular.

Fireball's computer replaces many of the mechanical, scoring, conventional electronics and sensing devices of a standard pinball machine. It's a dramatic change in pinball devices and the start of a new consumer electronics revolution.

With the first paragraph I create *interest and excitement* for this product. With the second paragraph I start to weave the *drama* of the product and the differences between Fireball and conventional pinball games.

Then I go into the next block of copy and explain why and how the game is *different, how to play it* and some of the *unique features* made possible by the computerized electronics.

Logically, a reader who had read this far would want to know a little more about how the game was constructed, the quality of the product and the many new features. Therefore, the next block of copy has this information.

Okay, you are really interested in purchasing this game. But you say to yourself, "How can I justify it? I'd love to get this Fireball game. Emotionally I'm hooked, but how can I justify purchasing it?"

So the next block should *justify the purchase.* I used cost comparisons with what you pay for a TV set, pool table or your stereo system. I plant the seed about its practicality when guests pop in and how Fireball will be the hit of any party or family gathering. It's here that I'm giving the prospects the logic they need to make that emotional purchase. I even suggest that a business might purchase one as a way to entertain employees at work and claim it as an investment tax credit and depreciation expense—all tax-saving measures. I knew I had to provide all the logic possible for this $650 purchase.

By now the customer is saying to himself, "Okay, I want to get the unit and I can justify the purchase, but what if I use it, get tired of it and it sits in the corner like that exercise device that's gathering dust?"

So I go into the fact that it has *lasting play value.* And I describe several reasons why people won't get tired of it.

The customer is now thinking to himself, "Hmm. I like the product, I can justify it and I can see that it will have lasting play

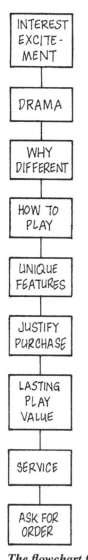

INTEREST EXCITE-MENT

DRAMA

WHY DIFFERENT

HOW TO PLAY

UNIQUE FEATURES

JUSTIFY PURCHASE

LASTING PLAY VALUE

SERVICE

ASK FOR ORDER

*The flowchart for copy sequence goes in one direction— down.*

value, but what if I buy this big pinball game and suddenly the computer poops out?" I then raise the *service* question in the ad copy and answer it. The point of each of these blocks of copy is that they are logically placed as if to anticipate the next question a prospect is going to ask—all in an environment that you have created and all flowing logically to the last part of the ad when you *ask for the order.*

## Flowing in a Logical Sequence

When you work with copy long enough, the flow is automatic. You don't need to do flowcharts, as you can instinctively sense the next question and answer it. And that is the special skill that a good direct response copywriter has over a one-on-one salesperson. We sense the questions, answer them—and we do it on a mass scale.

You still might find it helpful to create a block diagram of your ad after you've written it to see if it flows properly and raises the right question at the right time. How do you want to sequence your questions in your copy? What kind of environment do you want to weave through the early part of the text? What are some of the questions you would surely be asked about the product if you were a salesperson and you were selling the product face-to-face?

It's really all common sense. Looking at your copy as it flows out onto a computer screen or onto a piece of paper is the mechanical part of this process but not the important part. It's the common sense you use to anticipate the sequence of what will be asked next and how your copy should flow that really counts at this stage of the copywriting process. This brings up my next axiom.

*The ideas presented in your copy should flow in a logical fashion, anticipating your prospect's questions and answering them as if the questions were asked face-to-face.*

**Axiom 13**

By now you understand the basic concepts of good direct-marketing copywriting. You understand the importance of becoming an expert on the product you are going to write about. You know that the more you learn about a product or service, the greater the chances you'll come up with that unique copy angle or product position or big idea.

But there are some other tips I can give you that will help generate that concept you want to develop. First, state the problem. It might be as simple as "I want to sell this pinball game." Then, once you have stated the problem, restate it in a different way: "I would like to introduce my prospect to the unique aspects of this pinball game." Then restate it again: "I want to make the pinball machine easy to buy and seem like fun."

It's that last restatement that makes the pinball game seem to come alive and is closer to the copy approach I've actually used. During problem restatements (and you could list dozens of them), all the knowledge that you've gained about the product seems to come together to give a new perspective.

## Prepare That Big Idea

Once you've restated your problem and you have the statement that you like best, sit down and list your big ideas or concepts. List several concepts. Then pick the one or two that make the most sense.

Visualize your concept and see how it might be incorporated into the ad. Think again about your problem restatement and whether your concept seems to be consistent with it. Then stop. It's time to incubate.

After you've slept on it for a while, start writing. First write your headline—an attention-getting blockbuster of a headline short enough to grab the reader's attention. Then write the subheadline—so compelling and curiosity-building that your prospect must read the first sentence. And finally, write the first sentence of the copy—short, to the point and strong enough to carry you into the next sentence—and then it's down the slippery slide.

Block-diagram your ad. What do the first few paragraphs do for the ad? What is the emotional appeal? Are you anticipating those questions and answering them to the satisfaction of your prospect? Are you frank and honest in those answers?

## Try Patterning Your Ad

Another approach is called "patterning." Simply pick an ad written by somebody you admire and whose product or service is similar to yours and use their ad as a pattern or style from which to write. If they use a long headline, make your headline long. If they use a lot of captions, then you create a number of captions. Capture the feel of the ad, but be careful. Do not copy the person's layout too closely so that people reading the ad might think at first glance it was from the company you were copying. This exercise is only to give you a format or guide from which to write. If you copy the layout too closely, you are violating the rights of the person who wrote the ad.

The main points in this chapter are the basic steps and the thought processes you go through as you construct your ad. The key point is that you don't have the prospect in front of you, so you have to anticipate the questions the prospect will ask in almost the same order the prospect will ask them.

This flow is important. But there is also a critical part of the copywriting process that really separates the best copywriters from the rest. It's called the editing process and we cover it in the next chapter.

This chapter holds one of the most valuable secrets to effective and persuasive copy, for it is in the editing process that you turn that raw emotional outpouring of thoughts and ideas into a polished, harmonious, resonant tuning fork that will vibrate perfectly with your prospect.

It's like the story of a diamond. When a diamond is found it looks like a piece of coal or carbon. Take that black, ugly stone and polish it and it soon becomes the world's most beautiful gemstone.

Remember that lecture I referred to earlier in Chapter 11 that I gave at New York University? I mentioned to the students that if everybody in the class completed a writing assignment, my first draft would probably be the worst in the class. Poor grammar, atrocious spelling and disjointed sentence structure might be the way an English teacher would describe it.

But it is what I do after that first draft that makes the difference. It's the difference between just plain copy and a polished advertising message—from copy that doesn't move prospects to copy that moves prospects so strongly that they reach into their collective pockets and exchange their hard-earned money for your product or service. It's the difference between earning a salary as a copywriter and earning millions of dollars as an effective copywriter/entrepreneur.

## The Secret to Editing

Is there a secret to editing? Once again, it is a mental process that almost parallels that of the copywriting act itself. It requires lots of practice, although you will find it easier to do than writing the copy itself. In fact, it is a lot more fun. Look at the act of writing the first draft as giving birth. It may be a painful, long process or it can go quite quickly with little pain. Then compare the editing process to raising the child—the caring and nurturing required to ensure a healthy, happy child.

You wouldn't want your child to go out into the world in funny clothes, unable to communicate or relate with others, would you? You therefore have to mold and nurture that child as you prepare to present him or her to the rest of the world.

Editing is a nurturing process. And just as there is no perfect way to nurture your child, there are many different approaches to editing copy that are certainly acceptable. I strive for one result when I edit, and this can be summed up in the following axiom:

**Axiom 14**     *In the editing process, you refine your copy to express exactly what you want to express with the fewest words.*

Now this sounds rather simple, doesn't it? But it is the true essence of the editing process. You want to maintain the same emotional feel, the same thought process, the same vibration that you had in mind when you wrote the copy. It's just that you want to do it in the fewest words.

This may mean that you rearrange the words you wrote to make the thought more direct. Or it may mean cutting out words that have little contribution to the overall feel of the ad. It may mean substituting new words that express your thoughts better. And it may even mean adding words to clarify a thought. But the goal in writing ad copy is to express the thoughts you want to convey in the most powerful way but with the fewest words.

I remember the feeling I had writing my book *Success Forces* in 1980. Since it was a book format and I was not under the same constraints as when I wrote my advertising copy, it was an easy process. In fact, it is a lot easier writing anything other than direct response advertising copy. You have the freedom to use as many words as you wish to express a thought or feeling. And you have no space restrictions.

## Copy Has Space Restrictions

But with advertising copy you do have space restrictions. Your copy has a very focused purpose—to motivate your prospects to exchange their hard-earned money for your product or service. And everything you do or write must lead to this one goal.

Let me give you one example from an ad that I wrote. We'll look at my first draft of the initial two paragraphs, which contained 66 words, and then the final draft, which contained 43 words. We'll then study the two versions and certain lessons will emerge. The ad was for a bathroom scale, and here's the first draft:

Losing weight is not easy. Ask anyone.

And, if you've tried it, you know that part of a good weight reduction program is your bathroom scale. A bathroom scale is like a report card. It's a feedback mechanism that tells you how well you've done. In fact, one of the few pleasures of losing weight is stepping on your bathroom scale and seeing the positive results.

Now let's take the same ad and condense it to reduce the word count while still maintaining the same meaning and emotional feel.

Losing weight is not easy. Ask anyone.

One of the few pleasures of losing weight is stepping on your bathroom scale and seeing positive results. Your bathroom scale is like a report card—a feedback mechanism that tells you how well you've done.

In the second paragraph there is a reduction from 59 words to 36. With nearly 40 percent fewer words, the meaning and emotional appeal of the second version is exactly the same as the first or even better.

Apply this percentage to a full-page ad with 1,000 words and you can see the difference the editing process can make. In fact, at this point, let's look at the advantages.

## Advantages of Fewer Words

With less copy, your ad will look less imposing to the prospect and he or she will be more likely to read it. The second advantage is that you are making the slippery slide even more slippery by making it shorter. Your prospect will get to the bottom of the slide much faster, yet still get the full impact of your sales message.

The preceding example was given to my seminar class and they spent about 20 minutes coming up with their own edited versions of the ad. Many of them were excellent and some were even shorter than my version. Of course, the copy was taken out of context; they didn't have the rest of the ad and couldn't see far enough into the ad to see what my environment, goal and emotional appeal for the product were, so this might not be the perfect example. But it brought out many of the principles of good editing. The following are five of the principles they learned:

## Some Principles of Editing

1. **Look for any "that" words.** For example, in my first draft I used the words, "And, if you've tried it, you know that. . . ." The words up to and including "that" can very often be eliminated. In this example, I could eliminate eight words.

2. **Edit for rhythm.** Make sure that you vary the length of sentences so they don't sound monotonous. I discuss rhythm later in this book, in Chapter 18.

3. **Consider combining sentences.** Note that in the edited version, I combined the two sentences that read, "A bathroom scale is like a report card. It's a feedback mechanism that tells you how well you've done." I condensed it into "Your bathroom scale is like a report card—a feedback mechanism that tells you how well you've done." I saved only one word by doing this, but it made sense to combine the sentences and eliminating even one word is a good move.

4. **Eliminate unnecessary words.** Look at the word "the" in the phrase "and seeing the positive results." The word "the" can easily be eliminated without changing the meaning so that the final sentence will read, "and seeing positive results."

5. **Rearrange thoughts so they flow better.** Note that in the first draft, the flow of the copy pointed out that the scale was a report card and the second thought was that part of the pleasure of a weight loss program was stepping on a scale and seeing the positive results. By reversing these two thoughts, I made the ad more emotional by focusing on the pleasure of using a scale when losing weight and then I explained why. This sounds a lot better and more logical from a flow standpoint than the first draft.

## Take as Long as You Need

Sometimes editing is like raising and nurturing your child and you need to take a lot of time. You may end up doing 10 drafts before you get to the final draft. Other times it may flow right out of your mind with hardly a correction.

When Frank Schultz, the grapefruit marketer, attended my

seminar and wrote his famous grapefruit ad, it was so close to perfect that it didn't need much editing at all. When Joe Karbo, who wrote *The Lazy Man's Way to Riches,* attended my seminar, he told the class that after his ad was written, other than two words that needed correction, the ad was perfect. In contrast, other seminar participants who had a great deal of copywriting experience spent many hours editing their ads.

And the same holds true for me. I've written ad copy that flowed right out of my brain through my pen, or later my computer, and never had to be edited much. Most of the time, though, I would have to go through several drafts before I was satisfied. And then there is the experience factor. The more you write, the less editing you have to do. The easier the flow out of your brain, the better you are at expressing the emotional feel of copy and the excitement that each word represents.

*You want to remove the unnecessary words and still have the ad make sense.*

The novice copywriter will usually need the editing process to craft and polish an ad, whereas the experienced copywriter has many of the editing mechanisms programmed in his or her brain. The copy seems to flow out through a filter that comes only from experience.

However, the need for editing is sometimes unpredictable regardless of your experience. You could produce copy that needs plenty of editing or you could end up with excellent copy that never needs much at all.

## Read the Periodicals

I'm always amazed at the lack of editing I see in many of the periodicals I read. Phrases like "Finally, it is important to note that . . ." can be totally eliminated and not affect the flow or understanding of what follows. Another example: "Fortunately or unfortunately as the case may be . . ." is not really required to make the information that follows clearer. Many of the articles written in periodicals contain these unnecessary preliminaries that fill up space but mean very little. In writing effective copy you can't afford to be too wordy.

If you'd like a little practice, take a look at the examples that follow and edit them yourself, or read any periodical and edit the copy by seeing how many extraneous words can be eliminated. Or write a draft and practice this critical skill.

**Example 1:**

About the only redeeming feature of this product is that we don't have huge quantities to sell. The importer is afraid to order too many for fear that nobody in their right mind would buy it let alone sell it. So we only have a few hundred to sell as part of this test program.

**Example 2:**

I was sitting in an office in New York City talking to a very successful friend and businessman whom we'll call Stuart. I told Stuart that I had to make a very critical decision in my business. I needed some guidance and advice.

When I started writing a great deal of copy in the 1970s, I would use a legal pad and ballpoint pen and write my draft in longhand. I would then give it to my secretary, who would type it out for me in rough draft form, usually double-spaced.

I would then make my editing corrections and hand it back to my secretary for her to retype. And this process would continue for several drafts until it was in a final form for the typesetter.

## Computers Are a Great Help

When computers with word processing programs first came on the scene, I resisted using them. I was used to writing the copy in longhand and to switch to a computer and keyboard seemed difficult. But I made the transition sometime in the early 1980s on an Apple II computer and I haven't looked back since.

Writing copy on a computer makes the editing process very easy. Word processing allows you to pick words or entire sentences and drag them to another place in the copy. Sophisticated spell-checkers whiz through copy and correct your spelling even as you type. Thesauruses, grammar-checkers and all sorts of editing aids are built into every decent word processing program. Today, I never have to give a draft to a secretary. I type it in draft form first on the computer and then do all my editing, often before I even print my copy. The computer has done more for my copywriting and editing than any other single factor, and it is making a difference for copywriters everywhere.

Another technique that will help you in the editing process is time. If you can put aside your copy after you edit it and look at it the next day or even in a few days, you will often discover things that you never saw before. If time is critical, put the copy down for a short while and then get back to it. The key is to allow time for your subconscious mind to digest what you've done and pick out the areas that need work.

Many other rules for editing can be found in English textbooks and style books. There are also other books on writing that cover this subject very nicely. In fact, it was a book I read in college that really opened my mind to the importance of editing in the copywriting process.

Finally, after you think you have that perfect final draft—a draft so well edited that you can't possibly make one more correction—ask somebody who is a professional editor or an English major to correct the English and grammar that you missed. This does not mean that you have to accept all of the changes. Sure, you want to correct the spelling and the dangling modifiers and any other instances of terrible grammar that may negatively impress your prospects. But then simply weigh each one of the changes and if you feel that any interfere with the style of your writing and your original version does not violate grammar or spelling rules, then ignore them. The point is, don't be intimidated if you don't feel comfortable with somebody else's suggestions to change your writing.

## The Use of Commas

A good example is the use of commas. There are two schools of thought—one that uses a lot of commas and the other that does not. I do not believe in too many commas as they take up space. And as a copywriter you don't have much space to work with. So I use commas where the rules of grammar are clear that they are needed for clarification. I don't use commas in places where I am not violating any grammatical rules or where they are considered optional. For example, when three items are grouped together, such as "apples, oranges and tomatoes," I don't use a serial comma after "oranges."

I would have both my sister Judy, who is a high school teacher, and Mary Stanke, my associate at JS&A, proof all my copy. I didn't accept all their changes but I certainly paid a lot of attention to them.

It is important that you do make your copy as free from error as possible. If you don't, it reflects badly on the integrity of your offer. It raises doubts in the minds of your readers. They may think, "If this guy can't get his grammar straight, how do I know he runs his business right?"

A good example of how a prospect thinks is reflected in a letter I received from an irate reader of one of the airline magazines in which we ran the ad for our Consumers Hero club. We received the following:

> Dear Sir: Despite the intended conversational tone of the attached advertisement, no license within consumer-oriented ad writing permits the type of glaring poor grammar usage circled in paragraph five of your copy. "We better not" may occur in sloppy, colloquial speech, but it is not acceptable in writing. The phrase should read, "we'd better not," of course.
>
> I cannot believe that your ad agency would permit such poor proofing in an ad which finds its way into the hands of a sharp consumer such as the type which pays the kind of money required to purchase an airline ticket today, and thus is inflicted with this bad grammar in a captive audience magazine like the attached.

The above individual took the time to write us about a simple grammar error. How many others saw it and didn't respond? And whenever we do make a mistake, our readers do usually find it.

One editing error was actually quite funny. In copy describing a blood pressure unit, I wrote, "blood pressure can be very dangerous" instead of "high blood pressure can be very dangerous." Nobody picked it up. Sometimes I'm amazed at what the public misses and what they complain about, but the fact remains that in the editing process you really do want to be as thorough as possible.

What I have conveyed in this chapter is simply how important the editing process is, the value of editing in terms of the final copy, and some of the logic I use in the editing process.

Now you're ready for some interesting, subtle and sophisticated insights into copywriting. By now you understand the entire copywriting process, can write an ad and edit it. In Section Two, I give you some of the significant insights I've gained during years of experience.

# Section Two

Section Five

Now comes the fun part. In the following chapters you'll find not only insights and tips on how to write copy but also revelations of what has worked exceptionally well during my 30-year career as a copywriter.

This section contains only five chapters. But packed into these chapters is the heart of this book—the basis for the copy I write and many of my copywriting secrets. It's an education that cost me millions to learn and you're going to learn it for the simple price of this book.

In my seminar promotional outline, I listed several topics that would be presented, one of which was "The 64 Points Every Ad Should Cover." And very often, my seminar participants, in anticipation of coming to the seminar, would sit down and in advance list some points to see if they could guess what I taught in the course.

Typically, they knew maybe six or seven of the points. And typically, they were amazed at what they didn't know. You've already learned the first 10 of these points, the graphic elements of an ad, in Chapter 4. You're now about to discover the rest— 23 copy elements and 31 psychological triggers to buying. And from the other chapters in this section you will further build the base you need in order to write incredibly effective copy.

So study this section completely and continue to build your solid copywriting foundation.

Remember our discussion about graphic elements in Chapter 4? We explained that each of these elements was designed to get prospects to do only one thing—read the first sentence. And we explained how important the first sentence was in your copy.

And if we know that all those graphic elements are designed to get you to read the first sentence and eventually all of the copy, then the next thing we should address is the nature of the copy elements in an advertisement.

In this chapter, I will cover all the copy elements and their relationship to the advertisement—23 concepts that you should review for each ad you write.

**1. Typeface:** This element is really important. If you're a graphic designer, you know that each typeface has its own personality, emotion and legibility. And that's the point of this subject. You've got to determine the combination of personality and legibility that will make your ad easy to read and inviting. Since we are talking about copy here, we are talking about only one style of type, called "serif" type. Serif type has short protruding lines whereas the other style of type, called "sans serif," doesn't. The type used for the text of this book is serif type. Why? Because in legibility tests, serif type produced greater comprehension than sans serif type and by a 5 to 1 margin. I didn't discover this until well into my writing career, but now all my ads are printed in serif type. This was one test I wish I had known about earlier.

Another important factor is the legibility of all your typefaces in other parts of your ad such as the headline, subheadline and various headings. Fancy type might look elegant to the type designer, but if it can't be read it has no value. It's like talking to a foreigner and finding the words difficult to understand. The most important role a typeface has is to allow the greatest comprehension possible, and the second role, less important by far, is to convey the image of a company.

**2. First Sentence:** This we discussed in Chapter 4 as the purpose of all the graphic elements of an ad—to get the prospect to read that all-important first sentence. Keep your first sentence short, easy to read and compelling enough to cause the reader to read the next sentence.

**3. Second Sentence:** This sentence is almost as important as the first. You've got to maintain interest, so you must also create another sentence with a compelling reason to cause your reader to want to continue. You must continue this momentum throughout the first and second paragraphs. Put aside any facts, benefits or product features. Your only goal is to get the momentum going and create that buying environment.

**4. Paragraph Headings:** In Chapter 4, paragraph headings are mentioned as one of the graphic elements in a print ad. They are supposed to make the copy look less intimidating, and thus encourage the reader to read all the copy. But paragraph headings are also a copy element that needs to be addressed in this chapter as well.

Paragraph headings could introduce material in the paragraph that follows or they could have absolutely nothing to do with the copy underneath or the copy in the entire ad for that matter. Remember, they are designed to break up the copy and make it look less intimidating. They have little to do with selling or presenting your product. They simply make the copy look more inviting so your reader will start the reading process.

When a reader looks at copy that appears like one continuous paragraph, subconsciously it looks a lot more difficult to read than copy that is broken up into neat little chunks headed by various paragraph headings.

Use paragraph headings to break up copy in the middle of columns but not at the very end or beginning. Avoid placing paragraph headings right next to each other in two adjoining columns.

As I just mentioned, your paragraph headings could say anything. I once ran an ad for a radar speed indicator, and as a test I used the most outrageous paragraph headings you could think of. They included "Scrambled Eggs," "Working and Playing" and "Success and Good Things." Even though the headings had absolutely nothing to do with the ad copy, they drew absolutely no attention. Nobody ever asked me what the headings meant or commented that they were not consistent with the copy. But had I misspelled a word in the body of the ad, I would have heard plenty about it.

The primary purpose of paragraph headings is to get the reader to read the copy by making the copy look less intimidating.

A secondary purpose might be to arouse curiosity. Maybe my "Scrambled Eggs" paragraph heading did just that—created curiosity and caused somebody to start reading the copy to find out what scrambled eggs had to do with the product I was offering. Although I've never tested to see if this was the case, my experience with paragraph headings tells me that curiosity does play a minor role but the main purpose of these headings is to make the copy less intimidating.

**5. Product Explanation:** Sounds simple. Sounds basic. But you'll be amazed at how many ads leave out the simple step of explaining what the product does. A rule of thumb here is to explain a complicated product in a very simple way and explain a simple product in a very complex way.

For example, I once sold a smoke detector. At the time it was a very common household product whose function was clearly understood by the consumer. In short, the product was simple. In the ad I wrote for an expensive brand, I told a story about the inside workings of my smoke detector. I described the gold contacts (which every other smoke detector had) and even explained how the comparator circuit functioned to determine if there was smoke in the room. Even though this smoke detector cost $10 more than the average market price, it was a big success. The ad illustrates a way to present a simple product in a complicated way. You should sell a simple product that is clearly understood by the consumer in a more complicated way and a more complicated product in a very simple way.

When I first explained the computer to my customers, it was always a very simple explanation of what it could do for them. My ad was not about the technology inside (although some reference was made to the inside) but focused on the simplicity of the product and its use. At this time, consumers were just getting into computers. They were new, seemed complicated to use and indeed many were. By explaining computers in very simple and basic terms without getting too complicated, I was able to ease them into a purchase.

Later, as consumers understood more and the products became a commodity, explaining them in greater detail proved more effective.

In addition to the concept of simple versus complex, you should always check your copy to make sure you have explained all of the features. Ask yourself, "Did I explain the product sufficiently to my prospect?" You might ask a number of people to read your copy to see if they understand the product and its features. Look at the questions they raise and see if you've addressed them fully in your copy.

**6. New Features:** Highlight those features that make your product or service new, unique or novel. This might appear to be the same as the copy element "Product Explanation" that we've just discussed, but it is different. Here you are revealing not just the features of the product, but the features that distinguish it from anything else on the market.

**7. Technical Explanation:** Regardless of the product or service, each ad can be enhanced with a technical explanation. We all like to buy something from an expert—somebody we like, respect and trust. Buying is indeed a process of trust. The buyer's thought process might be, "I trust that you really know your subject and fully understand the product category and have described your product to me properly and will give me something of value that I want in return for my hard-earned money."

Trust is always enhanced when the seller has become an expert at what he or she is selling. Let's say the seller says, "I have studied everything I could on competitive products and know everything there is about the product I am selling, so I know that what I am offering you is the best product at the best value." You would naturally have a great deal of confidence that this seller's product is indeed good.

You might also be impressed if the seller, in describing the

I DON'T UNDERSTAND ANY OF THIS TECHNICAL STUFF .... BUT, HEY, IF THEY UNDERSTAND IT, THE PRODUCT MUST BE **SUPER!**

*A technical explanation will build confidence in the prospect.*

product, used words that you didn't understand. Why? Because it would appear that the seller really was an expert about the product. This is not deception. A seller must become an expert on the product in order to talk about it in technical language.

In a mail order ad, technical explanations can add a great deal of credibility, but before you write them, make sure you indeed become an expert. If not, the consumer will see right through the ploy.

A good example of this technique is expressed in the following caption I wrote for a picture of the integrated circuit in a watch:

> A pin points to the new decoder/driver integrated circuit which takes the input from the oscillator countdown integrated circuit and computes the time while driving the display. This single space-age device replaces thousands of solid-state circuits and provides the utmost reliability—all unique to Sensor.

Very few people would be able to understand the technical commentary. In fact, when I sent the ad to the manufacturer for approval, he called my attention to the caption under the picture and said, "What you wrote there is correct but who is going to understand it? Why did you even use it?"

Providing a technical explanation that the reader may not understand shows that we really did our research and if we say it's good, it must be good. It builds confidence in the buyer that he or she is indeed dealing with an expert. Incidentally, the watch was one of our best-selling products.

Another example of a technical explanation appeared in the outline of a seminar. Jimmy Calano of CareerTrack came up to me after I explained the reasons for a technical explanation and said, "Joe, do you realize that the outline of one of my seminars is, in fact, a technical explanation? By using technical terms that not too many people understand until they come to the seminar, they sense that we know what we are talking about."

Yet another example is an ad written by Frank Schultz after attending my seminar. His product was grapefruit and he was explaining how he graded them:

> Even after picking there are other careful inspections each fruit must pass before I'll accept it. I size the fruit. And I grade it for beauty. Sometimes the fruit will be wind scarred. I won't accept

it. Or sometimes it will have a bulge on the stem that we call "sheep nose." I won't accept it. You can see I really mean it when I say I accept only perfect Royal Ruby Reds.

In many of my ads, catalogs, direct mailings and infomercials I convey thorough knowledge not only of what I am selling but of the entire universe of products available. I convey the thought process I went through in picking the product I chose and why it is better than anything similar at a particular price point. And the consumer appreciates the effort I took, feels more confident in the purchase and consequently is motivated to reach into his or her pocket and exchange hard-earned money for my product or service.

**8. Anticipate Objections:** This is a very important element to consider when writing copy. If you feel that your prospect might raise some objection when you are describing a product, then raise the objection yourself. Remember, you're not in front of the consumer and you have to sense what the next question might be. If you sense that there might be an objection and you ignore it, it's like ignoring that consumer. You won't get away with it. The consumer is too sharp and will not buy.

A good example of anticipating objections is in that ad we saw earlier in Chapter 16 for that expensive electronic pinball game from Bally Manufacturing. The average consumer would raise the question about service. We resolved it in our ad.

Another example of raising an objection is in my ad offering a thermostat for the home. If you remember from Chapter 8, I looked at the product and saw that it was really ugly. It didn't have a good design at all. In fact, it would turn me off if I were a consumer. So I raised the objection at the very beginning of the ad, calling it the worst-looking product I'd ever seen. I later justified the product by calling attention to its spectacular features, but only after I had raised the design objection myself.

Often products that require installation concern consumers. It is then that you have to raise the question about installation yourself and not hide from the facts.

**9. Resolve Objections:** Just as you have to recognize objections, it is your opportunity and duty to resolve the objections, too. You must be honest and provide alternative solutions or dispel the objections completely. With the pinball game, we talked about the modular circuit boards that you simply snap out and exchange if service is required. More on this later in copy element 14, "Service." In 2006 Gillette introduced its new five-bladed vibrating Fusion razor, which uses a small AAA battery located in the handle of the razor. A consumer might be wondering, "How long will the battery last?" But Gillette's excellent approach was to both raise the question and answer it with the statement, "For best performance, change the battery every six months."

**10. Gender:** Who is the consumer? Male, female or both genders? Are they female golf players, lady pilots or professional women? Make sure there are no sexual or sexist comments that would offend any group, and know your target audience so that you can communicate in their terms.

I once ran an ad for gold chains in my catalog. It was in the form of a story about a salesman named Bob Ross who tried to convince me to sell gold chains. I resisted until he showed me a picture of his cousin who could model the chains in the ad. I quickly accepted the product after seeing a picture of Bob's cousin. The ad copy was considered by many to be one of my most creative approaches to selling a product. The chains had nothing to do with the core products we had been selling—electronic gadgets. However, I did get a few letters as a result. A woman in Egg Harbor City, New Jersey, wrote:

> Dear Sir: Your friend, Mr. Bob Ross, may regard himself as a successful salesman, but unfortunately he comes across in your ad as a consummate asshole.

The letter then went on to point out the achievements of women in many technical fields, the military, air traffic control, sports and leisure, racing and several other professions in which women now play a very active role. She finally concluded:

> Perhaps a long, hard look at the person or department responsible for the ad on page 37 is in order. Apparently he has to "come a long way, baby" to catch up to the Twentieth Century. Cordially wishing you immediate bankruptcy, I remain,

And with that she signed her name. It was a two-page single-spaced letter that included a copy of our mailing label.

Was I really insensitive to women? Did I demean them in my ad copy? I've reproduced the ad in Chapter 33 and it is called "Gold Space Chains." See if you agree.

It is also important that you recognize the differences between men and women in terms of what is important to them. Women are generally into color, fashion, family, home and relationships. Men are more likely into sports, military combat, machines, earning money and supporting their family. Sure, their roles overlap tremendously today. Women are assuming the roles that men once had exclusively and men are doing things today that years earlier would have been considered feminine. Being aware of the differences (and sometimes the lack of differences) is the most important point here. And this awareness can help you harmonize with your target audience by understanding how to communicate with them and knowing what might offend them.

**11. Clarity:** Your copy should be clear, simple, short and to the point. Avoid big words that confuse those who don't know them and which often establish the writer as a pompous snob—unless, of course, you're trying to appeal to pompous snobs. Keep it simple. The clearer the copy and the more concise, the easier it will be for people to read and get on the slippery slide and stay there. The only exception to this rule is when you give a technical explanation, as described earlier in copy element 7 in this chapter.

**12. Clichés:** Avoid the obvious ones: "Here's the product the world has been waiting for," or "It's too good to be true." If you feel inclined to use a cliché, don't. Clichés seem to be used when you have nothing really significant or good to say and must fill up space. How do you know if you are writing a cliché? If it sounds like you're writing typical advertising copy some agency may have written 20 years ago, that's one clue.

Have I used them? You bet. My first several ads were replete with them. Back when I wrote them, I didn't know any better.

For example, in my 1972 ad for a desktop calculator, I stated, "It's the breakthrough the world has been waiting for!" Bad, isn't it? I wrote it then but would never write anything as trite today. The lead sentence for the first pocket calculator I introduced in the United States in 1971 read, "It's the most exciting new breakthrough in electronics since the transistor radio!" Ironically, at the time it may have actually been more truth than cliché.

**13. Rhythm:** Just as a song has a rhythm, so does copy. Humor writers know this well. If you can write good humor, you've already got the rhythm thing down pat. In fact, the most difficult copy to write is humor. Why humor? Because you have to know how to build up to a punch line and then deliver it. You have to know how not to be too obvious in your delivery and you've got to understand the art of timing. So what does this rhythm sound or feel like in advertising copy?

It has no distinct pattern: a short sentence, then a long sentence followed by a medium sentence followed by a short sentence and then another short sentence and then one really long sentence. Got it? In short, a mixture of sentence lengths that, when read together, gives a sense of variety and rhythm.

Think about how copy would sound if all the sentences were very short or very long or all had a distinct predictable pattern. Pretty boring. And that's the point of copy rhythm. Vary your sentences; vary their length to give your copy a rhythm.

Another rhythm technique is the use of what is called a "triad." Very often when I list examples or attributes of something, I use just three of them. For example, take the sentence, "I went shopping for a hammer, a screwdriver and a pair of pliers." In copy you list three items in a series with the last item preceded by the word *and*, and you create a nice rhythm within that sentence. In fact, when you read some of the ads in Section Three of this book, you will see how many of them have triads throughout.

**14. Service:** If you are selling an expensive product or one that is not easily returned for service, you must address the question of service and convey the ease of that service to the consumer. Often the mention of a brand name manufacturer is all that is needed to establish ease of service. But if there is a remote possibility that the consumer would still ask about service, then you must address this issue in your ad.

In selling our Bally pinball game by mail, we knew that a buyer might have concerns about the matter of service. What if the pinball game broke and required repair? It was large and expensive and the inconvenience of a broken game would be in the back of our customers' minds. We addressed that in the ad. The following is the subheading and paragraph we used to alleviate any customer concerns:

### A FRANK DISCUSSION OF SERVICE

Fireball is a solid-state computer with its electronics condensed on integrated circuits—all hermetically sealed and all pre-tested for a lifetime of service. Fireball is also self-diagnostic. Let us say something goes wrong with the system. Simply press the test button on the back panel of your machine and the exact problem is displayed on your scoreboard in digits. Check the instruction booklet and simply remove the designated plug-in circuit board, light bulb or part and send it to the service department closest to you for a brand new replacement. Even your TV or stereo isn't that easy to repair.

A full paragraph was used to cover the issue of service. And we sold thousands of pinball machines to people who ordinarily might not have purchased a unit because of their concern about service.

Another good example of how important service is to help sell a product took place during the height of the digital watch boom in the mid-1970s. The industry was expanding very rapidly but there were problems with the reliability of these space-age timepieces. Unlike mechanical watches, these new electronic timepieces had batteries, used sophisticated chips and circuitry and had a high defective rate.

I recognized this as a problem that had to be addressed in our copy. And since I look at problems as opportunities, I wondered, "Where is the opportunity in this serious and rapidly growing problem?" I then came up with the following copy to establish the quality of the product we were offering and our commitment to back it.

The Sensor 770 has an unprecedented five-year parts and labor unconditional warranty. Each watch goes through weeks of aging, testing and quality control before assembly and final inspection. Service should never be required, but if it should anytime during the five-year warranty period, we will pick up your Sensor at your door and send you a loaner watch while yours is being repaired—all at our expense.

Then later in a summary of the offer, we again played up the part on service.

> We have selected the Sensor as the most advanced American-made, solid-state timepiece ever produced. And we put our company and its full resources behind that selection. JS&A will unconditionally guarantee the Sensor—even the battery—for five years. We'll even send you a loaner watch to use while your watch is being repaired should it ever require repair.

We alleviated any concern about service in the copy of the ad. If the issue of service was raised in the minds of our prospects, it was now resolved. By showing such a strong commitment to service, we had overcome a major objection that we realized, in advance, could be a problem, and turned it into an opportunity.

Indeed when a customer's watch did not work, the customer would call us on our toll-free number and we would immediately send out a package containing a UPS call tag that allowed UPS to pick up the defective watch free of charge, a loaner watch and a postage-free envelope for the consumer to return the loaner after receiving the repaired watch.

This gave our company the opportunity to prove to our customers how consumer-oriented we were. Our customers were literally amazed at the way we followed up with our service program. And after they received their repaired watch, they even got a call from us to make sure everything was okay.

But that's not the point of this example. If service is a consideration in the subconscious mind of the consumer and you address it up front, you will melt any resistance to buying your product. The Sensor watch was one of our best-selling watches and the mailing list of watch customers became one of our strongest mailing lists for future offers.

Service in the selling process has been a critical factor in the success of a personal friend, Joe Girard, who is in *The Guinness Book of World Records* for having sold more cars in a single year than anybody in history. Joe's books on salesmanship are worth reading for their many insights, but the one factor that made Joe such an effective salesman (aside from the fact that he was a very personable guy) was the way he handled service. His customers' service problems became his. And each time he sold a car, Joe became that buyer's personal service representative. And Joe performed. Then when buyers returned for another car, they wanted to buy only from Joe. It wasn't price that made Joe's success, although that was important; it was his attitude toward service.

**15. Physical Facts:** In copy you must mention all the physical facts about a product or you risk reducing your response. I'm talking about weight, dimensions, size, limits, speed, and the like. Sometimes you might think that a certain dimension isn't really important or the weight may not be necessary. But it's not true. Give readers any excuse not to buy and they won't buy.

I remember running ads for products and then personally taking the orders on our toll-free lines. I did this because it was on the phone lines that I got many of my insights into the buying process. Here were my customers, motivated enough to reach into their pockets and pull out their hard-earned money for a product they trusted me to sell them. What a wonderful opportunity to peek into this process and hear the really subliminal reactions people made when they responded.

It was during my time on the phone lines that I learned that if you don't give all the facts, it gives your customer the excuse not to order. It may be a weight or dimension that you thought was irrelevant, but if you don't mention it, people will call and ask for it. And how many more customers didn't bother to call and check on it? Of course, they didn't order, either.

I remember an ad for a scale pictured on the floor. I didn't give the actual weight of the scale itself. "Who would care?" I thought. But my prospects did care and frequently asked. We eventually included the weight of the scale in the ad. I remember showing an object that was being held in my hand. I gave the exact dimensions but failed to give the weight because the weight was not really relevant. I got a lot of calls from people wanting to know the weight before deciding whether to buy.

The point: List the physical dimensions even in cases where you think they are not that important.

**16. Trial Period:** With mail order items, you must offer a trial period for any product that the consumer cannot touch or feel at the time of purchase. The only time you can make an exception to this rule is when the value is so strong and the product so familiar that the consumer is willing to take the risk. If I were selling a box of 24 rolls of toilet paper at a bargain price delivered to your home and it was a brand that you already used, then you wouldn't need a trial period.

Make sure your trial period is at least one month, or even better, two months. Tests have proven that the longer the trial period, the less chance the product will be returned and the more confidence the consumer will have in dealing with you and purchasing the item.

Let's say you receive a product that has a one-week trial period. You've got one week to make up your mind. You feel the pressure, so you examine the product and try to make the decision as quickly as possible. If you are unsure when the week is almost up, what do you do? You say, "I'm not sure, so I'm not going to take the chance," and you return it.

But let's say you have two months to make up your mind. No pressure there, right? You even have a pretty good feeling about the company offering the product. The company must be confident that you're going to like the product because it is giving you a two-month trial period.

So you put the product aside. You use it freely, not worried about having to make a decision, and then before you know it the two months are up and you've not even thought about returning it. Just knowing you could have returned it was enough to make you feel comfortable holding on to the purchase.

**17. Price Comparison:** Whenever possible, offering a price comparison to another product establishes value in the mind of the purchaser. This points out one of the really important considerations that motivate consumers to buy—namely that they are getting real value.

An example of a price comparison was my ad for the Sensor watch. I stated:

> The $275 Pulsar uses the LED technology which requires pressing a button each time you want to review the time. Even the $500 solar-powered Synchronar watch, in our opinion, can't

compare with the Sensor and its 5-year warranty. And no solid-state watch can compare to Sensor's quality, accuracy, ruggedness and exceptional value.

If you are selling an expensive item or something that is a good value when compared to another product, you should always consider a price comparison as a means of establishing the value of your product. If your product is the most expensive product being offered, then you want to suggest that it has more or better features. If your product is less expensive, then you want to focus on better value and use a price comparison.

But there's a word of caution. Your comparison must be totally accurate and be 100 percent fair or you could be sued by the company whose product you are comparing.

**18. Testimonials:** A testimonial is a good way to add credibility if it is from a very credible person or organization. This approach can be used not only in the copy but in the headline or photo. See if your ad copy could use a celebrity for a testimonial, but make sure the testimonial makes sense for the product.

When I was selling a space-age Midex security system, it made sense to ask Wally Schirra, the famous astronaut, to endorse my product. He did, and the product sold very well. If I were selling basketball shoes, Michael Jordan would be a natural.

Make sure that the celebrity matches with the product and adds credibility. The use of a celebrity who doesn't make sense for your product or doesn't add credibility could backfire, have the wrong effect and kill sales if the offer is not believable.

You can also use what I call a "reverse testimonial." That is where you don't use a spokesperson but you refer to your competitor's. For example, when I was selling the Olympus micro recorder, I stated the following:

**Headline:** Endorsement Battle
**Subheadline:** A famous golf star endorses the Lanier. Our unit is endorsed by our president. You'll save $100 as a result.
**Copy:** Judge for yourself. That new Olympus micro recorder shown above sells for $150. Its closest competition is a $250 recorder called the Lanier endorsed by a famous golf star.

**FANCY ENDORSEMENT**

The famous golf star is a pilot who personally flies his own Citation jet. The Olympus recorder is endorsed by JS&A's president who pilots a more cost-efficient single engine Beechcraft Bonanza. The golf star does not endorse the Lanier unit for free. After all, a good portion of his income is derived from endorsing products.

Our president, on the other hand, does not get paid for endorsing products—just for selling them. And his Bonanza is not as expensive to fly as the golf star's Citation. In fact, our president also drives a Volkswagen Rabbit.

I then continued to show how inefficiently the Lanier was sold (through a direct selling organization) and how efficiently the Olympus was sold (via direct marketing and through JS&A). The conclusion: savings of $100 for an even better product—all because we didn't have our product endorsed by an expensive spokesperson.

Another form of testimonial is from the man on the street—used primarily on TV. I've used them extensively in my BluBlocker infomercials. And finally, another one could come from those people who use your product and send you an unsolicited testimonial. Whatever testimonial you do use, make sure it is authentic and honest. The public will see right through a lie and the Federal Trade Commission (FTC) won't be far behind.

**19. Price:** Another important copy point to consider is the price. Should the price be obvious? Should it be set in large type? Small? These are important considerations and must be examined.

If you're selling a product or service at a very good price, then set the price in larger type. After all, you want people to see that benefit very clearly. If the product is expensive and it's not the price that will sell it, you want to underplay it. Don't hide it; just underplay it.

As I write my ad I have always anticipated the questions my prospects will ask. There is one exception. I never know when they are going to wonder about the price of the product. I have always felt that the point at which your reader will want to find out about the price could happen anytime during the reading process. It could happen before they read the ad. It could happen halfway through or it could happen near the end. You must, as an effective copywriter, answer the question when it is being raised by the reader.

By putting the price in a logical position in the copy—whether it be in the coupon, which is the ideal place, or in the copy highlighted with a bold typeface—you are answering the question that the reader asks without knowing when the reader is ready to ask the question. The reader simply scans the ad and if the price is in bold or in the coupon, the price will pop out and answer the question.

**20. Offer Summary:** It's a really good idea to summarize what you are offering the consumer somewhere near the end of your ad. "So here's my offer. Order two pots with Teflon coating and you'll receive the two pots plus our handy cookbook and video for the price of only $19.95." You'll be surprised at how many ads miss this important point.

**21. Avoid Saying Too Much:** This is probably the biggest mistake my students make. They say too much. There are really two issues here. The first issue is one of editing. It is normal to say as much as you can about a subject and then refine the copy to a point where it flows smoothly. This usually means editing and reducing the copy length until it has rhythm and it flows. This could take time and involves a few steps.

First, say to yourself as you go through the editing process, "Is there a simpler way of saying this?" Very often you can cut your copy down 50 to even 80 percent and still say the same thing. It's the difference between a salesperson who talks too much and one who is to the point and succinct. Wouldn't you rather be sold by the one who is to the point?

There is another issue involved with not saying too much, and later in this book in the "Mental Enagement" section of Chapter 19 I explain how not saying too much will actually enhance and even stimulate the selling process. Chapter 17 on editing also has ideas that will help you reduce your copy.

**22. Ease of Ordering:** Make it easy to order. Use a toll-free number, a coupon, a tear-off reply card or any vehicle that is easy to understand and use. My recommendation: Use a coupon with dotted lines. In tests, it usually generates more response because the dotted lines clearly convey at a glance that you can order the product from the ad.

**23. Ask for the Order:** Always ask for the order near the end of your ad. This is often forgotten by many copywriters. At the end of an ad, I state the following or something similar: "I urge you to buy this at no obligation, today." Have you ever met a salesperson who has already sold you and you are waiting for the salesperson to ask you for the order but he or she never does? It's happened to me. And it is one of the problems with a lot of inexperienced salespeople. You've got to ask for the order, and if you're doing it right, it should be at the very end of the ad where you've finished selling your prospect, you've summarized the offer and your prospect is ready to buy.

These 23 copy elements are points you want to consider when you are writing copy. Use this chapter as a checklist when you get started. Consider all of these points when you write an ad. Can some of them be eliminated? Possibly. But simply by using them as a checklist, you might discover a few deficiencies in your ad copy that can be corrected with my suggestions and might result in enhancing your response.

One of the other benefits of the list is to give you an insight into the relative importance of the various copy elements. Some, like the paragraph headings, have little purpose other than to make the copy less imposing. Others, like resolving objections, can make a dramatic difference in the credibility of your copy.

Use the convenient copy elements checklist located in Appendix C in the back of this book and make a copy to keep right next to your computer or desk when you are writing an ad.

But the really interesting part of my checklist is in the next chapter where you'll learn about the psychological triggers that need to be considered when you write an ad. You first learned about the 10 graphic elements and their purpose (to get you to read the first sentence of the copy) in Chapter 4. You have just learned 23 copy concepts and how they are to be used. Now learn the 31 psychological triggers—the underlying motivational messages that good direct response copy should convey, often in subtle but very effective ways. When I was teaching my seminar course, this was the part my students enjoyed the most. So read on.

The 31 psychological triggers are probably going to be the most interesting of the 64 points you want to consider when writing a direct response print ad or any kind of selling message.

The first part of the 64-point checklist involves the 10 graphic elements of an ad—those elements designed to get you to read the first sentence. The previous chapter covered 23 points to consider when writing the actual copy. But now get ready for the psychology that should be considered when writing your advertising message—concepts that took me years of failure, experience and gradual insight to understand and implement.

You may understand and relate to some of these concepts right away. Some you may not fully understand without experiencing them yourself. And finally, some will require a fairly detailed explanation.

If you've found this book informative so far, you will find this chapter fascinating. So let's start.

## 1. Feeling of Involvement or Ownership

I was once told this story by a master salesman who worked at a TV and appliance store. He was the most successful salesman this store ever had. He consistently beat out all the other salesmen. He had some very good sales techniques, but that wasn't what impressed me. It was the way he decided in advance who his best prospects might be.

What he would do was stand in an aisle watching customers walk into the store. He would observe them. If they walked up to a TV set and started turning the knobs, he knew that he had a 50 percent chance of selling them. If they didn't turn the knobs, he had a 10 percent chance of selling them. This was before remote controls.

Direct response advertising doesn't give you the opportunities of observing your prospects. You are not there to see any knobs being turned. But you can get them to turn the knobs by giving them a feeling of involvement with or ownership of the product you are selling.

In all my ads I try to make the prospects imagine they are holding or using my product. For example, in one of my earlier calculator ads, I might have said, "Hold the Litronix 2000 in your hand. See how easily the keys snap to the touch. See how small and how light the unit is." I create through imagination the reader's experience of turning the knobs.

In short, I take the mind on a mental journey to capture the involvement of the reader. I make the reader believe that he or she could indeed be holding the calculator and experiencing the very same things that I've described. It's mental energy creating a picture for the prospect, whose mind is like a vacuum waiting to be filled.

In your copywriting, let your readers take a stroll down a path with you or let them smell the fragrance through your nose or let them experience some of the emotions you are feeling by forming a mental picture from your description.

If I were writing an advertisement for the Corvette sports car, I might say, "Take a ride in the new Corvette. Feel the breeze blowing through your hair as you drive through the warm evening. Watch heads turn. Punch the accelerator to the floor and feel the burst of power that pins you into the back of your contour seat. Look at the beautiful display of electronic technology right on your dashboard. Feel the power and excitement of America's super sports car."

I would still explain all the special features of the car—the logic upon which to justify its purchase—but I would really play up that feeling of involvement and ownership.

This technique is used in many different ways. In direct response, it is often referred to as an involvement device—something that involves the consumer in the buying process. Sometimes it may seem silly. Have you ever received those solicitations that say, "Put the 'yes' disk into the 'yes' slot and we will send you a trial subscription to our new magazine"? I often wonder who invented that seemingly simpleminded and juvenile concept. Yet, as direct marketers will tell you, this type of involvement device often doubles and triples response rates. It's not simpleminded at all but rather a very effective direct response involvement technique.

The reader becomes involved in the solicitation. Similarly, your reader is either taking action or imagining taking action through the power of the words you write.

## The Involvement of TV and the Internet

TV and the Internet are great examples of involvement. You see, hear and can almost touch the product. It is no wonder that TV and the Internet are among the most effective ways to sell.

My own daughter, when she was four years old, clearly demonstrated how you can get involved in the sales message. There was a Peanuts Valentine's Day TV special and my daughter Jill was sitting and watching the show with her seven-year-old sister, April. My wife, who was watching as well, told me this fascinating story.

> Charlie Brown was passing out Valentine cards in a classroom and was reading off names of the recipients, "Sarah, Mary, Sally . . . Jill. Where's Jill?" said Charlie Brown. My daughter immediately raised her hand and said, "Here." She was so involved in watching the show that she felt like she was a part of it.

I use involvement devices quite often. An involvement device that ties in with what you are selling can be very effective. Let me give you a perfect example from an ad that I wrote. The results really surprised me.

The product I was offering was the Franklin Spelling Computer—a device that helped correct your spelling. It was a novelty when it first appeared and it sold quite well. Although I wasn't the first to sell it, I had a model that was a little more sophisticated than the first version.

I examined the product and felt it was priced too high. But the manufacturer would be pretty upset with me if I were to drop the price. So I tried an involvement device as a method of lowering the price.

First, I wrote an ad that described the product but with an

unusual premise. The ad that I wrote had several misspelled words. If you found the misspelled words, circled them and sent the ad with the misspelled words circled, you would get $2 off the price of the computer for each misspelled word you circled. My concept was simple. If you didn't find all the misspelled words, you paid more for the computer, but then again, the computer was worth more to you than to somebody who found all the mistakes.

I ran the first ad in the *Wall Street Journal* and the responses poured in. I also received a few phone calls from people I hadn't heard from in years. "Joe, I want you to know, I spent the last hour and a half trying to find all the words and I don't even intend on buying your damn computer. I normally don't read the entire *Wall Street Journal* for that length of time."

### I Even Made More Money

And the response was surprising. I anticipated that the readers would find all the misspelled words. In fact, even the word *mispelled* was misspelled. When the response was finally tallied, to my amazement, people only caught, on average, half of the words and I earned a lot more money than I had expected from the ad. And, of course, those who really needed the computer got real value.

The feeling of ownership is a concept that is pretty close to the feeling of involvement, but here you are making readers feel that they already own the product and you're letting them use their imaginations as you take them through the steps of what it would be like if they already owned it. An example might be, "When you receive your exercise device, work out on it. Adjust the weights. See how easy it is to store under your bed. . . ." In short, you are making them feel that they have already bought the product.

Advertising copy that involves the reader can be quite effective—especially if the involvement device is part of the advertising. Whenever you write an ad, keep this very important concept in mind. It can make direct response copy far more effective.

## 2. Honesty

If I had to pick the single most important point of the 64 points, I would pick honesty. Your advertising must be honest. This doesn't mean that if you are dishonest in your message you won't achieve a successful result. Give the consumer a price that's too hard to believe or a product that doesn't live up to its claims and you might be able to get away with it once, maybe even twice, but not for the long haul.

But this section on honesty is not about whether you can get away with being dishonest and for how long. It's about honesty as a psychological selling tool. First, let's start out with a very important premise.

Consumers are very smart—smarter than you think and smarter collectively than any single one of us. With all the experience I have in marketing products and with all the product knowledge I've gained over the past 35 years, you can take my word for it, the consumer is quite sharp.

The consumer can also tell whether people are truthful in what they are trying to communicate. And the more truthful you are in your advertising, the more effectively your message will be accepted by your prospects.

Try to lie in your copy and you are only deceiving yourself. Your copy will say what you think you wanted it to say, but it will also say what you thought you covered up. Even a reader who hurries over your copy can feel the difference.

When I wrote a JS&A ad, I would include many of the negative features of my products. I would point out the flaws up front. And of course, I would explain why the flaws really didn't amount to much and why the consumer should still buy my product. Consumers were so impressed with this approach and had such trust in our message that they would eagerly buy what we offered.

And it seemed that the more truthful and frank my ads were, the more the consumers responded. I soon realized that truthfulness was one of the best advertising lessons I had ever learned.

Consumers really appreciate the truth. And since they are smarter than you or I, you can't fake the truth. They'll pick out a phony statement every time.

I learned to make every communication to my customers truthful, whether it be on national television or in my print ads. And the more truthful I am, the more responsive my customers.

# 3. Integrity

Not too far from honesty is integrity. An advertisement is a personal message from an organization or an individual and is a direct reflection of the writer's personality and integrity. You can convey this integrity by the truthfulness of your message, the look of your ad, the image that you convey and even the typefaces that you use.

Integrity can be reflected by the choices you make in the layout of your ad. Is it clean and neat? Or is it shouting out at you with color bars running in different directions and headlines screaming and words underlined and pictures exaggerated? You get the idea. The integrity of the person delivering the message is always amazingly clear to the recipient. And this integrity is often reflected by the appearance of the advertisement and the copy you write. Show good integrity and your advertising message will be well received. Don't show it and join the ranks of those who are rarely successful.

# 4. Credibility

If you convey honesty and integrity in your message, chances are you've gone a long way toward establishing your credibility. However, credibility is not just honesty and integrity. Credibility is being believable. In an ad for a product whose price is exceptionally low, you've got to convey that the offer you are making, as great as it may seem, is indeed a valid offer.

Let's say you are offering something for $10 that everybody else is selling for $40. Your job is establishing credibility for your price. You might explain that you are buying a very large volume from the Far East and that you were able to buy the remaining stock from a major manufacturer for a very low price. In short, you've got to establish the credibility of your company and your offer.

Credibility also means truthfulness. Does the consumer really believe you? Rash statements, clichés and some exaggerations will remove any credibility your offer may have had.

One of the most important factors that could affect credibility is not resolving all the objections that are raised in your readers' minds, such as hiding something or avoiding an obvious fault of the product or service. You need to raise all objections and resolve them.

Products that require installation or assembly are good examples. If it is obvious that a product doesn't just pop out of the box ready to use, you must explain that it does require assembly. You might say something like, "To make it easy, we provide you with the tools. In our tests, it only took five minutes for somebody with very little mechanical skill to put it together." Once again, it is the anticipation of objections and their resolution that means so much to the credibility of an ad.

You are in essence sensing the next question the consumer may ask and answering it in a straightforward, honest and credible way. The integrity of your product, your offer and yourself are all on the line, and unless you convey the highest credibility in your ad, your prospects will not feel comfortable buying from you.

When I appear on QVC—the TV home shopping channel— it is easy to sell a difficult product that normally would require a lot of credibility. The reason: QVC already has a lot of credibility with their customers. If a product is being offered on QVC, it must be good. It must have the quality that customers have come to expect, and chances are the product will be bought by somebody who has bought products before from QVC and already feels that the company is a very credible concern. In short, I've piggybacked my product onto QVC's credibility, and the combination of QVC's credibility and my product's credibility is pretty powerful.

The effect of credibility also extends to the magazines or newspapers in which you advertise. If you advertise your product in the *Wall Street Journal*, you are piggybacking onto their credibility and their constant vigilance, making sure their readers aren't being taken advantage of. On the other hand, place that same ad in the *National Enquirer* and you then take on the lack of credibility that this publication has established in the mind of the reader. Again, credibility is affected by the environment in which you place your advertisement.

You can enhance credibility through the use of a brand

name product. For example, if I'm offering an electronic product by the name of Yorx with the exact same features as one whose brand name is Sony, which one has more credibility? The Sony would probably sell better if both were at the same price.

Adding an appropriate celebrity endorser is another effective way to enhance credibility. The name of a company can, too. For example, there was a company by the name of The Tool Shack selling computers. This company's name actually detracted from the credibility of the product it was selling. We once ran the same ad in the *Wall Street Journal* to test the effect of our JS&A name against a lesser-known name—Consumers Hero. In the test, the JS&A ad far outpulled the other ad. Only the name of the company was different. Sometimes a city or state can add credibility. That's why some companies located in smaller cities have offices in London, Paris or New York. The various ways of adding credibility should be an important consideration in crafting your advertising.

## 5. Value and Proof of Value

Even if you are a multimillionaire, you want to know that you are not being taken advantage of, and even more importantly, that you are getting value for your financial investment.

In an ad, the copywriter wants to convey, through examples or by comparison, that what the customer is buying is a good value. A typical example in one of my ads is where I compare my prices to products with similar features and point out that I'm providing a better value.

By positioning your product and comparing it with others or by proving the value of something even though the value may not be apparent, you are providing the logic with which the prospect can justify the purchase.

Simply educating the reader to the intrinsic value of your product is equivalent to lowering its price. In short, there is a value associated with the education you are providing your reader.

The buying transaction is an emotional experience that uses logic to justify the buying decision. You buy a Mercedes automobile emotionally but you then justify its purchase logically with its technology, safety and resale value. So justifying its value is something that the consumer wants to do before making an emotional purchase.

And with such intense competition in the world, there is a question in the mind of the consumer: "Am I buying the product at the best price?" Once again, you must resolve that question or you are not communicating effectively with your prospect.

## 6. Justify the Purchase

One of the questions people may think about while reading an ad is "Can I really justify this purchase?" Once again, it is a question that is raised and then must be resolved. If you don't resolve it, then you won't answer all the prospect's questions and this will give the prospect the excuse to "think about it" and, of course, never buy.

Somewhere in your ad, you should resolve any objection by providing some justification to the purchaser. Sometimes it's just saying, "You deserve it." And other times you might have to justify it in terms of savings (the price is a one-time-only value), health reasons (protects your eyes), recognition (the men in your life will love the way you look in it) or dozens of other reasons based on the wants and needs of your prospect.

People often tell me, "Joe, when I read your ads, I feel guilty if I don't buy the product." That's quite a compliment and probably due to the way I justify a purchase in the mind of the consumer.

The higher the price point, the more need there is to justify the purchase. The lower the price point or the more value the price represents, the less you have to justify the purchase. In fact, the lower the price, the more greed plays a role.

## 7. Greed

Greed in the form of attraction to bargains is a very strong motivating factor. I don't know how many times I've bought things even though I didn't need them simply because they were a bargain.

Don't hesitate to recognize greed as a very strong factor in either low-priced merchandise or expensive products offered at low prices. Too low a price may diminish your credibility unless you justify the low price. Many people are willing to risk dealing with an unknown vendor just to pay less and get more for their money. Providing the consumer with more than what is normally received for the price is a way of appealing to the consumer's greed.

In one of my earlier ads in the *Wall Street Journal,* I offered a calculator for $49.95 and the manufacturer got really upset with me. "That product should have sold for $69.95 and now I have dealers all over the country calling me and complaining," screamed the manufacturer.

"Don't worry," I said. "I'll correct it." So I ran a small ad in the *Wall Street Journal* announcing my error, raising the price from $49.95 to $69.95 and giving consumers just a few days to respond at the old price. Even though the size of the ad was considerably smaller, it outpulled the previous one as people rushed to buy the calculator within those few days at the $49.95 bargain price.

Greed is not a technique that can be employed all the time. But it should be recognized as an effective element that plays on everybody's weakness.

When you lower the price of a product, you usually end up with more unit sales. Keep lowering the price, and you'll continue to generate more unit sales than before if the price drop is big enough. Go too low and you'll have to add a little justification for the lower price as it will start raising credibility issues with your prospects.

Greed is really not a very positive human trait. But it exists and it is a force to consider when communicating with your prospects.

## 8. Establish Authority

There's always something that you can say about your company to establish your authority, size, position or intention. The consumer loves to do business with experts in a particular area.

That's why the trend is away from department stores that sell general merchandise to category stores that sell a specific line of products. These stores have more expertise, knowledge and authority in a specific category.

For example, for years I would call JS&A "America's largest single source of space-age products." What I was really doing was establishing the authority of JS&A as a major supplier of space-age products. The words "single source" really meant that we shipped our products out of a single location. We may not have shipped more space-age products than Sears or RadioShack, but we shipped more out of a single location and we specialized only in space-age products.

Establishing your authority is something that should be done in each ad regardless of how big or how little you are. For example, "America's largest supplier of specialized products for the chimney sweep industry." (One of my seminar participants was actually in the chimney sweep industry.) Or even if you are the smallest, you can always say, "The hardest-working bunch of guys in the advertising business." If you really examine your company, you will find something you can say that establishes your authority and expertise in what you are selling.

Then, after you establish your authority, there is going to be the temptation to stop using the phrase that established your authority. I know that when we had run our phrase for almost six years I wondered if we really needed it. But there were always those first-time readers who caught the ad and needed that reassurance that they were dealing with an authoritative company in the field in which they were contemplating a purchase. That phrase gave them the confidence.

Sometimes it is easy to establish authority by virtue of the name of the company. American Symbolic Corporation was a company I set up once whose name sounded like it was a very big operation. Jack and Ed's Video doesn't sound very big at all. Computer Discount Warehouse gives you a pretty good idea of their authority. It has name recognition, plus it tells you what the company is through its name.

### People Respect Authority

People naturally respect a knowledgeable authority. Let's say you want to buy a computer. You might first check with the expert in your neighborhood who is known as the neighborhood computer genius. Let's call him Danny. He has established his authority and you feel quite comfortable going to Danny to get advice. He'll then tell you what he thinks you should buy and from whom. And chances are, he'll recommend some retail outlet that has established itself with some level of authority. It might be the cheapest computer company or maybe the company that provides the best service. You'll seek out the type of authority you need.

Sometimes the authority does not even have to be stated but can be felt by the copy, the layout or the message of an ad. Establish your authority in the field of the product or service you are selling and you'll find that it will make a big difference in your copy's effectiveness.

Let me give you a personal example of something that really illustrates the point. As I was about to walk into a local business supply store in Las Vegas, a young lady came running up to me and said, "Please, could you help me?"

I was a little surprised by the suddenness of her approach and, in fact, first thought that there was some kind of emergency. "Sure, what's the problem?"

Almost with tears in her eyes, she answered, "I'm about to buy a computer and I've picked out the one I like the most, but I need somebody to tell me if I've made the right choice. If you know about computers, could you come in the store with me and give me your opinion?"

I agreed and went into the store with her. The girl explained that she was attending college at UNLV (the University of Nevada at Las Vegas) and since this was her first computer, she needed reassurance from somebody who knew computers that this was a good and wise purchase. She told me how most of the people in the store really didn't know that much about computers. I looked over the computer and, having pretty good knowledge about home computers, told her that she had indeed made a wise choice and that the computer was also a good value. I pointed out some of the technical features that would help her in her schoolwork, and although she didn't have any idea of what I was talking about, she felt that she was making the right choice because I said so.

### Nobody Wants to Make a Mistake

Relieved, she thanked me, and then was off to buy her new computer. As she was walking away, she looked over her shoulder and said, "I've worked hard for my money and I didn't want to make a stupid mistake."

Before you bought a computer, you may have first called somebody who was a partial expert on computers to ask for an opinion. You, too, wanted reassurance and confidence about the purchase you were making—that the money you were about to exchange for a computer was going to be spent wisely. The same holds true when you buy anything of value. You just want reassurance. If, however, you can trust the sales organization as the experts, then you won't need any outside expert opinion as the young student needed in the preceding example.

Even after you buy something, you often seek confirmation that your purchase was a good one. The late direct marketing consultant Paul Bringe once wrote: "One of the first things we do after making a sizable purchase is to seek assurance from others that our decision was a good one. We tell our family, our neighbors, our friends and our business associates and wait for their approval."

One of the surprises I had while taking orders on our phone lines at JS&A was the number of customers who stated something like, "I bet that's one of your best-selling products." In many cases, it wasn't. But in every case, whenever I mentioned that the product they had just purchased was indeed a very popular product, there was always a comment like, "I just knew that it was." People need reassurance that they have made the right purchase.

# 9. Satisfaction Conviction

When you saw this heading, you might have thought we would be talking about the trial period. Indeed, a trial period could be defined as a form of satisfaction conviction. "If you aren't totally satisfied with my product within one month, you may send it back for a full refund." But that isn't what we mean here. Sure, every direct response offer should have a trial period. After all, the consumer needs to touch and feel a product to make a decision about whether to keep it. So the trial period provides the buyer with a level of confidence. The consumer can change his or her mind if it is not exactly what he or she is looking for.

But a satisfaction conviction is more than a trial period. It basically conveys a message from you to your prospect that says, "Hey, I'm so convinced you will like this product that I'm going to do something for your benefit to prove how incredible my offer is."

If your potential customer, after reading what you are going to do, says something like, "They must really believe in their product," or "How can they do it?" or "Are they going to get ripped off by customers who will take advantage of their generosity?" then you know you've got a great example of a satisfaction conviction.

Let me give you an example. When I first offered BluBlocker sunglasses, I said in my TV advertising, "If you're unhappy with BluBlockers, I'll let you return them anytime you want. There is no trial period." A lot of people thought to themselves, "That must be a good product or otherwise they wouldn't make that offer." Or they may have said, "Boy, are they going to get ripped off." In either case, I conveyed a conviction that my customer was going to be so satisfied that I was willing to do something that is rarely done.

In one ad, I stated, "If you aren't happy with your purchase, just call me up and I'll personally arrange to have it picked up at my expense and refund you every penny of your purchase price including the time you took to return the product."

### Testing a Satisfaction Conviction

Once I was able to test the power of a satisfaction conviction. In an ad I wrote for the company called Consumers Hero, I was offering subscriptions to a discount bulletin showing refurbished products at very low prices. But rather than just mail the bulletin to prospects, I formed a club and offered a subscription to the bulletin. I tested various elements in the 700-word ad. I changed the headline and tested it and improved response by 20 percent. I changed the price and saw little change in total response. The lower the price, however, the more orders I received. But when I changed just the satisfaction conviction, the response rate doubled.

In one ad, I said, "If you don't buy anything during your two-year subscription, I'll refund the unused portion of your subscription."

In the second ad I stated, "But what if you never buy from us and your two-year membership expires? Fine. Send us just your membership card and we'll fully refund your five dollars plus send you interest on your money."

In the first ad, you see a basic, simple trial-period type offer. In the second version, however, you see an offer that goes well beyond the trial period and can be classified as a satisfaction conviction.

In the test, the response doubled even though the satisfaction conviction was at the very end of the ad. This meant that people read the entire ad and then, at the very end when that important buying decision had to be made, the satisfaction conviction removed any remaining resistance to buying into the concept.

If you have gotten the reader into the slippery slide and all the way to the end of an ad, it's that last part of the ad where you've got an awful lot to do. Think about it. You've got to explain the offer to the prospect, why it's a good offer and why he or she should buy the product, and then you've got to do something dramatic to push him or her over the edge—all within the very last part of your sales message. It's like a salesperson asking for the order and then also saying, "And if you buy this from me now, I will do something that few salespeople would do to ensure your satisfaction."

The right satisfaction conviction is important, too. The ideal satisfaction conviction should raise an objection and resolve it, as I've indicated in the previous chapter, but in resolving it, go beyond what people expect.

It was effective in my Consumers Hero ad because it tied perfectly into resolving any last-minute resistance. First it raised the objection—"What if I don't buy from your bulletin over a two-year period?" And then I resolved it with a satisfaction conviction—something that went beyond what people expected.

But be careful to use a satisfaction conviction that makes sense for the offer. You wouldn't want to raise an objection and then satisfy it with the wrong resolution. Make sure any objection is indeed satisfied by the correct resolution. In short, it's got to make sense.

The satisfaction conviction is a critical part of the sales message and few realize its importance. Yet, if you can create a powerful satisfaction conviction, this simple device will do a great deal for the success of your offers.

# 10. Nature of Product

This is one of the really important keys in determining how to sell a product. First, you have to realize that every product has its own unique personality, its own unique nature, and it's up to you to figure it out.

How do you present the drama of that product? Every product has one very powerful way of presenting itself that will express the true advantages and emotion that the product has to offer and motivate the largest number of people to buy it.

Remember the Midex burglar alarm that I sold for many years through full-page ads in national magazines? What was the nature of that product and how could I motivate people to buy it? I explained that in Chapter 2.

I used the security system as an example of the nature of products. This was an unusual product because it had a unique personality. The product category itself had its own profile. By realizing the nature of every product and playing to its strengths, you will end up with a very powerful and emotionally dramatic presentation.

Think about other examples. What is the nature of a toy? It's a fun game. So you bring out the enjoyment. What is the nature of a blood pressure unit? It's a serious medical device that you use to check your blood pressure. Note the word *serious*. What is the nature of a burglar alarm? It's a serious product that should be easy to install, work when it is supposed to and provide protection to concerned homeowners. Very often, common sense is all you need to understand and appreciate the nature of a product.

Realize that you must understand the nature of the product you are selling or you won't effectively sell it.

# 11. Prospect Nature

In selling, it is important to understand not only the nature of the product you are offering but the nature of your prospect as well. When I was in college and thinking about joining a fraternity, I had an experience that really points out the value of understanding this very important trigger.

Of all the fraternities I could have joined in college, I chose the worst one. Why? After spending time visiting various fraternities, I had figured out the nature of why guys join a fraternity in the first place.

I reasoned that with this knowledge, I could single-handedly take the worst fraternity on campus and turn it into the best one, simply by coming up with an effective marketing plan to dramatically increase membership. My approach would take into account the nature of my prospect (the student) and, using this information, seduce that student into wanting to join my fraternity at the exclusion of all others. I would thus, by building a large membership, transform my fraternity into a top-rated organization, regardless of how bad it had been when I joined. This may seem like a rather naive plan, but I was convinced that I personally could make a difference.

After joining and going through the initiation period, I got sworn in, went before my fraternity brothers, and laid out my plan—"Operation Survival" as I called it. I explained that guys join a fraternity for two psychological and motivating factors: One was as a vehicle to meet girls and the other was to experience the camaraderie and brotherhood of a group of guys. I showed that an illusion could be created to capture this effect of social interaction in a fraternity for the sake of acquiring new members or pledges. The goal was to have more guys wanting to join our fraternity than any other on campus. And we needed this big infusion of new faces or our fraternity would surely die—that's how bad this place was and how badly we were doing attracting new members. It truly was Operation Survival.

My plan was simple and consisted of two parts. The first part was to invite the most beautiful and sexy girls to act as hostesses for our get-acquainted events. I didn't want the active brothers' girlfriends to act as hostesses as was usually the case. No, these gals had to be world-class—girls the guys would talk about for days after our event.

The second was the way each brother had to introduce a fellow brother to a prospective member. I insisted that the brother should say to a prospect something very loving and warm about his fellow fraternity brother. I said, "Put your arms around your brother and tell the prospect what a wonderful person your brother is and how much you genuinely admire and love this guy."

The plan was not as easy to execute as it might seem. First, no world-class gal on campus wanted any part of my fraternity. Second, the guys hated each other, and expressing love about a fellow brother whom you hated seemed a rather difficult gesture, if not impossible. But I did a few things that made it work.

We hired four of the most beautiful strippers from the local strip clubs. They were young, sexy, and welcomed the opportunity to assume roles as sexy university coeds and hostesses for our three planned get-acquainted parties. I then rehearsed the guys and made them put their arms around each other, expressing this new brotherly love that was so foreign and repulsive to them. They could barely stand it. But the charade worked.

Not only did we end up with the biggest pledge class in our history, beating all the other fraternities, but some of the guys actually got closer to their fellow brothers, and an entire new spirit spread throughout the fraternity. There was such a buzz around campus about the girls who were acting as our hostesses that by the time we held our third party, we didn't have room for the crowd that we attracted. In fact, the strippers enjoyed their experience so much that they invited some of their beautiful girlfriends to join the fun. The guests were so impressed with the love, brotherhood, and display of beautiful women that when it came time to join, they were literally begging to sign up.

I had understood the psychological trigger of my product (the fraternity) and of my prospect (the young man looking for a place to find love and social interaction). The key in this case was the power of knowing the *nature of the prospect*—those emotional aspects of the prospect that would respond best to a planned pitch. Operation Survival was a huge success and transformed my fraternity into one of the best on campus—all from a simple marketing plan and in a few short weeks.

Let me cite a few more examples to illustrate this very important principle. If I was selling a home, I would get to know the motivations of my prospects and what they are looking for in a home. I would find out their history. I would ask them about their other home-buying experiences and what their hobbies are. I would gather as much information about them as possible and then I would develop a sense of what emotional needs they might have.

Understanding their needs and the nature of the prospect in general would give me enough information to craft a very effective sales presentation that, ideally, would match the nature of my product with the nature of my prospect.

The prospect has basic emotional needs that your product or service will solve, regardless of how sophisticated or simple your product offering is. Examine those emotional needs. It is from the perspective of emotion that you will reach the core essence of your prospect's motivation. And it is from this essence that you will get all the clues you need to uncover the way to that prospect's heart and soul and eventually to his or her pocketbook.

## 12. Current Fads

There are always a number of fads taking place at the same time. One might be a clothing fad, another might be an unusual expression made popular by a TV show or commercial, or a fad might be a popular trend.

There are also fads in direct response. On TV right now, the hottest products are exercise devices. There was a time when real estate shows were popular. Be aware of the current fads so you can determine the hottest product categories and also the new language of our time. You want to recognize them and harmonize with them.

A good example of recognizing fads and knowing what to do with them comes from an experience I had with Richard Guilfoyle, a direct marketer from Boston. He had a strong sense of history and prided himself on creating replicas of historic American objects—Paul Revere's lantern, a statue of George Washington at Valley Forge, a salt and pepper set from the time of the Revolutionary War. In 1975 his company was doing quite well.

And no wonder. The country was about to celebrate its bicentennial anniversary, and this class of merchandise was being recognized as a way of celebrating the birth of our nation 200 years before. Sales were brisk. Richard was capitalizing on this current fad for American Revolutionary period products.

Then the bottom of his business fell out. Sales plummeted and he couldn't figure out why. And it all happened just prior to July 4th, 1976—the date of the bicentennial celebration.

When he attended my seminar, he was really quite disappointed with his business. What happened? I suggested that maybe it was because people were associating his merchandise with the anniversary of the United States. Since that date had already passed, his sales reflected this perception.

But Richard insisted that this wasn't the case. "My products have true historic significance and have nothing to do with the bicentennial." Could I simply look at his copy and help him improve it?

After looking over his copy, which was actually quite good, I saw clearly what the problem was. He had not recognized that consumers perceived his products as part of the excitement of the bicentennial and not as a part of American history that they could save and own.

He then showed me a few ads he had prepared as a result of attending my seminar. One of them was for a necklace with a small replica of a Paul Revere lantern that had a diamond in the center representing the light. It was a beautiful piece of jewelry.

I read the copy and said, "You have a winner here. This ad will do well—not because of the historic nature of the necklace but because of the beautiful piece of jewelry that it is. You're now selling jewelry, Richard, not good old Americana."

Sure enough, the ad was a huge success and he soon realized how a powerful fad can grow and fade.

## Fads Generate Publicity

I used fads as a way of generating publicity when I was doing public relations for a few of my clients. One owned a ski resort and was trying to increase the awareness of snowmobiles at his resort. At the time, during the mid to late 1960s, the women's lib movement was new, strong and vocal. I suggested that the resort owner ban women snowmobile drivers and issue a press release proudly announcing the fact. He did and the publicity went national. He rescinded his ban and snowmobile sales grew dramatically from the national publicity and attention.

At the same time, one of my accounts—Jerry Herman, owner of the Spot pizza restaurant near Northwestern University in Evanston, Illinois—wanted national publicity, too. Women were in the middle of an unusual fad—throwing their bras away and going braless. I suggested to Jerry that he design a bra-shaped pizza and he, too, got national publicity. While these publicity stunts might seem a bit silly in retrospect, back then they were effective because they tied into a fad of the times.

A fad can die just as quickly as it can grow. So you must capture the moment early enough and get out right after the fad peaks. The people who came out with radar detectors when they became a fad did exceptionally well. A few of them attended my seminar and wrote great ads and built their companies into very successful entities.

One of the companies selling radar detectors—Cincinnati Microwave—sent three of their top people to my seminar before it really took off and became a $140 million company with over $40 million in profits.

But be careful. I can tell you stories (I should say nightmares) that show how dangerous fads can be to your financial health. During the Watergate scandal, I once introduced "The

Watergate Game—a game of intrigue and deception for the whole family." But no store would carry it because of the controversy and I lost my shirt. I once created the Batman credit card to capture the Batman fad of the 1960s and printed 250,000 of them only to be denied a license to sell them.

But as you can see, knowing how to recognize a fad and capitalize on it can be a very powerful tool if your timing is right. This brings us very nicely to the next topic.

# 13. Timing

How many times have you been too early with an idea or too late? I've heard complaints from many of my students who have failed because their timing just wasn't right.

Timing certainly has a lot to do with fads. You want to be involved at the beginning of a fad and not enter in the middle or the end. That's smart timing. But there are products that have just been introduced too early or too late, and that relates to timing, too. When do you introduce a new product? Is America ready for it? And how do you know?

The answer really is quite simple: Nobody knows. That's why I always test every product that I sell first. The consumer will tell me if I'm too early or too late or right on target.

When crime increased, it was good common sense to offer burglar alarms. When the O.J. Simpson case unraveled, there were plenty of opportunities to capitalize on it and the media sure did.

President Carter went on television in 1980 and reprimanded Americans, accusing us of running up too much debt. "Stop using your credit cards" was his suggestion. And millions of Americans did just that. Direct response rates plummeted overnight. Tests we had previously run that showed great promise were coming up as losses. Our timing obviously was bad but through no fault of ours. Knowing the cause of the problem helped us keep our sanity.

It's just as important to know when the timing is bad. We came out with a product called the Bone Fone, a portable radio worn around the neck. It was perfect timing until a product called the Walkman came out and killed our new product. Timing. It can kill a product or make it.

I once ran a media test on an electronic blood pressure unit we were thinking of putting in our catalog. I thought it would do well and when the results were presented to me, I was amazed at how well it had done. Armed with a great deal of confidence, I placed a major national advertising campaign in all the magazines we normally advertised in—spending almost $300,000 at the time. But even before the ads started to run I discovered that the report I thought was so good was actually produced in error. The product did not do well in the media test and in fact did quite poorly.

Since I had already placed the advertising, I braced myself for the bad response. But my timing proved to be coincidentally right on target. About the same time as the ads started to run, the American Heart Association started running a major advertising campaign suggesting that Americans take their blood pressure regularly. Our sales jumped and what was destined to become one of our biggest losses turned into a nice profit. And we even won the Life Extension Award from the Life Extension Association for our work in alerting the public to the need for measuring their blood pressure regularly.

# 14. Linking

A very critical technique that I have used in mail order ads is a process called linking. Basically, it is the technique of relating what the consumer already knows and understands with what you are selling to make the new product easy to understand and relate to.

One of the easiest ways to explain this trigger is to describe how it works in a fad—a craze that captures the public's consciousness and quickly creates strong demand, awareness or behavioral changes. The demand can be for a product such as for the Beanie Babies in the 1990s or the citizens band (CB) radios back in the 1970s. It can be simply the strong awareness of a new or different product or concept, such as the Viagra introduction in 1998, or it can be for behavioral changes, such as women throwing away their bras during the women's liberation move-ment of the late 1960s.

There are also fads within specific industries. For example, in the exercise industry there might be a fad for abdominal de-vices; on infomercials, there might be a glut of business opportu-nity shows.

Usually the fads come and go quickly. But the importance of the fad examples is to show you the process of linking on its most basic and obvious levels. Then I'll take it deeper to give you a sense of how linking can be used to effectively sell any product or service.

For example, I used the awareness of a presidential act as a way of selling products. When it was discovered in 1973 that Nixon was using phone tap equipment to record all his phone conversations, there was enormous publicity about it. I immedi-ately put together a JS&A offer for a system with which anybody could tap their phones and ran it in the *Wall Street Journal* under the headline "Tap Your Phone."

That ad was a mistake. The FBI showed up at my door and the *Wall Street Journal* threatened not to run my ads any more. Even worse, I didn't sell many of the systems and lost money on the ad. You see, what Nixon did was illegal and so my offer encour-aged illegal activity even though I had done nothing illegal myself.

In contrast, I caught another fad at just the right time. I of-fered a walkie-talkie right at the height of the citizens band (CB) radio boom in the United States. By calling my walkie-talkie a Pocket CB because it broadcast on one of the CB frequencies, I was able to capture a major chunk of the CB market.

The minute there is a lot of publicity about something and it has the potential to turn into a fad, you could have a great oppor-tunity to link it onto something that you're doing either to get publicity or to promote a product.

Fads are very powerful. And you now understand the basic concept of linking. But how does this help you as a copywriter?

Whenever I sell a new product or a unique feature of a new concept, I use linking. I take what is familiar to the prospect, re-late it to the object I am selling, and create a bridge in the mind of my prospect. Because of this linking, the prospect needs to think a lot less to understand the new product. The product is easier to relate to the needs of the prospect. Everybody wins.

### Linking a Body Part

My ad for a smoke detector was an example of this process. The headline read: "The Nose." I talked about the smoke detector not as a smoke detector (many such devices were already being sold) but as a nose that sat on your ceiling and sniffed the air. When it smelled smoke, it set off an alarm. I took the very human and simple concept of a nose—a part of the body whose function is well understood—and then linked it to an electronic device.

In the ad I also used linking to express quality. For example, I talked about the integrated circuits using gold for the contact points. My prospect was then able to link the expense and quality of gold to this product to arrive at a quality link and justify its higher price. In actuality, every integrated circuit used gold for its contact points, so this wasn't revolutionary, but nobody had taken the time to explain it to the consumer.

I have used linking in many other ways. For example, I had a product that was a remote car starter. You pressed a button on a remote control device and your car automatically started. I called it "The Mafia Auto Gadget." Can you see the linkage with this product? No? Well, I explained it in the ad. The Mafia often used explosives activated by a car's ignition to eliminate competition. Because this device started the car for you at a distance, it eliminated the fear and concern for any Mafia member. Of course, the market was also broadened to include those people who simply liked the convenience of prestarting their cars on hot or cold days and having the cars reach a pleasant temperature before they got in. But the positioning of the product was done with a link that the consumer could understand—the Mafia.

Today, such a device might be linked to the terrorist car bombings in Iraq or a threat to homeland security—both strong but unpleasant trends. I doubt the product would be popular today, not to mention the poor association this link would make.

This is also a perfect example of why it often doesn't pay to copy a successful campaign of the past. But that is another issue.

I could give you many examples. The main point to remember about linking, though, is that it should relate the product or service you are selling to something that is easy for your prospect to identify with so that you bridge the mental gap in the mind of the prospect.

Usually products are simply improved versions of previously sold products. You need to relate the older product to the new version to explain the differences.

One of the hardest things to use linking for is a miracle product—a product that is too good to believe. For example, I was selling a pill to be put in the gas tank of your car; it would improve gas mileage and clean out the engine, and had 10 times the fuel additives of super unleaded fuel. It was truly an amazing product and difficult to link to anything that existed in the marketplace. We used the phrases "vitamins for your car" and "tuneup in a pill" as a few of our links.

Linking is a basic human emotional system of storing experiences and knowledge and then recalling those experiences and linking them to something we have to deal with on a daily basis or that is in the public's consciousness. We often link. When President John F. Kennedy died, I was in the military in Frankfurt, Germany, and his assassination took place in the evening Frankfurt time. I remember where I was at that precise moment and remember the confusion and the personal pain I felt. I linked every image and emotion to that moment in time. Do you remember where you were when you first found out about the attacks on September 11th?

## 15. Consistency

As a direct marketer, I have determined that the most important thing you can do to turn a prospect into a customer is to make it incredibly easy for that prospect to commit to a purchase, regardless of how small that purchase may be. It is therefore imperative that the commitment be simple, small, and in line with the prospect's needs.

Once the commitment is made and the prospect becomes a customer, the playing field suddenly changes. There now exists a level of commitment and consistency, directed in your favor, to encourage future purchases.

A good example of this can be seen at a car dealership. The salesperson tallies your purchase, gets approval from the general manager, and then has you sign the paperwork. As she is walking away to get the car prepped and ready for you to drive away, she turns to you and says, "And you do want that undercoating, don't you?" You instinctively nod your head. The charge is added to your invoice. "And you'll also want our floor mats to keep your car clean as well, won't you?"

Or how about the times when you order something from a catalog and say to yourself, "Since I'm going through the trouble or ordering, let's see what else they have that I might like," and you end up ordering more.

Once a commitment is made, the tendency is to act consistently with that commitment. The customer nods his head.

A good example of this phenomenon was told to me by Jon Spoelstra, the former general manager of the Portland Trailblazers basketball team and president of the New Jersey Nets. One of his primary jobs was to sell tickets. "I would personally visit a prospect, sell him a simple yet basic ticket package, start to leave, and then turn around just as I was about to walk out the door and offer something else. Very often my customer would simply nod his head and say under his breath, 'Yeah, sure, add that to it, too.'"

One of the important points to remember is to always make that first sale simple. Once the prospect makes the commitment to purchase from you, you can then easily offer more to increase your sales. This is equally true for products sold from a mail order ad or from a TV infomercial. I have learned to keep the initial offer extremely simple. Then, once the prospect calls and orders the product I am offering, and while the prospect is on the phone, I offer other items and end up with a larger total sale. An additional sale occurs over 50 percent of the time, depending on my added offer.

Once you've committed to the original purchase, you are

poised for a course of action consistent with what you have already undertaken. In the case of buying, you are now primed to buy more by virtue of the original commitment to buy.

# 16. Harmonize

An important lesson I taught at the seminar was learned from the story of how the late Bobby Darin, a popular singer of the 1950s and 1960s, became famous.

As a young singer in New York, for a long time Darin tried unsuccessfully to break into the music business. He would go from record company to record company trying to convince them to make an album of him singing old popular standards.

He was rejected. Nobody believed that the music industry would accept old popular songs from an unknown young singer. Besides, the hot music at the time was good old rock and roll sung by black artists and called the Motown sound.

Darin was quite frustrated, so he took things into his own hands. Did he cut his own album by himself? No, he didn't have the money. Did he convince a record company to record him? Yes, but not the songs he so desperately wanted to record. Instead he sat down and wrote a tune that fitted or harmonized with what the public was buying at the time.

The tune he wrote was called "Splish Splash," and the lyrics started out, "Splish splash, I was takin' a bath, 'round about a Saturday night." It went on to tell a story about what happened when he took that bath. The song was good old Motown rock and roll and he easily sold this music to a record company, which recorded it with Darin singing the lead. "Splish Splash" became a smash hit and sold millions of records. In the recording, he even sounded like a Motown recording artist.

Darin recognized what the market wanted and was buying at the time, and he created something that harmonized perfectly with that market, even though his song was far from the music that was in his heart. He made the practical choice to put aside his desires, put aside his ego and goals, and just cut a record that would sell and earn him the recognition he needed to record the type of music he really wanted to record.

Despite the hit record, which became a million seller, he still couldn't interest any record company in recording him for a pop album. So he took all his earnings from the success of "Splish Splash" and made the album himself. One of the songs he recorded was his version of an old Kurt Weill song called "Mack the Knife." Not only was his album a smash hit, but "Mack the Knife" became a multimillion-selling single throughout the world. Bobby Darin went on to be known not for "Splish Splash" but for the music he loved best—popular jazz oldies.

### Lessons from Bobby Darin

There are many lessons to be learned from this one example. First, realize that often you must go with the established way of doing things in order to accomplish your goals. You've got to pattern yourself after what is working and then harmonize with the marketplace. Once you have an established reputation, it's easier to try something different that you yourself want to do.

So first you meet the needs of the market to raise the capital *you* need and then you go for your dreams. Once you've raised your own funds, you can do anything you want. You can pursue a course of action that nobody else would believe possible.

I also use the Bobby Darin example to convince people who come to me with a concept or idea that seems really too far out of the mainstream that they have to harmonize with the marketplace. In some cases, their product needs a slightly different twist to work, even though that is not what they envisioned for the product. The change usually involves removing a component or making the product cheaper or presenting it in a totally new and simple way. Let me cite one perfect example.

It was 1973 and the president and national sales manager of a calculator company, APF, came to me with their new product. They were all excited about it and felt that they had the greatest and most exciting breakthrough in electronics since the calculator was invented.

So confident were they that they were willing to pay for the cost of my test ad. "Joe, this product is so hot that you'll sell millions," said the president of the company.

At the time, prices were still quite high for calculators, so $69.95 was a very attractive price back then for a good desk calculator with a large display. APF had sold their calculators successfully at $69.95 but felt that with their latest innovation, they had the ultimate product for my company—truly a revolution in electronics (or so they thought).

"What's the innovation?" I asked. The company president and his national sales manager unwrapped a special box to show me their prototype.

The calculator was the same calculator they had been selling for the past year but with a new feature—a clock that ran in the calculator display when the calculator wasn't being used. "What do you think?" the president beamed. "We plan on selling this for $99.95."

I didn't like the idea. I explained that the consumer felt that a calculator was a serious business tool, turned on when it was needed and turned it off when it was not. I had been selling them for almost two years and had a pretty good sense of the product and its emotional appeal. Putting a clock into the display and keeping the calculator on all the time was not in harmony with what would impress the consumer and therefore it would not be successful. Increasing the price was a mistake. If I had a choice, I would have offered the product for less, or about $39.95, in order to get rid of their inventory. I just felt that it wouldn't sell.

The company president didn't believe me. "What?" he blurted out. "It costs more to make than the standard model and it's so revolutionary—why should we even consider selling it for less?"

I agreed to write an ad to prove my point. "I will write a great ad and let you approve it. I will then run the ad in the *Wall Street Journal*. We'll measure the response and if it's successful, we'll create a nice advertising campaign for you."

I sent APF the ad and they loved it. "If this doesn't work, I'm getting out of the calculator business," said the president. And so I ran the ad.

It failed miserably. The product was closed out at $39.95

shortly thereafter. When you are not in harmony with the market, the marketplace doesn't respond. Taking a product and making it harmonize with the prospect is simply a matter of good listening and observation. It doesn't take genius. It takes a good eye and ear, and a little intuition helps, too.

It is important that your product harmonize with or fill the needs of your prospect. If it doesn't, it is up to you to figure out how to change it so it does. It might mean showing it in a different color, removing or adding an accessory—the point is that the customer is the king. Your goal is to harmonize not only with the marketplace but in particular with your customer.

# 17. Desire to Belong

The desire to belong is a strong motivational factor in marketing but it is often not appreciated. Think about it.

Why do people own a Mercedes? Why do they smoke Marlboro cigarettes? Why do certain fads catch on? It could be that these people buy a specific product because they subconsciously want to belong to the group that already owns or uses that specific product.

In the case of Marlboros, the smokers subconsciously want to join that group of smokers who have responded to the rugged western image the cigarette's ad agency has created.

The people who buy a Mercedes often want to belong to that special group of Mercedes owners. Do you think it's because of the special braking or suspension system? Forget it. They're going out and spending megabucks to buy something that's maybe slightly better than many of the other automobiles. The other cars can take you to the same places at the same speed and yet these people—all very intelligent—will go out and spend plenty more to buy a Mercedes.

And the list goes on. You name a product that has an established image and I'll show you a consumer who, somewhere in his or her subconscious value system, wants to belong to the group of people who own that product. Fashion, automobiles, cigarettes, gadgets, whatever the category—the consumer who buys a specific brand has been motivated to buy that brand by virtue of the desire to belong to the group of people who already own that brand.

When Volvo discovered that its customer base had one of the highest educational levels of any of the car manufacturers, they publicized this fact. They then noticed that when the same survey was conducted a few years later, the percentage jumped even higher. The increase was caused, in my judgment, by the association that other highly educated new buyers wanted to make with the Volvo owners—they wanted to belong to that group.

Some students have said to me, "Well, what about hermits? Don't tell me they have the desire to belong."

And my answer has been that they want to belong to the group of people who are hermits. To identify with the group doesn't necessarily mean you have to be with anyone or be very social. And maybe the key word here is *identify*. The Mercedes owner wants to be identified with the class or group of people who also own a Mercedes.

Owning a Rolls-Royce in California in the 1970s was the ultimate status symbol. I couldn't believe how impressed people were with other people who owned one. Being a Midwestern boy and not having grown up on the car-conscious West Coast, it was culture shock to realize how much a Rolls meant to somebody from the West Coast. Yet when you look at the car, it is one of the most conservative and old-fashioned-looking automobiles on the road today.

The desire to belong to and identify with a group of people who own a specific product is one of the most powerful psychological motivators to be aware of in marketing and copywriting. But one of the best examples I can give was a personal experience, which leads me to my next psychological point.

## 18. Desire to Collect

There must be a natural instinct in the human race to collect, as I learned from my marketing experience.

If you are selling a collectible, it's pretty easy to understand that this urge exists and therefore, as a direct marketer, you need to capitalize on it. But often overlooked is the fact that it can be used to sell any other product, too. Let's take the watch buyer. An enthusiastic watch buyer is your perfect prospect for another watch.

When I was selling watches in print, I would send mailings to those customers who had previously ordered from me and offer them other watches. I received a great response. My best list for watches consisted of my existing watch owners. Now you would think that if you had a watch, what would you need another one for? Wrong. Many people actually collect them. They'll have several watches, several pairs of sunglasses, several pairs of jeans, a library of videos or compact disks. The list is endless.

I'm always amazed at the number of dolls collected by QVC viewers. Some of the viewers are older women, long past childhood, yet among QVC's most avid collectors. And they have dozens of dolls.

Small car models are also sold on QVC. They are some of the most popular products. And not to be outdone, there must be thousands of viewers who own many BluBlocker sunglasses—often in several different styles.

The point is, when selling, whether in print or on TV or the Internet, recognize that there is a very large segment of the population who, for whatever reason, has an emotional need to collect a series

*You'd be amazed at what people collect.*

of similar products. These products bring great joy and satisfaction and in some cases utility.

And think about those who collect the real cars. Many who can afford them have collections that range up to hundreds of full-sized automobiles. What kind of emotional need are they fulfilling?

One of the ways that direct marketers optimize on the collecting instinct is by sending, free of charge with their very first shipment, some sort of device to hold the collection.

I can remember ordering a series of silver airplane tails with various airline logos embossed on them from the Franklin Mint. I started collecting them to see how the Franklin Mint conducted its program rather than from any interest in collecting airplane tails.

I received a beautiful chest with cutouts for each of the silver tails. And they came once a month and each month I put one more tail in the chest. I looked at my collection each time I put in a new tail and felt the pride of knowing that my tail collection was growing. Finally, I had enough to fill the chest so that when guests came over, I could display my entire tail collection. I finally sobered up and stopped collecting. It was costing me a small fortune, and after all, the only reason I had started was for the research. And the collection was kind of silly to begin with. The airlines were either merging, going out of business or changing their names so fast that even the Franklin Mint couldn't keep up.

But it was this experience that convinced me that there were lots of opportunities for selling to collectors.

# 19. Curiosity

If I had to pick the one major psychological reason that makes direct marketing so successful today, it would be curiosity. At retail, a customer can touch and experience the product first-hand and then decide. A mail order customer can't do that. The product might look good and do exactly what the customer expects it to do, yet there is always that level of curiosity that makes the product attractive to the prospect. "What is that product really like?" might be the typical thought of a prospect.

When I sold BluBlocker sunglasses on TV, I deliberately created an enormous amount of curiosity. I had my subjects—ordinary people we would find on the streets—try on a pair of BluBlocker sunglasses. I would then videotape their reactions. Some of the reactions were great and when I presented them on TV, the viewers were wondering, "What was it like to look through these glasses—that pair of sunglasses with the orange lenses that was making everybody go wild?"

I didn't take the TV camera and look through a pair. That would have destroyed the curiosity and would not have given the true picture of what the sunglasses would do for you. (Your brain adjusts to the color shift when you look through the lens, whereas the TV camera does not.) Instead, I enhanced curiosity by not showing the view. The only way you could look through them was to buy a pair. And buy the public did—almost 8 million pairs from a series of commercials that ran for six years.

Curiosity also works well with books. You can tease prospects by telling them what they will find out by reading your books. In fact, the strongest motivating factor in selling books is curiosity, followed only by notoriety and credibility.

Because a prospect can't touch or experience the product, curiosity is the strongest motivating factor in mail order. Immediate gratification is the strongest factor in retail. So if I recognize that fact and can deliver your product promptly—let's say with FedEx—I'm capitalizing on the curiosity in mail order and coming close to the retail advantage.

I've sold products relying completely on the factor of curiosity. In 1973 I offered a pocket calculator without ever showing a picture of it. By creating such compelling curiosity about that product, I sold thousands of them. Sure the price was good and the product was great, but without showing the product or even mentioning the brand name, I was still able to make the selling message very compelling.

How do you use curiosity in selling your products? First realize that when you sell books, curiosity is the key motivating factor and you should use it as your prime selling tool. But realize also that there are many other products that lend themselves to holding back part of the story in order to arouse curiosity and create a demand.

Show too much, tell too much, and you run the risk of killing whatever advantage you have using mail order as a medium.

A friend of mine, Steve Dworman, who publishes an infomercial trade newsletter, was fascinated by my success using curiosity as the main selling tool in my BluBlocker commercial. He thought to himself, "Could the same technique be used to sell something that was impossible to sell on TV in a direct response commercial? Like perfume?" So he organized the shooting of a commercial using curiosity as its main motivating factor.

In the commercial, everybody was raving about the perfume but there was no way the TV sets allowed viewers to sniff it unless they bought Steve's product. The commercial generated enough curiosity to work.

How many times have you said too much, shown too much or failed to use the power of curiosity? It is one of the leading motivating factors in all direct response marketing.

# 20. Sense of Urgency

You might have already figured this one out. You've almost sold the prospect. The prospect believes in your product and is ready to buy. But like many of your customers, this one says, "Well, let me think about it."

It is a proven fact that when this happens, chances are the prospect won't buy. And the reasons are really very logical. First, in time that excellent sales message you wrote will most likely be forgotten. Second, if you're lucky and it isn't forgotten, it won't have the same impact it had when it was first read. That old saying, "Out of sight, out of mind," holds true in a case like this.

Therefore, to avoid the delaying tactic, you've got to provide prospects with an incentive or reason to buy now. In fact, if you do your job right, customers have to feel guilty if they don't buy right now. But how do you do it?

First, here's what you don't want to do. The prospect has spent a lot of time with your ad and you've convinced him or her to buy. The one thing you don't want to do is blow your integrity at the very end of the ad by making a statement that is not true. A statement like, "If you don't respond within the next few days, we'll be sold out," or some other deceit will turn off the prospect. So be careful. Whatever you say at the end should be the truth and should be crafted to maintain the same integrity that has been expressed throughout your ad.

Now, what can you do to provide a sense of urgency? Some ads reek with a sense of urgency and nothing has to be said. For example, I once ran a retraction for an ad that said that the price listed for a calculator was the wrong price and that the new price was $20 higher, but you had a few days to purchase the product at the old price before the new price went into effect. That approach was an integral part of the concept and provided a sense of urgency that was obvious and very real.

You can also convey a sense of urgency by offering limited editions. "We have only 1,000 sets and this will be our last advertisement" can be persuasive and motivate the buyer to act right away.

You might have a great ad with a good sense of urgency but a fatal error might still kill your ad's effectiveness. What is that fatal error? Omitting important information that the buyer needs in order to make that buying decision. Then the buyer has the excuse, "There's a question I have but I'm too busy to call and find out the answer," or a similar reason. In short, even a great sense of urgency can be wasted if you leave out some critical information from your ad copy.

You can use the sense of urgency in many different ways— low supplies, closeout opportunity, price rise, product shortages, limited-time price opportunity or limited-edition opportunity. How about "Buy now so you can start enjoying the benefits of my product tomorrow." Or even "Buy one during the next three days and you'll get a second one free."

Another way to provide a sense of urgency is through your shipping methods. "We'll ship your purchase via FedEx if you order by (a certain date)." Or "Since you are one of our customers, you can buy this wonderful product prior to our national introduction if you order by (a certain date)."

We used to run all our new product introductions with the phrase, "National Introductory Price." This didn't mean that much but it raised the possibility that the price was the introductory price and later might go up. In actuality, the prices of calculators and electronics always went down, so we eventually dropped that phrase.

The number of possibilities is limited only by your imagination. The sense-of-urgency statements always go at the end of your advertising. And if there are two critical locations in your advertising, they are the very beginning and the very end. And it is at the end where the sense of urgency and several other important concepts meet and must be considered and blended seamlessly together.

# 21. Fear

Fear is one of the great motivators that will cause us to take action. Give a person a reason to act based on the fact that they may lose the opportunity to buy something and they will usually act in a positive way toward your offer. As just discussed, sense of urgency is an important psychological trigger.

A part of the sense of urgency is based on fear. Your customer fears that he or she will lose out on the opportunity of buying a product or service because it won't be available in the future or it won't be available at the same price. But fear can be a motivating factor in other situations as well.

For example, when a new flu virus or strain threatens, this would be an opportunity to sell products that build the immune system or products that may help prevent the disease. People are buying these products because they want to protect themselves from the virus, which today is a real and present danger. They fear the consequences if they don't buy something to protect themselves. Even though it is easier to sell something that cures a disease than it is to sell a preventive, this rule is often violated when fear is a major factor.

### Fear of Crime

Another example is the purchase of a burglar alarm or even a gun. There might be an outbreak of crime in a certain city and residents who are fearful they might be attacked or robbed will take action to protect themselves and their homes.

There are products that play to our fear of aging. Creams, lotions and pills offering a fountain of youth are bought because people fear the aging process and are concerned about what others think of their looks.

It is common to hear of people who take action and show irrational behavior based on their fears. The stock market is a good example of irrational behavior when it comes to a person's fear of losing money. When the market crashes and is near the bottom of what is called a bear cycle and the economy looks extremely grim, consumers start dumping stocks fearing that the market will continue to collapse and they will lose more money. In reality, this usually is the best time to buy stocks. Or when the viability of the dollar is questioned, many investors, out of fear, protect themselves and buy gold coins or hoard cash.

Fear can be a great motivator if used carefully in response to some perceived danger or loss that one might have to face.

# 22. Instant Gratification

This is a big advantage at retail. Think about it. At retail, you pick something up, hold it, touch it and look it over completely. You can make your decision to buy and then you can take it home with you where you can enjoy and use it immediately. You don't have that advantage in mail order.

So to compensate, you should convey to your customer either the advantages in ordering from you via mail or the assurance that you ship promptly and that the customer will have his or her purchase within a few days.

The effort by direct marketers to provide that instant gratification—shipping promptly—has made mail order one of the fastest methods of distribution in the United States and has thus taken a great deal away from the retail industry. I can call a computer mail order company and order a piece of software on Monday morning and use it by Monday evening. That's so much easier than running to the store, parking, finding the right department and then having to deal with the salesclerk. It's no wonder direct marketing has taken a dramatic bite out of many of the traditional retail categories.

The mail order computer industry created giants such as Dell Inc. and Gateway 2000 that specialize in next-day delivery.

And so if you have a product and want to capitalize on the main advantage that a retailer has, find a way to ship your merchandise out quicker, deliver it faster and provide better service than any retailer could ever offer.

# 23. Exclusivity, Rarity or Uniqueness

These are very strong motivating factors for the right product or the right situation.

The concept is to basically let prospects feel that they are special if they buy a particular product—that they will belong to the very small group that can be envied for owning this very limited item.

The emotional appeal of this approach is quite strong. Everybody likes to feel special. Most people would like to belong to a rare group that owns a product that few people can own and enjoy.

By limiting the number they produce, some marketing companies have come up with a very strong appeal for consumers. The Franklin Mint—a multimillion-dollar business—was built on the premise of the limited edition, first with coins and then later with everything from plates and cups to model cars and dolls. Anything you could collect and they could limit was fair game for the Mint.

The thought behind the limited edition is also to provide value. As people build various collections of things, the objects grow in value if others start collecting the same goods too. Soon, the collections come to the attention of the mass market and that attracts more collectors. Then the value of the collections really starts to grow.

Those collectibles that have a limited circulation or a limited number in circulation grow in value even more. And there's always the story of somebody discovering an heirloom in the attic worth a small fortune. There are exceptions, of course—silver airplane tails, to name one.

One of the appeals of an exclusive item is the possibility of extra future value implied by limiting the circulation of that product.

The power of exclusivity was driven home to me in October of 1980 when I was in Minocqua, Wisconsin. It was right after I had given a seminar.

At the seminar site, for the enjoyment of the participants, I kept a stable of six snowmobiles. Whenever I would give a seminar during the winter, I would have these machines available for my students during their breaks. Riding snowmobiles was a lot of fun and everybody loved to drive them. Then one day the president of Mattel Electronics, Jeff Rochlis, broke his arm in a bad snowmobile accident. That ended our snowmobile program.

I now had six snowmobiles in my garage with not many people to use them. Out of curiosity, one day I visited the local snowmobile shop—the same place that had sold me the six that I owned. I obviously didn't need any more but I wanted to see what small improvements were added in the new models.

I walked into the shop and asked the salesman, "Well, Paul, what's new for this year?"

Paul took me over to a snowmobile that was propped up on a small riser and pointed to it. "This baby is our new oil-cooled model that goes over 100 miles per hour and sells for $2,600."

At the time, snowmobiles were selling for under $1,000 and their top speed was around 40 miles per hour so this new model was obviously special. But regardless of how special it was, I already had six and I certainly did not need any more. I turned to Paul and in a matter-of-fact way said, "Who could possibly want a snowmobile that could go 100 miles per hour and cost $2,600? How ridiculous."

Paul chuckled, "Well, there are only going to be six sold in the entire state this year. We've been allocated only two of them and we already have one sold."

I then quickly blurted out, "I'll take this one." Yes, I ended up buying it. I wanted to be one of the few who owned this powerful new machine. I wanted to feel that I was part of a unique group and that I was special. And even though I didn't need any more snowmobiles, I ended up buying it and I was proud of the fact that I did.

It was this incident that made me realize the power of exclusivity, uniqueness and rarity.

# 24. Simplicity

You must keep your advertising copy simple. The positioning of your product must be simple. Your offer must be simple. In short, you want to keep your entire presentation as simple as possible while still getting across your message.

There are times when you want to turn something simple into something complex. We talked about that in the previous chapter under the topic "Product Explanation." But that rule applies to marketing issues, and here we are looking at the basic psychological motivator of simplicity.

What does this mean in terms of your advertising copy? I like to tell my students to focus. Focus on what you are trying to accomplish and eliminate things that either complicate your presentation or aren't necessary.

This doesn't mean you write copy that is so simple a third grader can read it. That's not what we mean by simple. The copy should be able to be read by the less educated people as well as the more educated and come across clearly. It is not good style to write either "up" or "down" to anybody.

The use of big words to impress is one example of writing up to somebody. You're trying to impress with your use of words while somebody else who might not be familiar with your fancy words will be lost. Use simple easy-to-understand words. Words are, after all, stories—emotional images—each having an impact sometimes greater than we think. Using simple words has the greatest impact. Using words that everybody can understand has a greater impact than words that most people have difficulty with.

And keep your layouts simple. Tests have confirmed that things like color bars across an ad, fancy type that is difficult to read and lines that draw your eyes away from the copy can hurt comprehension. Fancy typefaces may look good but they often give the lowest comprehension scores.

## Simplicity Is a Powerful Tool

If you have a tendency to complicate things, you're not going to succeed in writing good direct response advertising copy. Be aware of this important point as you decide which typeface to use, how you want to present your product and the offer you want to make.

A good example of how simplicity works in direct response happened to me when Murray Raphel, a dear friend and a great public speaker, approached me. He had been in touch with the people who had developed the Swiss Army watch and wondered if I would be interested in marketing the product in the United States. Yes, I was. A meeting was arranged in which I was going to see the line of watches.

At the meeting I was presented with three styles and three colors in each style for a total of nine different watches. One was a men's style, the second was for women and the third was for children. The colors were black, red and khaki. I examined the watches, learned the history and in general became very knowledgeable about the watches themselves. Then came the big question.

"Mr. Sugarman, you've examined the watches. What do you think?"

I looked over the watches, thought for a few minutes and answered, "I'd like to run just the men's watch in black in the *Wall Street Journal* to test the concept."

The watch company executives looked perplexed. "Why don't you offer all the styles? Look at how many more people you'll reach if you offer nine different styles. You'll reach women and children in addition to men and you'll give them all a color choice."

I told them that in my experience, keeping it simple was the best approach and that offering a customer too many choices was a very dangerous thing to do.

But no matter what I said, they would not agree. "Logic says, Mr. Sugarman, that offering more of a choice will result in more sales."

I then came up with an idea to prove that I was right. I offered to run two separate ads in what is called an "A/B split." That is where the *Wall Street Journal* will print two separate versions of the same ad—version A and version B—to be delivered in the same area at the same time. So one home will get one version of the ad while the next-door neighbor might get version B.

*These two ads were practically identical with ad A (top) offering nine different models and ad B (bottom) offering only one.*

This was a very good way to test two different ads to determine the winning approach.

I offered to do the test and ran the two ads with almost identical copy and graphics. One of the few differences was that in ad A, I showed the men's watch along with the child's watch for size perspective, whereas in ad B, I showed just the men's watch. I then listed each one of the choices—nine in all—in ad A and just one in ad B.

When I finished the ads, the A version actually looked better than the version with only one choice. When both versions ran, the ad that featured only one men's watch outpulled the other version that featured nine models by a surprising 3 to 1 ratio. In short, for every watch we sold from the ad that featured the nine styles, we sold three in the other ad that showed just the one black watch.

I knew almost instinctively that to give the consumer a confusing array of choices meant that the consumer would back off and not buy.

When would I show all these nine watches? Later, in my catalog. Once I've located those people interested in Swiss Army watches, I would then show them all nine models in the catalog. By the time the catalog reaches my customer, he or she has been qualified as a watch buyer. I can now offer a larger selection.

Another good example of the power of simplicity occurred during the production of a half-hour TV commercial I was doing for a pill that reduced wrinkles and improved the skin. Called Miracell, the product was truly revolutionary. I had been taking it for a few months and noticed dramatic results. We did two double-blind studies that proved that the product really did work. But there was one major problem.

For maximum effectiveness, you had to take two pills a day for the first three months and then reduce the intake to one pill a day.

This violated my principles of simplicity and I was very concerned that the consumer was going to be confused. You make it easy initially to buy a continuity product and then later you raise the price. For example, the first video in a video series offered on TV may cost only $5. It is a simple offer and it isn't very expensive. You then buy the video and to get the rest of the series, you must pay $19.95 a month to receive a video each month for the next 12 months.

I was going the opposite way. For the first three months, pills would cost double what they would cost during the fourth month and beyond. And here I was recommending taking two pills a day for three months and then one pill a day for the rest of the time. Prospects might find it really confusing and hold off buying.

So I did two things to ensure the success of this show, which we had already spent hundreds of thousands of dollars to prepare. The first was to have the host in the show verify the dosage and tell how the program worked even after I had explained it. We devoted almost three minutes to explaining the complicated offer in order to answer all anticipated questions.

But somehow I knew that the first offer was too complicated. And so I prepared an alternative offer just in case. For the second version I shot additional footage with just a simple offer: "Miracell costs $25 a box and a box lasts one month." That was it. It was very simple and very easy to understand. I knew that I would have to supply my customers with a double dose for the first three months, so three boxes would be at my own expense if this second version of the ad worked and the complicated first version did not.

Sure enough, after testing, the version that worked was the simple one; it outpulled the first one by a very large margin. We ended up giving away an enormous amount of product in order to keep the offer simple and make the program simple as well.

Simplicity in direct response is critical and quite necessary. These are just two typical experiences from my many years of direct response marketing in various media.

# 25. Human Relationships

It is always important to relate the product or service you are offering in human terms. How the product will fit, how it will feel, how it will look—these are just some of the ways you can relate. That may seem pretty obvious.

But there are other ways that copy or graphics can bring a human element to an advertisement. And let's look at why this is important.

Buying is an emotional human experience when we exchange our hard-earned money for a product or service. And because we worked hard for that money, the act of buying represents more than just handing over our money. Buying something becomes an emotional event.

### Resonating with Your Prospect

Now let's consider for a moment a physical device—specifically a tuning fork. I'm talking about the ones that look like a U-shaped piece of metal. Clang one of the metal tines and you hear a vibration. Take two tuning forks and if they are of the same frequency and you hit just one, the other one will start vibrating even though it did not come into physical contact with the first one.

Taking this experiment one step further, if you take several tuning forks and put them together and hit them all, they will create a harmonic frequency all their own. And if you just happen to know what that combined frequency is and have a tuning fork that matches that frequency, then, it too, will start to vibrate in resonance with all the other tuning forks.

In creating a direct response advertisement, it is important that you create a condition where your customer is in perfect harmonic resonance with your copy. We talked earlier in this book about getting the prospect to start nodding his or her head in agreement until the close. And the close becomes easier because the prospect is already nodding yes in agreement. It then becomes easier to say yes when that final question is posed: "May I have your order?"

If you look at all the elements of an advertisement as a series of tuning forks that must resonate with your reader, you've got a valuable picture of the dynamics that take place during the selling process.

One tuning fork might be the headline, another might be the picture, another might be the caption, and on to the first sentence and through the copy to the final offer. In a print ad, the vibrations must be conveyed through the elements in the advertisement.

In order to create these positive vibrations, you first must interest the prospect in reading your copy and then you must really "tune in" and relate to your prospect.

You can add a human element by relating a story in your copy. Stories hold people's interest. This technique is the next trigger discussed. Or you can use a byline and write copy in the first person using a conversational tone. This makes your copy a more direct communication from one individual to another. Using humor in a light, inoffensive way will also develop a relationship with your prospect. The humor can relate a story in a folksy way as in my "Pet Plane" ad in Chapter 29 or it can bring out the "humanness" of the person marketing the product or service as I've done in my ad for the Magic Stat thermostat in Chapter 28.

Another approach is to use a picture of a human hand holding a small product. The hand adds size and perspective to what is being presented and also adds that human element.

You can use attractive models. People like to relate to pretty women or handsome men even though they may not themselves be attractive. In a subtle sense, they want to belong to the group of people in the picture. Conversely, you don't want to use a picture of yourself if you think some of your readers may respond negatively to it. Especially if you look like a bearded villain from some B-rated movie.

In short, in your advertising you want to use as many positive human elements as you can without risking any negative vibrations from emotional reactions.

And if you do your job right, your advertisement will have its own vibration—so much so that some people will be able to pick up that vibration and feel that they almost know you.

## 26. Storytelling

*Telling a story is a powerful tool to create a bond between you and your prospects.*

People love stories, and one of the really good ways to relate to your prospect is to tell a story. Just as a picture is worth a thousand words, a story can be invaluable and often creates an emotional relationship or bond that keeps your prospect riveted and listening. Stories create human interest. In childhood, stories read to us by our parents were the way we fantasized or even saw the world. In short, we've been primed for stories ever since we were very young.

Think of the public speaker who starts his speech with a story or uses stories throughout his presentation. It makes for an interesting presentation and often holds the interest of the audience. In fact, very often, after I've been listening to a boring speaker and my mind starts to wander, I become alert when I know a story is about to be told.

### Stories Have Lessons to Teach

Stories usually have lessons to teach or experiences to share or even endings that can excite, surprise or bring out emotion. And so it is with good copy. If you tell a story in your copy that is relevant either to selling your product, to creating the environment for selling, or to getting the prospect to read your copy, you are using this wonderful and powerful trigger in a very effective way to sell your product or service.

Finally, some stories add a unique human element that allows you to relate to and bond very closely with your prospects.

Kathy Levine, formerly one of QVC's top salespersons, wrote in her book, *It's Better to Laugh* (Pocket Books, 1995), "I realized early on that selling is a matter of capturing people's attention and holding it with a good story."

The most interesting salespeople I know always have a story to tell. It is their way of relating to their customers and entertaining them as well. One in particular has a repertoire of hundreds of jokes—each targeted to his prospect, to the selling environment and what he has to sell. As you can imagine, he is very effective.

My most successful advertising campaigns all used stories as the basis for my presentation. Here is one example of this technique from one of my most successful ads. I wrote an ad for BluBlocker sunglasses that will give you a flavor of how a story can be very helpful in creating human interest that will cause your prospects to read your entire message.

**Headline:** Vision Breakthrough

**Subheadline:** When I put on the pair of glasses what I saw I could not believe. Nor will you.

**Byline:** By Joseph Sugarman

**Copy:** I am about to tell you a true story. If you believe me, you will be well rewarded. If you don't believe me, I will make it worth your while to change your mind. Let me explain.

Len is a friend of mine who knows good products. One day he called excited about a pair of sunglasses he owned. "It's so incredible," he said, "when you first look through a pair, you won't believe it."

"What will I see?" I asked. "What could be so incredible?"

Len continued, "When you put on these glasses, your vision improves. Objects appear sharper, more defined. Everything takes on an enhanced 3-D effect. And it's not my imagination. I just want you to see for yourself."

The story continues as I personally look through the sunglasses and learn more about them from Len. It uses a conversational tone, but still covers all the important points about the sunglasses, the danger from ultraviolet (UV) rays, and the advantage of screening out blue spectrum light rays. A story is used very effectively to build curiosity and cause the reader to read all the copy, and eventually to read the final sales pitch.

That ad for BluBlocker sunglasses launched a multimillion-dollar company that eventually sold 20 million pairs of sunglasses and has recently celebrated 20 years in business.

When writing copy for your product, think about using a few stories that might be of interest to your prospect and assist in the sale of your product: stories about a new development and how you discovered it—stories about yourself that would be of interest to your prospects.

Timing is also important in the storytelling process. It is nice to start with a story, because it holds attention and engages the prospect. Telling stories is an art form and using it effectively in a print ad grows with experience. Simply being aware of its potential and its effectiveness is a good start. You'll be surprised at how many stories you'll be able to come up with once you put your mind to it.

A good story should capture a person's attention, relate the product or service in the copy and help you bond with the prospect.

## 27. Mental Engagement

Have you ever gone to a movie and known how it was going to end after watching the first few minutes? Or a movie where every action can be easily anticipated? These movies tend not to be very enjoyable.

However, the opposite is true when you watch a movie that keeps you in suspense until the very end when it reaches a credible but surprise ending. Any movie that is not predictable is more enjoyable. I recently saw a movie called *Inside Man* about what I thought was a bank robbery but turned out to be what I least expected. And the identity of the robbers was also a surprise at the end of the movie. I loved that film.

What forces in our minds make us perceive one movie as a lot better than another?

I have a theory that I strongly believe comes pretty close to the answer: The more the mind must work to reach a conclusion that it eventually successfully reaches, the more positive, enjoyable, or stimulating the experience.

I taught this concept at my seminar for many years, and one day one of my students brought me a copy of a media newsletter that confirmed what I had been teaching. The article claimed that a missing element was responsible for advertising failure—a lack of whole-brain appeal.

It then went on to explain how science is rapidly discovering that different parts of the brain perform different functions. Some brain researchers suggest that human beings experience the most pleasure when all these parts of the brain are engaged in agreeable levels of stimulation and activity.

The four brain parts discussed were those that control thought, intuition, sensation, and emotion. The article suggested that advertising that pleasurably engages the senses, emotions, and thought process, as well as our innate intuition, will tend to be successful.

Advertising that merely grabs the attention of the senses will tend to be only temporarily attractive. Most advertising tests today reflect the power of day-after recall but fail to predict the response from whole-brain advertising.

Let's look at how whole-brain advertising applies to writing effective advertising copy. If you make your copy too obvious, the reader feels either looked down on or bored. Provide a little suspense so that the reader has to come to a conclusion on her own using intuition, thought, sensation, and emotion, and you've got a very good force working for you. Let me cite an example from an ad I wrote on digital watches.

The ad was for an alarm chronograph digital watch for which we were charging $99. At the time, Seiko was the standard of comparison for this type of watch. Seiko was the first out with the new technology. The following paragraph from the ad best exemplifies what I'm talking about:

> The Seiko chronograph alarm sells for $300. The watch costs jewelers $150. And jewelers love the item, not only because of the excellent reputation of the Seiko brand, but because it's probably America's best-selling new expensive digital watch. And Seiko can't supply enough of them to their dealers.

Now, note what I didn't *say* but what was still rather obvious. Read the quote again to see if you pick it up. Give up? What I didn't say was that the jewelers were making a small fortune each time they sold a Seiko. I didn't have to say it, yet the readers could come to their own conclusion all by themselves using their intuition, thought, and emotions. Had I made it too obvious, by adding the line "and jewelers are making a small fortune," it would not have been as powerful. The mind had to work a little to reach a conclusion through its own thought processes. And when the reader compared our $99 watch with the Seiko, it appeared that the jewelry stores and Seiko were soaking the consumer.

This is a very subtle but powerful concept. It's the difference between talking down to prospects and making prospects feel you are talking directly to them. And it is one of the most difficult theories to understand.

### Working Hard Brings Appreciation

To get a better appreciation for the theory, think back in your life to times when you had to work hard to achieve something and how much more you appreciated what you achieved. I remember all the work I had to go through to get my instrument rating after getting my private pilot's license. It took me months of flying and study, not to mention thousands of dollars in expense. When I finally received my instrument rating, it was a thrill.

In contrast, when I took my commercial rating test, it was simple. Not that much study, very little flying, and within a few weeks I had the rating. Sure, I was proud that I was finally a commercial pilot, but nowhere near as proud as I was of my instrument rating. Working hard for a successful conclusion results in a great deal of personal satisfaction.

The same holds true for the mind and the thinking process. Anything that causes the mind to work hard to reach a conclusion creates a positive, enjoyable or stimulating effect on the brain. The opposite is true if the mind does not have to work because the conclusion is obvious.

You appreciate that sale to a difficult client a lot more than a sale that is a pushover and takes only a minute. When a very difficult product is given to me to sell and I am successful, I get great pleasure from the achievement. But give me a really easy product—something that is already in demand—and I don't have the same feeling of satisfaction.

*Anything that causes the mind to work hard to reach a conclusion creates a positive, enjoyable or stimulating effect on the brain.*

## Vague Descriptions Encourage Thinking

When Ernest Hemingway described beautiful women in his books, he was never very specific. He used general terms and let his readers imagine the women.

If you make your intentions too obvious, the prospect will feel either patronized or bored. Make the prospect think in order to come to a conclusion, and you create a very stimulating mental effect.

Too often we write too much. We reveal too much of the pitch without allowing the prospect's mind and intelligence to become engaged. Simply realizing how this powerful psychological trigger works will help you craft copy that causes your prospects' brains to experience an enjoyable and stimulating time by allowing them to reach—on their own—the conclusions that you want them to reach.

# 28. Guilt

Have you ever received mailings from charities that include a small gift? The gifts are usually address stickers, colorful stamps or some other inexpensive token. Or how about those mailings with surveys that include a dollar bill or a reply envelope with a return stamp? In both cases you may have experienced a slight touch of guilt. After all, you've received something of value and you feel an obligation to take some action in return, such as sending in a donation or answering the survey. These are good examples of the use of guilt. But how do you use this technique in a print ad when you can't include stickers or a dollar bill?

Many people have told me that after they read one of my ads, they not only are compelled to buy my product, but would feel guilty if they didn't. Instead of giving them stickers or a dollar bill, I give the reader plenty of compelling information and reading entertainment—so much so that they sense an obligation to respond. In a print ad, often the mere repetition of seeing an ad in several magazines works to create a slight sense of guilt.

Repeated mailings also create guilt. Keep sending somebody mailings and after a while, they may feel guilty that they haven't responded. I used this technique when I sold ski lifts for a company called Ski Lift International. Each week I sent out a small mailing with a premium gift enclosed. One mailing would have a button, another an unusual mailing piece and still another an involvement device. After a while, many of the recipients felt guilty and responded. Some even apologized for not responding earlier.

# 29. Specificity

Being specific in your explanations is very critical and can establish your credibility. Let me first give you an example. If I were to say, "New dentists everywhere use and recommend CapSnap Toothpaste," it sounds like typical advertising lingo—puffery designed to sell a product. It's so general that it will probably cause a viewer to discount the statement I have just made and maybe everything else I say. But if I said, "Ninety-two percent of new dentists use and recommend CapSnap Toothpaste," it sounds much more believable. The consumer is likely to think that we did a scientific survey and that 92 percent was the result.

When people perceive certain general statements as puffery or typical advertising babble, those statements are at best discounted or accepted with some doubts. By contrast, statements with specific facts can generate strong believability. In an ad I once wrote for a collectibles company I created called Battram Galleries, I stated the exact cost of running the ad and the exact cost of the product. I clearly demonstrated through specific figures that we weren't making any profit from the offering. It was so successful, it was oversubscribed. I've used this technique on video as well.

In my BluBlocker infomercials, I state the specific reasons why screening out blue spectrum light rays improves your vision. I explain that blue light rays focus in front of the retina (which is the focusing screen of the eye) and not on the retina as do the other colors. So when you block blue light, you block those rays that don't focus on your retina and therefore objects appear clearer, sharper and more defined. I'm specific. It sounds believable. And the statement is a lot better than just saying, "BluBlocker sunglasses let you see clearer, sharper and with more definition."

If you're describing a product that is designed for the circulatory functions of the body, you can talk about "242 miles of blood vessels" instead of "miles of blood vessels." When you talk about the bottom of your feet, instead of saying, "There are a lot of nerve endings at the bottom of your feet," you can say, "There are 72,000 nerve endings at the bottom of your feet." You are stating a fact as opposed to a general or vague statement. You are more believable.

### You Sound More like an Expert

There's one other benefit to being specific. By being specific you sound like you're an expert on your product—you've really investigated it and are very knowledgeable. And, this too, builds trust and confidence.

People, in general, are very skeptical about advertising and often don't believe many of the claims stated in ads. But when you make a specific claim using the exact facts and figures, your message is much more credible and often trusted.

# 30. Familiarity

The Kowloon section of Hong Kong is an exotic part of the city. Its storefronts, hordes of people and many sounds and smells make for a very unique and exciting place to visit. It is different. And when you are in Kowloon, America seems awfully far away.

I was walking down the street absorbing the energy of the area and stopping occasionally to look in a store when suddenly, right in front of me, I saw one of my American suppliers walking down the sidewalk.

What a surprise! It was a wonderful feeling to see somebody I knew in a foreign place like Hong Kong.

Although previously I hadn't been that friendly with the supplier, I suddenly felt close. I asked if he was available for dinner and I made an appointment for that evening to get together and spend some time with him. As a result, he ended up selling me a lot more than I normally would have bought. The contrast of seeing somebody with whom you are familiar in a totally foreign setting creates a strong attraction. And so it is with advertising.

### An Ad as an Old Friend

If somebody is reading a magazine and sees your advertising format—something they have seen many times before—and recognizes your logo or company name, there is a feeling of familiarity. They see a friend in an environment of foreign advertisers and to them you're not foreign. You are familiar and as a result there is an attraction to your offering just as I was attracted to my supplier in Hong Kong.

Advertise enough times or sell a product whose name is familiar to your prospect and you will create the same attraction. That is why brand names are so important; that is why the familiarity of a shopping environment is also important.

When I first appeared on QVC, the home shopping channel, we sold out our entire inventory of BluBlocker sunglasses within minutes. When our sunglasses first appeared on retail shelves in the Walgreens drugstore chain, they quickly sold out within a few days. In short, our product was well known to the consumer. Each time we introduced our product to a familiar shopping environment, the combination of brand name familiarity and a familiar selling environment caused an immediate sellout.

The words *familiar* and *familiarity* have the word *family* in them. People feel most comfortable within their own family. They feel confident and trusting and allow themselves to be more vulnerable. So it is with anything people are familiar with. They trust a brand name, are more confident that they are buying the right product and are more inclined to do so.

One of the biggest mistakes traditional advertisers make is to kill campaigns they have been using a long time because they are tired of them. "Fly the friendly skies of United" and "You deserve a break today, at McDonald's" are but two examples familiar to consumers. In addition, consumers often sang along during these commercials. Too often in traditional advertising, the client gets tired of the commercial long before the public does.

In direct marketing, a decision to drop a commercial approach is not arbitrary. You keep running your product or service ad until the public tells you when to stop by virtue of lower sales. The orders simply stop coming in or you have replaced your ad with something that pulls more response. Good direct-marketing technique calls for continually revising or tweaking your ad until it does better. But you never drop a campaign because you are tired of it. Drop it only when the public stops exchanging their hard-earned dollars for your product or service.

Now the traditional agencies will tell you something like, "Well, we asked a focus group what they thought about our slogan and they said that they were getting tired of it, so we are going to pull it." This is a major fallacy, too. There is no real way to test the effectiveness of a commercial except by virtue of sales. Focus groups only tell you what they think you want to hear and not how they would act themselves. If the product isn't selling, then look at the campaign. Maybe it isn't even the campaign but rather competition or some other element in the marketing mix.

### Use Familiar Words

There are certain words that are more familiar to most people and to the human consciousness. For example, if you ask somebody to give you a number from 1 to 10 right off the top of their head, chances are the number 7 will be chosen more often than any other number—often dwarfing the next choice. Therefore, using the number 7 in a book title such as "The Seven Ways to Improve Your Relationships" or "The Seven Spiritual Laws of Success" is utilizing the most common and familiar integer of the first 10. You are therefore vibrating with the familiar and harmonizing with your reader.

Ask somebody for a color off the top of their head and the answer will be "red" the majority of the time. Ask them to name a piece of furniture and the answer will likely be "chair." There are familiar words that can create a very subtle harmony with your reader and it's up to you to find them and use them. Where do you find them? Many books have been written on the effective use of words that really draw response. Books by David Ogilvy or John Caples are good ones to read. A list can be found in Appendix D. There are some powerful words such as *sale* or *free*. And then there are the not so obvious words—the ones that relate specifically to your product and which you, as a passionate devotee of your product, inherently already know. Finally, there are words that aren't in your own consciousness and aren't singled out in any books but will be discovered only by testing. Sometimes, changing just one word in a thousand-word ad will double response.

As a copywriter, be aware of the powerful force of familiarity to make a person comfortable with your product or service. Realize the importance of a familiar brand name, a logo that appears many times and becomes well known, a layout that people instinctively know is yours, familiar phrases (not clichés) and words that your public can harmonize with—all of these reinforce the bond that familiarity creates between you and your prospect.

## 31. Hope

Hope can be a great motivator in the buying process. A woman buys a new face cream that offers the hope it will make a difference in her wrinkles. An intense golfer buys a new golf ball that offers the hope it may take a few strokes off a golf game. In short, there is an implied possibility that using a product or service will provide a future benefit. The future benefit is not assured, nor is it guaranteed; it is a dream, a fantasy or, at the most, a possibility. The hope replaces the reality of an already-delivered benefit or guarantee that you receive when you buy other products such as a radio or a computer. Let me cite a few personal experiences and describe how hope applies to specific products.

I was introduced in 1996 to a very successful scientist. He had supposedly invented a formula that cured a great many human ills. The formula contained what he called "biological repair machines" that went to the source of a malfunction in your body and repaired it. If an organ was damaged, these miniature "machines" would repair the organ even if it meant regenerating a new one.

You placed a few drops of this product under your tongue twice a day and it was absorbed into your body.

In a discussion with the scientist, it occurred to me that if people took this product they would never die, if indeed it repaired any defective body part. He agreed. "I'm taking it and honestly feel I am getting younger. Look, my gray hair is starting to turn black again."

The scientist continued claiming that there was no reason why his formula couldn't keep us alive until the age of 300. This sounded incredible to me. If this was true, this man had indeed discovered the fountain of youth.

The scientist appeared to be very credible. He had several Ph.D.'s, and I honestly thought he was one of the smartest people I had ever met. He had three manufacturing facilities in different parts of the world. He had a reputation that extended all the way to Europe and Asia, and he told me how he helped an Asian country cure many of its citizens of a specific form of cancer.

His discovery of the biological repair machines came to him from uncovering formulas that were hidden in coded ancient artifacts and through the process of what he called "sacred geometry." He had apparently cracked the code and opened up a wealth of information. He spent two hours showing me photograph after photograph to substantiate the information he had received from the artifacts.

I had a health problem that was not serious but, for whatever reason, doctors did not know its cause or cure. The problem was a few small growths beneath the surface of my skin. They were not cancerous, others hardly noticed them and they posed no health threat. But they were there and they were not normal.

### Surgery Was the Only Way

The only method doctors had for eliminating these growths was to cut open the skin and surgically remove them—a relatively easy procedure that was done on an outpatient basis.

I was told by this scientist that indeed his formula could eliminate the problem completely. "In just a few months they'll be gone," he said. In short, I received from him an explicitly clear time frame during which my growths were going to melt away and disappear. The promise wasn't in the form of a hoped-for result or a dream or even a possibility. It was a definite warranty that they would disappear.

I was so impressed by him and his discoveries and he seemed so credible that I decided to put his product to a test. A 750 milliliter bottle (the size of a wine bottle) of his formula sold for $600. It was rather expensive but it lasted a long time as you used only a few drops each day and it was less costly than the surgical procedure.

### A Few Months Go By

After a few months, I noticed that the growths were not gone as I had been promised. I was then advised to buy his stronger formula—the one with a higher concentration of biological repair machines. I did, at a cost of $2,000. There was still no improvement after two more months.

I was then told that there was a $20,000 bottle that would do the job (boy, they saw me coming) and believe it or not, I was tempted to get a bottle. I didn't.

Note: In all fairness to the scientist, there were clinical studies done on rats with his formula by a credible pharmaceutical company and there were very positive results with the rats. The research is continuing now on humans and he may have indeed created a powerful new medical concept.

What did I learn from this experience? The doctor should have simply told me about how his formula improved his life. I trusted him. He had all the credibility I needed for me to ingest this foreign substance into my body. What if I could live to 300 years of age? What if indeed I could become younger? I would have gladly taken the formula and continued purchasing bottles of it with the hope that I was right about him.

### Scientist Made Fatal Error

But the scientist made a fatal error. Had he not made any claims to me about specific expected results, I would not have been disappointed but would have continued taking the product waiting and hoping that the stuff would kick in and dissolve those growths. I would, on the basis of hope, have continued taking it and buying more. But once a specific promise was made and I saw that the formula didn't work within that time frame, I immediately refused to invest further. The scientist's credibility was questioned even though he may have had a great product.

When using the psychological trigger of hope, you must avoid the trap of making a specific claim that can be measured or guaranteed. You want to allude to what the product is used for without making any promises of an exact outcome.

There are other products people buy repeatedly, on hope. Let's take vitamins, for example. Can people tell if taking vitamins makes a difference in their health? Yes, some can. Interview a bunch of people and they'll swear the vitamins are making a difference. Capture those interviews on TV and they are very impressive. Then prospects, impressed with the results shown on TV, start buying the product and continue to buy it regularly with the hope that it is making a difference in their lives. But the key here is not to make a specific promise but rather to imply results through testimonials.

How does this apply to selling in print and on the Internet? There are some products that are sold using hope as a strong motivational tool. You need to determine the nature of your product and find something that you can imply about a future result without stating a specific guarantee (particularly if you want to stay in business for a long time).

Many product categories lend themselves to the power of hope. The entire health food industry is a good example, including vitamins, food supplements and even brain enhancers. Lowering your golf score, finding a new relationship, preventing wrinkles, impressing your date—all are good opportunities to recognize the psychological trigger of hope at work.

### Focus on Credibility

One aspect to focus on when you create an ad using the power of hope is credibility. If you present yourself as a credible person representing a credible company, then what you say will elicit a feeling of confidence on the part of your prospect. Then, whatever you say your product did for you or for your previous customers will be taken as a possibility for your prospect, and the power of hope will compel your prospect to order. And re-order. It might be a book on relationships and how the information changed your life and those of previous readers. It might be a formula you take to live a long life and how wonderful you feel. Whatever you are selling, with the proper credibility, you will automatically engage the power of hope to sell.

This chapter is very important in your understanding of the underlying reasons why people buy. Some of the 31 psychological triggers to buying may not have been obvious to you before. Nevertheless, an awareness of each of these points will give you a tremendous boost in becoming a great copywriter.

One of the least understood reasons why many products fail is due to one aspect of human nature. Understand this aspect and not only do you hold the key to creating a successful direct response ad, but you will also understand clearly why some products just plain don't sell.

The key to successfully marketing certain products lies in the nature of that product and the way that product is viewed in the marketplace. The guiding principle can be summed up very clearly: Always sell the cure and avoid selling prevention.

Now what does this mean? Let me explain. If you were my prospect and I tried to sell you a magic pill that contained an extract of carrots and various tinctures of leafy vegetables because it would help prevent cancer, chances are it would be a difficult sale. However, if you suddenly discovered you had cancer and I said to you that I had a magic pill that would cure the disease, you would be not only willing to try it, but willing to pay considerably more. In the first instance, you might be willing to pay $20 a bottle to prevent the disease but in the other you might be willing to pay $1,000 if it would cure the disease.

## Human Nature at Play

The preceding is an extreme example. But let's take something less extreme. You're a traveling salesperson and stay at hotels a lot. Somebody tries to sell you a spray that you put on your feet before you go to sleep to prevent athlete's foot, which might come from walking on a floor that hasn't been cleaned thoroughly. You ignore the sales message because you rarely get athlete's foot, and besides, it's a bother to use. The next week you get athlete's foot and you're at the corner pharmacy trying to find the strongest thing they've got to cure it.

The two situations illustrate two general principles. The first: It is human nature to think you're never going to get the disease or affliction that the preventive can prevent, so it becomes a very tough sell. The second: If you do get the disease or affliction, you're willing to pay a whole lot more for the cure than you were for the preventive and it's easier to sell.

I have been talking in medical or health terms. But this theory also applies to several other products and concepts. I'll go into those in a moment, but let's examine the first step in breaking through the cure/preventive theory and see if you can make the appeal of the preventive as strong as the appeal of the cure.

It can be done, but only if you can position the product to make the preventive the cure. Let me cite an example:

When the Midex burglar alarms were first sold by JS&A in the late 1970s, it was definitely a product that was more of a preventive. However, I also knew that there were people who were recently robbed or whose neighbors were recently robbed, and to these people, the Midex alarm was more of a cure. Think about it. At first they thought, "Naw, our neighborhood is safe. I don't need one." And then after their neighborhood was robbed and they needed a cure, "Boy, I'd better get one of those Midex alarms or else I may be next." And of course, there was the prospect who had just been robbed: "Where did I see that ad for that burglar alarm?"

HELLO... BURGLAR ALARM COMPANY? I NEED ONE... QUICK!!

*The consumer waited until he felt threatened before he bought.*

I also knew that if I advertised in a professional manner and explained the quality and value of my product and its quick and easy installation, as opposed to using the scare tactics expressed through quoting crime statistics, I would attract a different kind of customer. I would attract the person not quite threatened but concerned—a person to whom the product did not currently represent prevention or a cure. In short, it was for somebody who hadn't been robbed and whose neighbor hadn't been robbed, but who realized that there was a problem out there. This last group would save my ad, and when they needed it, they would take it out of their files—often after several months—and call. This actually did happen a lot.

Twenty years ago, The Club automotive steering wheel locking device would have been a tough sale. Back then, car theft was not as big a problem as it is now. But with the increase in drug traffic today and with thousands of cars being stolen every hour, The Club has become more of a cure against your fear of having your car stolen.

The big rage in health food and disease prevention a few years ago was the melatonin craze. This is a hormone secreted naturally by the pineal gland—a pea-sized object at the center of the brain. It is supposed to help prevent aging. With millions of baby boomers turning 60, it became a very big product—more of a cure than a preventive.

## Many Products Make Powerful Cures

When I sold my wrinkle pill, Miracell, it, too, was a cure. If you have wrinkles, you are a great prospect for wrinkle creams and treatments. They represent cures, not preventives. And think about it. Don't the preventives like creams to moisturize your skin and sunscreens to avoid sun damage cost a lot less than the cures? But some of the effective wrinkle eliminators cost plenty for a small jar. Miracell sold at $25 for a month's supply.

Insurance is another preventive. "Keep your family from going through hard times after you die." What could be tougher than thinking you're going to die someday? But the older you get, the more you think about it. And remember the story about my friend, the insurance salesman, who always tried to sell me insurance and finally succeeded when my next-door neighbor died suddenly at an early age? I couldn't wait to sign the papers.

You must first make a decision when evaluating a product. Is this product a preventive or a cure? Can the product be positioned as a cure rather than a preventive? Is the market trend changing the perception of your product from being a preventive to being a cure? Or do you simply have a preventive that does not have a broad enough market?

If you've got a cure and the market is large enough, you've

got a powerful product. If you've got a preventive, think in terms of how you can change it into a cure. Let me show you how this can be done.

## Make a Preventive a Cure

Another pill I have been selling for the past few years, called simply "The Pill," is a fuel-conditioning treatment for automobiles. It is a pill you put in your gas tank, and it is both a preventive and a cure.

First, as a preventive, it helps you avoid engine problems by cleaning out your engine before anything serious happens to your car from impurities that could lodge in your fuel injectors. It reduces pollution to help you pass the many mandatory emissions tests conducted throughout the United States, and it prevents you from having to visit the repair shop. Again, these are the preventives.

But when I go on TV at QVC to present The Pill, I don't talk that much about what it prevents but rather what it cures. It cures engine knock, it eliminates ping, it saves up to 10 percent on gas. If you flunk your emissions test, use The Pill and you'll pass the next time. In short, I emphasize the curative aspects of the product and underplay the preventive features. And The Pill is truly a miracle product. (I swear, it really works.) This brings me to my next point.

Notice how I have to swear that The Pill really works. Selling truly breakthrough products is the toughest marketing job in the world because people find it difficult to believe that these products really work. And belief is one of the strongest motivational factors in human nature. If your prospect believes in something, he or she will move mountains to obtain it, but if he or she doesn't believe in something, you won't move that prospect an inch.

In this chapter you've learned that you sell the cure, not the preventive, that preventives don't sell very easily and that some products can be changed from preventives to cures. You've also learned that you can charge a lot more for a cure than you can for a preventive. And finally, I've demonstrated that you can successfully market a product that is both a preventive and a cure by emphasizing its curative aspects while underplaying its preventive aspects. So let's summarize what you've learned in a simple statement that we can refer to in the future:

*Selling a cure is a lot easier than selling a preventive, unless the preventive is perceived as a cure or the curative aspects of the preventive are emphasized.*

**Axiom 15**

The information presented in this chapter will be very helpful for you in evaluating products in the future. Simply understanding that the cure/preventive factor exists will help you to select and then position your next product for selling.

You've gained a tremendous amount of knowledge reading this book. And in Section Three you will use this knowledge to evaluate my mail order ads and those of others who attended my seminar.

But how are you going to rate yourself in the future? Is there some measure you can apply to your writing to determine if you are communicating at the level you need to in order to reach your audience?

Well, fortunately there is a way, thanks to Robert Gunning, who created the Fog Index for newspaper writers to help them avoid so-called foggy writing and determine for themselves the grade level of the copy they were writing. In short, were they writing with enough clarity so that a fifth grader could understand their copy or must a reader be in high school or even college to understand it? The lower the grade level, the wider the audience.

## Reaching a Mass Market

For example, if I wanted to reach a mass market, I would keep my ad copy simple and my sentences short and I wouldn't use big words. On the other hand, if I wanted to reach a very upscale audience, I might use bigger words and longer sentences.

Best-selling books are written for the 8th to 10th grade level. *Time, BusinessWeek* and the *Wall Street Journal* are 11th grade level. The Gettysburg Address and *Reader's Digest* have a 10th grade level in common. And for the most part, the average American audience reads between the 11th and 12th grade levels.

The following are the steps for determining the Fog Index, or grade level, of the copy you write:

1. Take a sample of your copy—start with 100 to 125 words from the very beginning of the ad.

2. Count the words in each sentence. Dates and numbers equal one word and independent clauses count as separate sentences (e.g., "We studied, and we learned" would be two sentences).

3. Divide the total number of words by the number of sentences to get the average sentence length.

4. Count the number of long words (those of three or more syllables), but:
   - Do not count short-word combinations like *pawnbroker* or *yellowtail*.
   - Do not include proper names.
   - Do not include verbs that have become three syllables by adding *ed* or *es*.

5. Divide the number of long words by the total number of words in the selection to get the percentage of long words.

6. Add the average sentence length to the percentage of long words.

7. Multiply this total by 0.4 to get the grade level.

Now let's use as an example the Vision Breakthrough ad we discussed in Chapter 19 under "Storytelling." The ad is presented in full in Chapter 32. I will take the first 102 words of copy, and show you how to determine the grade level.

I am about to tell you a true story. If you believe me, you will be well rewarded. If you don't believe me, I will make it worth your while to change your mind. Let me explain.

Len is a friend of mine who knows good products. One day he called excited about a pair of sunglasses he owned. "It's so **incredible**," he said, "when you first look through a pair, you won't believe it."

"What will I see?" I asked. "What could be so **incredible**?"

Len **continued**, "When you put on these glasses, your vision improves. Objects appear sharper, more defined.

I have put the three long words in bold type. There are 102 total words in this selection and 11 sentences. This means that the average number of words per sentence is 9.3.

The next step is to divide the number of long words (3) by the total words (102) to get the percentage of long words: 2.9 percent.

Now add the average sentence length of 9.3 words to the percentage of long words, which is 2.9, and you have the number 12.2. Then multiply the number 12.2 by 0.4 and you end up with the number 4.9. In short, this ad started out being understandable to a very large segment of the market by virtue of the fact that it was quite comprehensible to anybody reading at about the fifth grade level and above.

Incidentally, the next block of copy in that same ad had about the same reading level. The third block of copy jumped to 7.2, but by that time the reader was well into the copy. I would suggest that you take different 100-word blocks from different parts of your ad to see how consistent your style is.

Try this with one of your ads or with one of the many ads in Section Three. It is an easy way to determine the level of comprehension of your writing and it will also make you aware of the effect that multisyllabic words and long sentences have on the comprehensibility of your ad and the level of reader that will resonate with your copy.

The ad that we just tested was one of JS&A's most successful. And it seemed that with many of my ads, the greater the clarity, the broader the appeal and the greater the response. After you've tried it with some of the ads in this book or other ads, you'll be amazed at how easily you will be able to guess the Fog Index from reading just the first few paragraphs of any ad.

Clarity is one of the most important factors in writing copy, and the Fog Index gives you an insight into how important short sentences and simple words can be. But don't be obsessed with achieving low Fog Index scores at the expense of common sense. You need to vary the length of sentences and use three-syllable words when you need them and realize that every audience is different.

**O**ne of your reactions to having read the steps involved in writing copy might be that there are a lot of things to keep in mind as you craft your ad. And indeed there are.

But if I were to reduce everything down to a simple seven-step formula, I would suggest the following, keeping in mind that you have read this book and have comprehended its principles.

**Step 1:** Become an expert on the product or service you are planning to sell. I have gotten more great ideas delving into discovering everything I could about a product or service than I have from any other resource.

**Step 2:** Know your prospect. You might become an expert on your product or service but if you don't know your customer, you're at a big disadvantage. What will motivate your prospect to become a customer? Who is your typical prospect? This will give you insight and also spur lots of good ideas.

**Step 3:** Write your headline and subheadline. They must grab the reader and create enough curiosity to cause the reader to get to the first sentence. I like headlines that are short. "Vision Breakthrough," "Pocket CB," "Pocket Yellow Pages"—all are concise and yet create enough curiosity to get you to the subheadline. Subheadlines should be around 16 words, and first sentences should be as short as possible.

**Step 4:** Write the copy. Don't worry about sentence structure, grammar, punctuation—just start writing and keep writing. Let all your ideas and thoughts flow into the computer and above all don't worry about making mistakes. The main idea is to take everything that is in your head about the subject and dump it into your hard drive. If you write your copy by hand or with a typewriter, write with the same abandon. However, you're a lot better off writing your ad with a computer, especially when it comes to editing.

**Step 5:** Edit your copy. Go through it and correct the spelling, grammar, punctuation and sentence structure. Eliminate extra words not necessary to express your thoughts. Tighten things up.

**Step 6:** Incubate. Stop editing, put the text aside and take a walk or do something pleasurable. You'll be amazed at what getting away from your text will do for you. If you can come back to it the next day, better yet. The more time between what you've just edited and taking the next step—all the better.

**Step 7:** Take a final look at your copy. You'll be amazed at how much more you're going to catch and how much more refined you will be able to make the copy with this final look. Of course you could easily repeat steps 5 and 6 and continue to edit until you are happy with your results.

These seven steps summarize what you as a copywriter will go through to write copy. It's really that simple. And if you've learned the principles of writing copy, each time you do this you will get better at it. That I can guarantee.

## You've Learned a Great Deal

You have learned what it takes to be a great copywriter in Section One. You have learned in Section Two what works and why it works.

In the first two sections of this book I have taught you most of the copywriting techniques I taught my seminar participants. You have learned techniques that took me many years to develop. You have learned concepts that I didn't discover and personally use until well into my career. And most importantly, you have learned from my failures—an education that has cost me dearly but that you do not have to experience on your own. Finally, you did not have to pay $3,000 to get this knowledge as my seminar participants did.

In Section Three we take all that you have learned and crystallize it into practical knowledge by examining many of the ads that were used as examples in our seminar. This is an important section, for here you see how all the pieces you have learned fit together. We also examine a few ads where the pieces didn't quite fit together and we show you how they could have been done more effectively.

In addition to examining a few ads from beginning to end, I also reproduce a few of the JS&A ads that show my principles in action.

If you've had a problem understanding any of the principles, this is where you'll get greater understanding and clarity. It was during this part of my seminar when participants would often comment, "Now I feel I can do a great ad myself." And they often did.

# Section Three

You've learned the principles and theory of copywriting and you've had a chance to see how it all works through my many personal experiences. Now it's time to show you how these principles actually work in some of the complete ad examples that follow. This is the fine-tuning you'll need to perfect your newly learned skills.

During the course of my seminar I showed slides of various ads to illustrate the theories I was presenting. In my first seminars, the ads were mine and those of my competitors—the very companies that were copying my format. But as the course continued and more and more of my students succeeded with the knowledge I gave them, many of the ads I showed at subsequent seminars were created by my former students themselves.

Finally, I used illustrations to show the best and the worst of mail order advertising and even non-mail-order advertising. By the end of the course, not only were my students able to tell me what was wrong with each of the ads that I showed but they were producing great advertising copy and even helping their fellow seminar participants in crafting and improving their advertisements.

Hundreds of ads were presented during the seminar—all on slides. Several of the classic examples were duplicated and passed around. For the book I have selected only a few of the best ads to illustrate the principles I taught—examples that will solidify everything you've learned so far and add even more to your insights and copywriting skills.

"But hey," you might wonder. "What about those famous JS&A mail order ads that were the hallmark of mail order advertising in the 1970s and 1980s? Don't they point out some really important principles and aren't they good examples of the best in copywriting?"

Shucks. Well, if you insist. Okay, I'll include some of those as well.

Starting in Chapter 28 are some of the JS&A ads that really drive home various points. Not only are they examples of successful copywriting but they are entertaining as well. The fact that I wrote them might come through in my enthusiasm and commentary, so please bear with me. Deep down, I'm really a modest kinda guy.

If your future is in TV marketing, these examples will help you understand marketing in that medium as well. For as you have already learned, my copywriting and marketing principles can be applied to any form of advertising communication.

But now it's time to solidify everything you've learned in Sections One and Two with some classic ad examples to prove many of my points.

This is a classic example of a mail order ad. There are some people who spend their entire career creating hundreds of ads, and then there is Joe Karbo.

Joe Karbo wrote only a few ads. He wrote the one I've featured here right off the top of his head. There was practically no editing involved. As he later claimed at my seminar, "I just sat down and wrote the ad in a matter of a few minutes and then looked back at it, made a few changes, and that was it."

The ad Joe created ran in hundreds of magazines for many years. In later years, it was rewritten to reflect more current mail order approaches, but it was basically the same ad. And it has become a classic.

First, a little background on Joe. Joe Karbo was discharged from the Army in 1945, and at age 20 with a wife and child, no money and only a high school education, he started his business career. Karbo was modestly successful in the scrap paper business and then he moved on to acting, followed by advertising, radio and finally television.

Karbo had his own TV show in Hollywood and, along with his wife Betty, was on the air from midnight to 8 A.M. Since sponsors were hard to come by, Karbo started a direct mail business and sold a variety of products on his show. Joe soon mastered direct response advertising and flourished.

In 1973 Joe formalized his personal philosophies in a book called *The Lazy Man's Way to Riches* in which he shared his beliefs and principles both on success and on direct response advertising. The ad shown is the one he wrote to market his book.

Let's examine the ad, as it will confirm many of the things

*This classic mail order ad sold 3 million books.*

you have already learned. We'll start at the headline and systematically work our way through the entire ad.

**Headline:** The Lazy Man's Way to Riches
**Subheadline:** 'Most People Are Too Busy Earning a Living to Make Any Money'

The headline is provocative. At the time, this was a novel approach and a novel headline. Prior to this, ads such as this were found only in the group of magazines classified as "income opportunity." Magazines such as *Income Opportunity, Success* and *Entrepreneur* had dozens of offers such as the one Karbo was making, but the category of advertising hadn't yet made it into the mainstream. Joe's was one of the first to break through. The headline grabbed you and got you to read the subheadline. And the subheadline got you into the copy.

Let's start with the copy and see if he is creating that slippery slide. First, notice how he gets you into the copy by the use of short sentences. Notice how short the first sentence is and how short all his sentences are. Also notice how he is identifying with his prospect—the guy or gal who is serious about succeeding and wants a good life but finds himself or herself working hard and not getting anywhere. The copy starts out as follows:

I used to work hard. The 18-hour days. The 7-day weeks.
But I didn't start making big money until I did less—a *lot* less.

The ad continues and you're compelled to read further.

For example, this ad took about 2 hours to write. With a little luck, it should earn me 50, maybe a hundred thousand dollars.

Remember, this was written in 1973 and the equivalent of a hundred thousand dollars today might be close to a half-million dollars. Once again, Karbo is building curiosity. What is he offering? Why will this ad earn him so much money? You've got to read further. Notice also that there are no big words, no complicated long sentences. He's leading his reader into the copy slowly and easily, building curiosity as he goes. He tells a story as he progresses.

What's more, I'm going to ask you to send me 10 dollars for something that'll cost me no more than 50 cents. And I'll try to make it so irresistible that you'd be a darned fool not to do it.

Here Karbo is establishing trust with his readers. His honesty is almost disarming. He tells you up front that he has something he wants to sell you for 10 dollars that costs him only 50 cents. He's also building curiosity. He's using basic and simple statements, and the copy has you slowly slipping down his slippery slide right to the next paragraph. Then note how he justifies the purchase.

> After all, why should you care if I make $9.50 profit if I can show you how to make a *lot* more?
>
> What if I'm so sure that you *will* make money my Lazy Man's Way that I'll make you the world's most unusual guarantee?
>
> And here it is: I won't even cash your check or money order for 31 days *after* I've sent you my material.
>
> That'll give you plenty of time to get it, look it over, try it out.

Note the flow of the copy. Again he builds on the reader's curiosity, justifying the $10 purchase even if he hasn't yet told you about the offer. Now you are really curious. He wasn't going to cash the check for 31 days, which at the time was a novel approach. It was what I call a "satisfaction conviction" because your reaction might have been, "Boy, a lot of people are going to rip him off. They're going to get his book, read it and then return it and get their uncashed check back in the mail." You already know how important a good satisfaction conviction can be from Chapter 19, and Karbo uses it here, early in his copy. He also shows a degree of enthusiasm and confidence in his concept that raises your curiosity even more. He continues.

> If you don't agree that it's worth *at least a hundred times* what you invested, send it back. Your *uncashed* check or money order will be put in the return mail.
>
> The only reason I won't send it to you and bill you or send it C.O.D. is because both these methods involve more time and money.
>
> And I'm already going to give you the biggest bargain of your life.
>
> Because I'm going to tell you what it took me 11 years to perfect: How to make money the Lazy Man's Way.

Again, Karbo is justifying the purchase without even telling you what it is. And he is justifying why accepting payment by check is the only way he'll sell it to you, giving you an economic basis for his decision. The curiosity builds. But instead of telling you about his offer, he now changes direction completely to establish credibility for his offer by presenting himself as an example of how successfully this program has worked.

> O.K.—now I have to brag a little. I don't mind it. And it's necessary—to prove that sending me ten dollars...which I'll keep "in escrow" until you're satisfied...is the smartest thing you ever did.
>
> I live in a home that's worth $100,000. I know it is because I turned down an offer for that much. My mortgage is less than half that, and the only reason I haven't paid it off is because my Tax Accountant says I'd be an idiot.
>
> My "office," about a mile and a half from my home, is right on the beach. My view is so breathtaking that most people comment that they don't see how I get any work done. But I do enough. About 6 hours a day, 8 or 9 months a year.
>
> The rest of the time we spend at our mountain "cabin." I paid $30,000 for it—cash.
>
> I have 2 boats and a Cadillac. All paid for.
>
> We have stocks, bonds, investments, cash in the bank. But the most important thing I have is priceless: time with my family.
>
> And I'll show you just how I did it—the Lazy Man's Way—a secret I've shared with just a few friends 'til now.

Here in these last paragraphs he is obviously whetting your appetite and telling you what the results of his system produced for him. But there is another very subtle thing he has done as well. He is trying to personally identify with his audience. He doesn't talk about driving around in a Rolls-Royce but rather a Cadillac. He talks about having a mortgage, which most of his readers, if they own their own homes, probably have. He keeps his wealth to a modest level, for if it was too far out of the reach of his readers, they would not be able to relate to Karbo.

He is also selling the sizzle, not the steak. He is relating a number of things, most of which sound pretty inviting to you and represent the results of buying his system—the many material things in life that most of his readers dream of having. He is identifying with his prospects. And then at the end of the list, he talks about the most priceless thing his system has created, "time with my family." All of this resonates with the reader, who by now can't stop reading and might be saying, "What does this guy have to offer that can make it possible for me to live the life of

Joe Karbo?" So you read on. You read the secret that he's shared with only a few friends.

In the next paragraph you find one of the truly important highlights of his ad copy. He is very subtly trying to expand the appeal of his offer to the broadest possible segment of the market. Think about it. If he said that one person made millions, you might not identify with what he is saying if you honestly didn't believe that you could earn millions. But you might relate to the little old lady who is now able to travel wherever she wants or the widow who is earning $25,000 extra a year. Or the guy who doesn't have much of an education.

As you read the following copy, see how he appeals to the mass market—probably the single reason that this ad had such widespread appeal and was not confined to just the income opportunity area. Also see where he again builds on his integrity when he talks about almost declaring bankruptcy—thus relating to many in his audience who may also be facing financial difficulty.

It doesn't require "education." I'm a high school graduate.

It doesn't require "capital." When I started out, I was so deep in debt that a lawyer friend advised bankruptcy as the only way out. He was wrong. We paid off our debts and, outside of the mortgage, don't owe a cent to any man.

It doesn't require "luck." I've had more than my share, but I'm not promising you that you'll make as much money as I have. And you may do better: I personally know one man who used these principles, worked hard, and made 11 million dollars in 8 years. But money isn't everything.

It doesn't require "talent." Just enough brains to know what to look for. And I'll tell you that.

It doesn't require "youth." One woman I worked with is over 70. She's travelled the world over, making all the money she needs, doing only what I taught her.

It doesn't require "experience." A widow in Chicago has been averaging $25,000 a year for the past 5 years, using my methods.

These last sentences are very important. In short, he appealed to a very broad segment of the opportunity market and even went beyond it to people who might not be looking for an opportunity but would find this message compelling. And Karbo comes across as being incredibly honest. Remember, he told you the cost of what he was going to send you and he seems to be very honest throughout his ad, even to the point of being disarming. Remember, honesty is a powerful psychological selling tool.

Now comes the closing pitch, with complete and total enthusiasm for his concept and his book. Once again, Karbo realizes that many of his readers have jobs and at this point in the copy are wondering if they will have to give them up to learn what he has to offer. He uses a little sage wisdom given to him by a wise man he met. And then he wraps up the entire ad with a question that builds the final level of curiosity to a point that compels you to respond in order to find out what this man has to offer.

> What *does* it require? Belief. Enough to take a chance. Enough to absorb what I'll send you. Enough to put the principles into *action*. If you do just that—nothing more, nothing less—the results *will* be hard to believe. Remember—I guarantee it.
>
> You don't have to give up your job. But you may soon be making so much money that you'll be able to. Once again—I guarantee it.
>
> The wisest man I ever knew told me something I never forgot: "Most people are too busy earning a living to make any money."
>
> Don't take as long as I did to find out he was right.
>
> I'll prove it to you, if you'll send in the coupon now. I'm not asking you to "believe" me. Just try it. If I'm wrong, all you've lost is a couple of minutes and an 8-cent stamp. But what if I'm right?

It is interesting to see the cost of a first class stamp back in 1973. Today as I write this book a stamp costs 39 cents, so the cost of his book relative to the cost of a postage stamp was equivalent to $50 in today's dollars.

Then you examine the coupon. But right above the coupon you first read a sworn statement from his accountant:

> "I have examined this advertisement. On the basis of personal acquaintance with Mr. Joe Karbo for 18 years and my professional relationship as his accountant, I certify that every statement is true." (Accountant's name available upon request.)

He also includes his bank reference. Once again, this really is very convincing as prior to Karbo, nobody had ever put anything like this in an ad. He was strongly establishing his credibility by using the bank's name as an indirect testimonial to his honesty—something his prospects needed in order to feel confident to reach for their checkbooks and send him their hard-earned money.

The coupon is a summary of the offer.

Joe, you may be full of beans, but what have I got to lose? Send me the Lazy Man's Way to Riches. *But don't deposit my check or money order for 31 days after it's in the mail.*

If I return your material—for *any* reason—within that time, return my *uncashed* check or money order to me. On that basis, here's my ten dollars.

He even has a small box you can check if you want his "material" sent by airmail for only one dollar more.

Note that he is sending "material" and not just a book. "Material" makes the program appear much more valuable—more like a course as opposed to a book. It has much more sizzle than just saying "book."

If you sent in your money, you received a wonderful book that actually looked like it cost about 50 cents to print. But it contained both a motivational message and the direct marketing techniques necessary to make money the "Lazy Man's Way."

Karbo ran these ads for several years. I had been establishing the fact in my national advertising that there was no such thing as too many words. By 1973 we were really cranking out our advertising, but mostly in the *Wall Street Journal.* One year later when we advertised in many national magazines, we noticed that Karbo's copy was expanding to include testimonials and more examples to cover the broad market he was trying to reach. The ads became more wordy with each passing year.

But it was Joe's very first ad—the first major mass market advertising campaign to come from the income opportunity area in many years—that was the purest example of what I was teaching in my seminar.

Joe Karbo attended my seminar in 1978. At my seminar he shared his background and told the story of how he wrote this one ad.

Joe died in 1980 from a massive heart attack. He was being interviewed at a local TV station near his home in California when the interviewer decided to unfairly attack Joe, thus changing entirely the premise of the interview. Joe's first reaction was a heart attack from which he never revived. Joe was survived by his wife Betty and eight children.

His work and efforts have been continued in an excellent recently revised version of his book (by Richard Gilly Nixon) including a workbook. Any student of mail order needing some really good motivation should purchase it. Please see the listing in Appendix D for this course as well as several other good direct marketing books.

The Karbo ad was a classic. It was his biggest and best shot in the mail order business and its significance was felt by the many millions who bought his book and later indeed profited by it. But if this seemed like a real fluke—a once-in-a-lifetime experience that would be impossible to duplicate—you're wrong. It is happening even as you read this, with other entrepreneurs using direct marketing as a method to market their products.

The next true story tells of somebody who never wrote print mail order copy before he sat down and wrote one of the classic long-running mail order ads of the decade, and he did it right after attending my seminar. Read on.

Frank Lewis Schultz is a farmer who grows grapefruit in the Rio Grande Valley of Texas. For years he had used a simple letter or direct mailing to build his customer base into a nice-sized business that sold grapefruit by mail. But something always seemed to elude him. He couldn't get print mail order advertising to work for him.

He realized that space advertising (the idea of reaching millions of people for the same price it takes to reach thousands by mail) sounded like a great concept. And along with reaching millions, he could add credibility to his company and more profit to his bottom line.

It all sounded great until Schultz hired one of the nation's most respected direct response agencies. The first ad bombed. So did the second. In fact, his gross sales didn't cover the raw cost of the ad space. Schultz was discouraged.

When I announced my first seminar in 1977, Schultz was one of the first to sign up. During the seminar, he was very quiet, but he seemed to be absorbing everything I had to say. I didn't know at the time that he had a degree in marketing from the University of California at Berkeley.

After the seminar, with the information fresh in his mind, he went to the local Holiday Inn in Minocqua, Wisconsin, and started drafting his first print ad.

He based it on both the successful letter that he had run for years and the information I had taught. And the result was sent to me in Northbrook, Illinois, upon my return home after the seminar.

The ad was great. It wasn't the very technical style of the JS&A ads, but it had a homespun feel that grabbed you at the

*It was Frank's first ad and it became a classic.*

start and drew you through the copy all the way to the very end. As Frank later said about the seminar and what he had learned about writing copy, "It was actually pretty easy because suddenly everything was clear. I knew what I had to say and how to say it. I learned that you don't have to be a professional copywriter to write effective copy."

When I received Schultz's ad, I called him on the phone and told him, "Your ad is great. I only have a few changes to suggest but they are minor. Your big problem is the headline." I suggested "Fluke of Nature" instead of "A Stroke of Luck from Mother Nature"—the one he had written. I suggested the subheadline: "A new grapefruit discovery may change your concept of fruit." I also suggested he take out a line, "The zesty flavor of Royal Ruby Red grapefruit juice will help start your day with a smile," as it seemed almost a cliché—something an ad agency might have written. And there were several other small changes, but again, they were minor.

There were two pictures captioned with copy explaining the offer, and of course all the elements were designed to get you to read the first sentence. Let's examine the copy as we did with the Karbo ad and see how Schultz captured the essence of what I taught, and in a very simple yet persuasive way. The copy starts out with a first paragraph that was printed in bold type to act almost as a subheadline, thus drawing you further into the copy:

> I'm a farmer. And the story I tell you is the absolute truth, as incredible as it may seem.

This is a classic opening for an ad. Remember we talked about how each word has an emotion and a story attached to it? What does the word *farmer* bring to mind? How about honesty, hard work and integrity? Simply by stating that he is a farmer, he has established a degree of credibility right from the start of the ad. And then look at the curiosity he creates right away in the second sentence. How could you not continue?

> It all started in a grove owned by Dr. Webb, our family doctor. One of the men who was picking fruit in the doctor's orchard came up to the Webb house holding six of the strangest grapefruit anyone had ever seen. A single branch of an ordinary grapefruit tree had produced these six unusual fruit.
> These were big grapefruit, unusually big. And they had a faint

red blush on their skin. When Dr. Webb sliced open the grapefruit, the fruit was a brilliant ruby red in color.

Dr. Webb decided to taste this strange new grapefruit. The fruit was perfect, juicy and luscious. It wasn't sour like other grapefruit either—it was naturally sweet without sugar.

For some reason, we'll never know why, nature had chosen to produce an entirely new kind of grapefruit here in our Magic Rio Grande Valley. It was incredible—men had labored for years to produce the ideal grapefruit, and had failed. But suddenly on a single branch of one tree in one grove, Mother Nature had done it all by herself!

The copy reads almost like a fairy tale with the use of the Magic Rio Grande Valley name and the story of this unexpected discovery. Schultz created this environment—all woven through a compelling and interesting story that holds your attention and keeps you reading. You can't stop now. You've got to see where this all takes you. Schultz now goes into more detail on the fruit itself. And he uses one technique that you would never believe could be applied to fruit. He makes his product a rarity—a limited edition to be shared by very few people. Read the following and see what I mean.

### YOU CAN IMAGINE THE EXCITEMENT

From the fruit on that one branch, grove after grove now produces our own Texas Ruby Red Grapefruit. When I say, "Not one man in a thousand has ever tasted this grapefruit"—you can easily understand why.

To begin with, Ruby Reds are rare. You can look for them in stores but I doubt if you'll find one. You may find pink grapefruit, but seldom if ever do you see the genuine Ruby Reds.

So you start with the rarity of Ruby Reds, and to get to ROYAL Ruby Reds you have to get rarer yet. Only 4 to 5 percent of the entire crop will qualify as a "Royal Ruby Red."

Schultz graphically brought out the true rarity of what he was selling. You can certainly do that with a collectible, but the simple way Schultz made his fruit rare was ingenious. After he told you that "not one man in a thousand has ever tasted this grapefruit," you might have thought he was going to pitch you on the fruit. Instead he started to explain what makes it even more rare. And it got so rare that it seemed quite plausible that few people indeed have tasted this fruit.

In the next passage, Schultz continues to build the story but now he makes his message a very personal one. It almost sounds like he goes right into the grove with his men to pick the fruit. He is personally involved in every step of the growing and picking process, and he uses this approach to make his message personal. Secondly, he even uses a technical explanation—something that really builds confidence in the expertise he brings to his farming. A technical explanation in selling electronics would make sense, but see how he does it here with a very nonscientific product—grapefruit. And he also gets you totally involved with the fruit itself. Your taste buds are activated and you can almost savor the grapefruit as you read the copy. He is actually using your sense of taste as an involvement device. Instead of turning the knobs of a TV set or clicking on the keys of a calculator to involve you, he's getting you to salivate. The copy continues:

> Each Royal Ruby Red weighs a pound—or more! Each has a rich red color, flowing juices, luscious naturally sweet flavor, and the ability to stay this way for many weeks.
>
> Why, we won't even consider harvesting a grove until I've checked out the fruit for tree-ripened maturity myself. I check for "natural sugar," low acid balance and high juice content. I check to see that the fruit is plump and meaty, and I even check to see that the skin is thin. Not only does each factor have to check out, but all the factors have to be in a proper relationship to each other before I'll harvest a grove.
>
> And when we pick the fruit, we're just as fussy. Every one of us takes a "picking ring" when we harvest. If the fruit is small enough to pass through this ring—we don't pick it! It simply isn't big enough to qualify as a Royal Ruby Red!
>
> Even after picking there are other careful inspections each fruit must pass before I'll accept it. I size the fruit. And I grade it for beauty. Sometimes the fruit will be wind scarred. I won't accept it. Or sometimes it will have a bulge on the stem that we call "sheep nose." I won't accept it. You can see I really mean it when I say I accept only perfect Royal Ruby Reds.

By now you can just picture Frank Schultz out in the grove with his picking ring rejecting wind-scarred grapefruit or fruit that has sheep nose. By now you are actually convinced that this fruit is very carefully selected—chosen not only for its juice content but also for its beauty. Beauty? Yep, beauty.

Probably the one thing that he uses with great skill is the

personal nature of his presentation. His company sounds small—as if it is made up of just Schultz and a few other pickers. And they all go out with their picking rings, spend the day gathering only the prettiest and juiciest grapefruit, and then return with their harvest for shipping to just a few of their customers the next day. It is a beautiful example of the personal one-to-one selling technique that you want to capture in print, and Schultz has managed to do this in a very simple and masterful way.

Think also about the nature of grapefruit. This is unquestionably a simple product and this chapter is a good example of my "simple versus complicated" rule. When something is simple, like a grapefruit, you make it complex. If it's complex, you make it simple. What could be more simple than a grapefruit? But look at how Schultz has brought out all the features and the complexities of his selection process and even his own expertise by telling you more than you've ever wanted to know about grapefruit.

Schultz is now ready for the pitch. The grapefruit could not get any better. It is rare, it is delicious, it is beautiful and it has value. It's now up to Schultz to make his customers reach into their pockets and exchange their hard-earned dollars for his grapefruit, and he makes it as simple as possible.

Frank does this by offering a sample shipment—a low-priced no-risk opportunity just to try his product. He makes it so simple that you begin to wonder if he's going to be ripped off. And what does that signify? That's right—a satisfaction conviction—something that is so compelling, you wonder if people are going to take advantage of him.

> When I realized that the Royal Ruby Reds were the ultimate fruit, I decided to form a club and sell only to my club members. In this manner, I can control my production to insure that nobody will be disappointed.
>
> But before I ask you to join my club, I want you to sample my Royal Ruby Reds for yourself, at no cost to you whatsoever. Let me send you a box prepaid of 16 to 20 Royal Ruby Reds. Place four of them in your refrigerator until they are thoroughly cool. Then cut them in half and have your family sample this unusual fruit.
>
> You decide whether or not Royal Ruby Reds are everything I say. You determine whether or not eating a Royal Ruby Red is the fantastic taste experience I promise.

> You decide. I'm confident that you and your family will want more of this superb fruit and on a regular basis, too. If the four Royal Ruby Reds make you say "yes," then keep the remaining fruit. Otherwise return the unused fruit (at my expense) and you won't owe me a single penny.
>
> But you are never going to know just how wonderful genuine Royal Ruby Reds are unless you place your order right quick.
>
> This way you are sure to receive your package containing 16 to 20 Royal Ruby Reds for you and your family to sample. But since the supply is strictly limited it's important to place your order now.

Note the use of the words "right quick." That's the way farmers talk, isn't it. And it is this homey-sounding copy that captivated his audience. In fact, Schultz asked me if he should leave it in. "It isn't really good English" was his concern. "By all means, leave it in," I suggested. "It sounds great to me."

His offer then went on to give the terms of the purchase. The first box was going to cost $5 less than the standard shipment—a further incentive to at least try his grapefruit. In fact, you actually didn't pay anything up front, as he also included a bill for $9.95. You paid only if you wanted to keep the shipment and you then were enrolled in his monthly club. His copy continued:

> Now suppose you do like Royal Ruby Reds—suppose you love them—can you be sure of getting more?
>
> You surely can. By saying "yes" to my first shipment you have the privilege of automatically joining my Winter Fruit Club. Please be assured you pay nothing in advance. But each month during the winter, I'll ship you a pack of 16 to 20 orchard-fresh, hand-selected, hand-picked Royal Ruby Reds.
>
> Every Royal Ruby Red you receive will pass my tough tests. Each will weigh a pound or more. Safe delivery is guaranteed. This fruit is picked, packed and shipped each month, December through April.
>
> You pay only after you have received each shipment. And you can skip or cancel any shipment, simply by telling me your wishes.

He summarized his offer. He restated most of the points he told you in the previous copy at the very end of the ad. And then he goes into the close:

> Remember, it obligates you to nothing except making a taste test of the best grapefruit that has ever been grown. And this taste test is on me!

Of course, as you can well imagine, when I say supplies are lim-ited—I'm not kidding! There's just so many club members I can accept before I must close my membership this year.

In this statement, he is giving you a sense of urgency that is both believable and true. Production is limited and getting your order in quickly is very important to ensure that you'll be part of the membership program. He also makes it sound risk free and easy to test.

So to taste this "miracle" grapefruit and have the opportunity to savor it each month during the growing season, be sure to place your order at no obligation, today.

Frank was pleasantly surprised when he ran his test ad in the *Wall Street Journal:* "Our cost per order was the lowest of any outside list we've ever used, and I realized that a single advertise-ment held the key to the rapid growth of our company."

But Frank Schultz didn't stop there. He continued to advertise in the *Wall Street Journal,* the *New York Times, Parade*, and *TV Guide*, to name only a few. "When you're a farmer you always worry about the crop. It's growing too slow—you worry. It's grow-ing too fast—you really worry," said Frank later in a letter to me.

"I find it to be about the same when a farmer gets into space advertising. The orders are coming in so good from our space ads, I'm beginning to worry. A high-class worry, I'll admit."

In December 1980, an article on Schultz appeared in *Texas Monthly* magazine. The story talked about his wonderful copy and how the copy made his business seem small and personal. Yet it also explained that the business was quite large by then. He harvested 26,000 tons of grapefruit in 1979 with only 4 per-cent passing Schultz's rigorous standards for Royal Ruby Red grapefruit. The rest were sold to the grocery chains. And he now had 80,000 customers in the 48 contiguous states. He owned 14,000 acres of orchards spread out from Brownsville to McAllen, Texas, and had hundreds of employees. He truly was a success story—all created from the power of his pen.

And yet, his customers visualized Frank with his picking ring out in the orchard picking those perfect Royal Ruby Red grapefruit free of sheep nose and wind scarring.

From time to time, Frank would send me some of the letters he received complimenting him on his copy. One came from Stanley Marcus, then the chairman of Neiman Marcus. Some were from other copywriters who recognized his ad as brilliant. And for many years Schultz ran the ads until they finally wore out.

I myself was in Schultz's grapefruit club for many years. And from my orders alone, he probably made back all the money he had spent on my seminar. If you'd like Royal Ruby Red grapefruit sent directly to your door, call Frank toll free—1-800-477-4773 between 8 A.M. and 6 P.M. Central time. But do it "right quick."

Victoria's Secret is now a major chain with 900 stores doing $2.4 billion in sales with a major catalog division that does $870 million by itself. But back in 1979, it consisted of just three small stores and a catalog—all founded by an entrepreneur named Roy Raymond. And that is when Barbara Dunlap attended my seminar.

The ad she wrote helps illustrate many of the principles you've learned in this book and also points to a few she overlooked. Let's start with the headline and subheadline. If you were a man or a woman reading through a newspaper, you might stop dead in your tracks if you saw the following:

**Headline:** Lingerie for Men
**Subheadline:** How a Group of Very Special Men Made It All Possible

Note that the headline was just three words—short, concise and certainly enough to get you to read the subheadline. Then notice that the subheadline did not give away the premise of the ad; you still don't know what it is. In fact, it might sound like some men got together and made the wearing of lingerie possible. You just don't know, so you keep reading.

Now read the first paragraph, which is in large type and actually draws you into the copy. Also note the storytelling feel of the first few paragraphs.

WE WERE ASTOUNDED! When we opened the doors of our new business, we thought most of our customers would be women. After all, beautiful designer lingerie is the kind of luxury a lady can't resist.

**How wrong we were.**

That first Valentine's Day, the men came in droves! Hundreds of men, who had secretly been dying to visit our boutique. At last, they had the perfect excuse—Valentine's Day gifts for their favorite ladies.

*The ad drew a lot of attention but missed a few major points at the end.*

### They loved the merchandise.

Can you imagine how shocked we were? All those men—milling about our Victorian boutique. Admiring the silk stockings and lacy garter belts from France. Totally smitten by the luxurious silk and satin kimonos from London. Crowding around the bra and bikini sets from Italy. They couldn't wait to surprise their wives or girlfriends with something truly special.

Once again as the story is told you can visualize the scene. You can almost see the merchandise and appreciate how the variety of merchandise is woven neatly into the story. But now a question might pop into your mind as you are reading this. And this very question is brought into the copy at precisely this moment.

### Weren't they embarrassed?

The truth is, they were. But not enough to keep them away! They had seen our exciting, full-color catalogue. A breathtaking picture book of beautiful women, wearing enticing creations. Besides, a few men became our first satisfied customers. And in a short time, they had managed to spread the good word. Victoria's Secret wasn't like shopping for lingerie in a department store. No matronly saleslady to make a man feel uneasy. No raised eyebrows or pursed lips asking about sizes. No racks of flannel and terrycloth to wade through. And no clunky, plastic boxes overflowing with boring white foundation garments.

There were a number of good issues just covered. First, Dunlap comes across as being truthful when she admits that the men were embarrassed. In short, she raises an objection in the paragraph heading ("Weren't they embarrassed?") and then answers it honestly. But then she brings in the fact that they were motivated by a full-color catalog that she refers to as a "breathtaking picture book." Here she very subtly brings in the catalog as the motivational factor that prompted all these men to come to the store.

Another objection you might raise if you decided to go to the store is the store environment itself and the human element in the store—the salesclerks. If you were a man, would you be embarrassed? Here in this same paragraph (which really should have been a new paragraph) she raises the objection and resolves it by pointing out that the store has none of the embarrassments found in a department store. In short, this is a store that would not embarrass a man at all.

In this ad, Dunlap first got your attention and raised all the objections that you might have if you were a man and wanted to buy lingerie for your wife or girlfriend in a women's lingerie store. In the next paragraph, Dunlap broadens the market from just a few men to all men, similar to the way Karbo broadened his income opportunity ad to include anybody interested in bettering his or her life. Here's what she said.

### The men in our life.

Since that first Valentine's Day, we've learned a lot about our male customers. Mainly, they can't be stereotyped. Some are conservative, some far from it. Some are rather old, while others are much younger. Whether doctors, accountants, salesmen or bankers . . . they all have one thing in common. They are true connoisseurs of beauty. They know how sensuous and lovely a lacy camisole or elegant gown looks on a woman. And what's more, they know how wonderful a woman feels to receive something beautiful and intimate from a special man. And it takes a *very* special man to shop from Victoria's Secret.

Not only does Dunlap include a broad range of men but she then compliments the men on their taste and understanding of women in general.

In the next paragraph we finally get the real pitch of the ad. Since the only Victoria's Secret stores were located in northern California at the time, the real purpose of this ad, which ran nationally, was to attract catalog customers from the other 49 states. So after the paragraph heading "Our luxurious photo album . . ." comes the pitch. Note the colorful and sensuous language, which only helps to create the environment for this ad.

If you're like our male patrons—sensuous and fashion-conscious in your own right—you've been dying to find a place like Victoria's Secret. However, if you live outside of northern California you won't find it. But for $2.00 you can have the next best thing. Our luscious, full-color catalogue of alluring designer lingerie.

### What if you don't like our style?

We guarantee you'll be the first man who didn't. But . . . if after you receive our catalogue, you find our fashions too sensuous or too luxurious for the lady in your life, you haven't lost a thing. Our lush, full-color catalogue is an elegant collector's item—a conversation piece your friends will adore! (Already, our customers are requesting previous editions of the Victoria's Secret catalogue.)

To receive your own personal copy, send $2.00 to Victoria's Secret, dept. W500 [*address went here*]. We'll send you our colorful catalogue of fashion romance via first class mail.

There was one main problem with this ad, and unfortunately it came at the most critical part—at the end. The objection some prospects might raise is, "What if I'm not pleased with the $2 catalog or any of the merchandise?" Nothing was indicated about their return policy. And a nice hook could have been to allow customers to use their $2 investment in buying the catalog toward the purchase of their first order. Or even allowing them $10 toward their first order.

From what I understand, the first ad was moderately successful in bringing in catalog requests, which in turn brought in sales. This was a two-step process—to scan the market for possible customers and then make them customers through the catalog. This is a very good application of a print ad and a good example of many of the principles.

The principles that you should particularly pay attention to are the excellent timing of the objections and how they were resolved and the beautiful use of words that told a story and created the perfect environment for the offer. The real offer was the catalog, but the story that was told gave men permission to get the catalog and buy from it—a lot less embarrassing than going into the store.

"Lingerie for Men" was brief, it was interesting and it flowed quite nicely. And although its ending could have been more compelling and more effective, it brought you through the copy like a slippery slide all the way to the very end. I would have also added a byline to the ad to make it even more personal.

The catalog Victoria's Secret published back in 1979 was a lot more sensuous than the catalog they put out today. If I had to classify it, I would say it was an upscale version of a Frederick's of Hollywood lingerie catalog. And indeed, both catalogs were quite popular with the men.

Two advertising people from Victoria's Secret attended my seminar before the franchise was sold to The Limited. The two women used their copywriting skills to write the colorful catalogs. They both claim that the seminar was one of the turning points in their careers and a major factor in the early success of Victoria's Secret. Tragically, Roy Raymond, Victoria Secret's founder, committed suicide in 1993 by jumping off the Golden Gate Bridge.

The lesson to be learned from this example is that you can write a great ad but then miss some important opportunities at the end. And the end of the ad is when the buying decision has to be made—it's a critical point in any advertisement.

In the next chapter, I give you an example of a company trying to resolve a problem without first raising it. It will clarify the important method of always raising an objection and then resolving it.

This is a good example of an advertising message that could have been quite powerful if it weren't for one fatal flaw. Let me explain.

I was flying back from Rockford, Illinois, in my own private plane. I was about 50 miles from the Pal-Waukee airport where I was scheduled for an instrument landing even though the weather was perfect for flying. The air traffic controllers were unusually quiet as I approached Pal-Waukee. It was a bright clear day—one of those rare days when you could see for miles.

As I got closer to Pal-Waukee, I could see off in the distance a big fire near Chicago's O'Hare airport. I landed my plane, parked and walked into the airport office where I learned from a television broadcast that American Airlines flight 191 had just crashed on takeoff from O'Hare and that all its passengers had died. That was May 25, 1979, and it was one of those memories that remains indelibly etched in my mind.

The plane that crashed was a DC-10—one of McDonnell Douglas's largest and most popular aircraft. Immediately after the crash, it was determined that there was a hydraulic problem that, under certain circumstances, could cause loss of control and consequently a crash. McDonnell Douglas quickly corrected the problem, but for a while all DC-10s were grounded.

If that weren't enough, the DC-10 was involved in two more crashes within a relatively short period of time. The last two were unrelated to any fault of the airplane, but the stigma of the American Airlines crash was still on the mind of the public. McDonnell Douglas realized that it had to do something to offset the negative publicity.

They picked Pete Conrad to act as spokesman in an advertisement to address the public's concern. But instead of raising the

*This ad had a major flaw. The entire first part was missing.*

objections of the plane crashes and then resolving the problem with the excellent copy that was written, the objection was totally ignored. The resulting ad was hollow. The following is the copy as it was written:

**Headline:** "The more you learn about our DC-10, the more you know how great it really is."

**Byline:** Pete Conrad, Former Astronaut, Division Vice President, McDonnell Douglas

**Copy:** I've watched airplanes and spacecraft take shape for much of my adult life. I'm certain that nothing made to fly has ever been designed or built to more exacting standards than our DC-10.

Eighteen million engineering man-hours were invested in this plane's development. That includes 14,000 hours of wind tunnel testing, as well as full-scale 'fatigue testing' for the equivalent of 40 years of airline service.

I'm convinced that the DC-10 is the most thoroughly-tested jet-liner ever built. Along with U.S. Government certification, the DC-10 has passed structure tests just as demanding, in their own way, as those required of U.S. Air Force fighter planes.

The DC-10 fleet demonstrates its dependability flying more than a million miles a day and serving 170 cities in 90 countries around the globe.

The ad then ended with a place to write McDonnell Douglas to get more information.

The copy was good copy—very persuasive in terms of building confidence in the plane. And all this was presented by a former astronaut to add credibility. But it lacked an important opening that would have made the copy many times more effective.

What if the ad had started out differently? If I were given the assignment of writing the ad, here's the way it would go:

**Headline:** DC-10's Big Secret

**Subheadline:** You've heard a lot of bad publicity about the DC-10. But here's something you may not have known.

**Byline:** By Pete Conrad

**Copy:** It was horrible. When American Airlines flight 191 crashed at O'Hare in Chicago last May 25th, hundreds of people lost their lives in what was considered one of the worst plane crashes in American history. The plane—a DC-10.

But as the facts emerged, it was learned that a series of coincidences resulted in a hydraulic malfunction that in all likelihood would never happen again. But it did happen. And in the subsequent weeks, a series of fail-safe systems were installed that make the DC-10's hydraulic system among the safest of any jetliner.

In addition, two other recent crashes of DC-10s were determined to be totally not the fault of the airplane but of the pilots. But because of the negative publicity generated by the American Airlines crash and these other two crashes, we have been even more diligent. All airlines are required to give each DC-10 a complete inspection every 50 hours instead of the required 100 hours of flying. The plane's hydraulic system is checked before each flight instead of waiting until a required inspection. And the plane's structural system is checked not only by each mechanic but by the pilots themselves. You couldn't fly a safer plane.

Then I would pick up the copy from the existing ad so it would continue,

I've watched airplanes and spacecraft take shape for much of my adult life. I'm certain that nothing made to fly has ever been designed or built to more exacting standards than our DC-10.

The rest of the original copy would follow. Do you see the difference? What I have done is to raise the real problem (or as I call it, the "objection") and then resolve it. Conrad's copy, which could easily go at the end of my ad, would then contribute to resolving the problem.

After reading my version of the ad, you would leave with a positive feeling about both the company and the message. You would think, "That was a sincere effort to dispel those false impressions on the safety of the DC-10." The message is an emotional presentation that shows concern, integrity and leadership.

Now compare that with the way the ad was originally written, which might have left you with the sarcastic impression, "Sure it's a safe plane. . . ." Or maybe, "They are just trying to cover themselves from all the heat they've been taking."

Keep in mind that the copy they had was very good. They just left off the entire front end of the ad and were avoiding the real issue—the events that actually happened that prompted their ad. They just spent most of their copy resolving the objection without acknowledging and addressing it directly.

The lesson to be learned here is to realize the importance of raising an objection, regardless of how embarrassing or detrimental it may seem, and then doing your best to resolve it. You'll find that the public really appreciates your candor, honesty and frankness and will respond to your message in a positive way, whether it be to buy your product, to develop a good feeling about your company or, as in the case of the DC-10, to restore confidence in an airplane.

$E$ven if you never wrote a piece of copy in your life, one look at this ad from Sony Video Communications and you would feel pretty much like the cartoon character shown in it. You'd feel like falling asleep.

The advertising agency that created this ad probably thought they had a very clever idea. Their concept—show the contrast between typical types of boring communications and a new, more stimulating video presentation (new back in the mid-1970s when this ad appeared).

In keeping with the theme, the headline in the ad was inadvertently boring in that it was hard to read with its dense capitalized type. The ad layout was boring. And finally, the copy was monotonous and did not follow many of my principles. So whoever created this ad was certainly being consistent with the theme in their presentation. It was boring.

But being consistent while going in the wrong direction is not a great strategy, either. Very few people would want to read a boring ad. There are thousands of ad messages out there on a daily basis, and to stand out you need a message that grabs people's attention and causes them to read your entire ad. And to get them to read your entire ad, you must use many of the techniques I've presented throughout this book, even if the ad you are creating is not a mail order ad.

In the Sony ad they are first trying to sell the concept of using video and then of using Sony video, once they have convinced their reader to try this new medium. My approach would have been to create a story of somebody who switched to video and saw a dramatic benefit—more sales, greater productivity or more awareness.

Here are the first few paragraphs to give you the sense of

*The theme of this ad was "boring." They accomplished their goal.*

how the copy flowed. The ad had no subheadline, no cartoon caption and started out with a very long and boring first sentence.

> Every day, American business spews forth a virtually endless stream of inter-office memos, conference reports, training manuals, brochures, telexes, phone calls, slide shows, letters, telegrams, direct mail pieces, annual reports, press releases and newsletters.
>
> The average employee is deluged with communication.
>
> And there is no way of telling how much of it is either ignored, forgotten, misplaced or summarily disposed of.
>
> In short, American business is in the throes of a vast and complex communication crisis.
>
> A problem that today—in an age of shortened attention spans and heightened communications costs—cries out for an efficient and imaginative solution.

The first sentence is too long and the copy is boring. But then again, isn't "boring" the theme of the ad? (I'm being facetious.)

The ad then tells how video is being used and what Sony has to offer the new and emerging industry. If you thought the first few paragraphs were boring, so was the rest of the copy. And since I get bored typing it into my computer for this book, I'm not going to include any more for you to read. Just trust me—it was boring.

Chances are, unless you were totally interested in video communications and were actively searching for everything you could find on the subject, you wouldn't even consider reading the entire ad.

And here's my final point. The ad was created by a professional ad agency using professional copywriters, layout artists and art directors. After reading this book, you could act as a consultant to that ad agency and improve its advertising by 1,000 percent and you may not even be a professional anything. The ability to write good advertising copy is not limited exclusively to professionals. Often even the most inexperienced person can write an incredibly effective ad. And certainly after reading this book, you can criticize even the most professionally prepared ads.

This JS&A mail order ad for the Magic Stat thermostat basically tells a story but with a unique twist. The story starts out with us hating the product, and then as the story unfolds, the product takes a quantum leap in our approval to become the best product on the planet. How I get there is an interesting process.

First I realized that the number one drawback in purchasing a thermostat is the installation. It's not one of those things that consumers relate to. It could be dangerous handling all those wires and there's a lot of extra expense in having an installer put one in. So one of the first good features we finally like in our story is the ease of installation. In short, we recognize that consumers don't like to be bothered with installation and we hit this feature early in the ad.

The copy itself raises many objections—the case design, the look of it and even the name. We realized that these would be some of the same objections consumers would raise when they looked at the product. And we resolved them one by one as we floated through the copy.

*I brought out the worst aspects of this product and turned them around.*

A good portion of the copy explained in a light sort of way the features of the product. And then near the end we built up the company selling us the product to add credibility and make the consumer feel more secure. Our competition, after all, was Honeywell—a company with an established name and reputation.

The Magic Stat ad ran in print for almost three years starting in 1983 and made the product into a very successful brand name. The company eventually was sold to Honeywell.

The following is the complete text of the ad:

**Headline:** Magic Baloney
**Subheadline:** You'll love the way we hated the Magic Stat thermostat until an amazing thing happened.

**Caption:** It had no digital readout, an ugly case and a stupid name. It almost made us sick.

**Copy:** You're probably expecting our typical sales pitch, but get ready for a shock. For instead of trying to tell you what a great product the Magic Stat thermostat is, we're going to tear it apart. Unmercifully.

When we first saw the Magic Stat, we took one look at the name and went, "Yuck." We took one look at the plastic case and said, "How cheap looking." And when we looked for the digital read-out, it had none. So before the salesman even showed us how it worked, we were totally turned off.

### REAL LOSER

So there it was—at first blush a real loser. But wait, we did find one good feature—a feature that led us to a discovery. The Magic Stat installs in a few minutes and no serviceman is required. Thermostat wires in your wall follow standard color codes. So when you install Magic Stat, you attach the red wire to the red location and the white to the white. That's play school stuff. And it's safe. Conventional thermostats installed over the past 20 years are generally only 24 volts, so you can either turn off the power or work with the "live" wires without fear.

### OK, LET'S TEST IT

The Magic Stat installation was so easy that the least we could do was test it. And that's when we made an incredible discovery. We discovered that the Magic Stat was probably the most consumer-oriented, technologically-advanced and most sophisticated thermostat ever developed on the face of this earth and in our galaxy for all times ever. What made us switch from hating the thing to loving it? Read the following:

The Magic Stat has six setback settings per day and a seven day program. That means that you could set it for 70 degrees when you get up in the morning, drop the temperature to 54 degrees when you go to work, raise it to 68 degrees when you return for dinner, raise it up to 70 degrees after dinner as you watch TV and then drop it down to 62 degrees when you go to sleep. Count them—five settings with one to spare.

In one day the Magic Stat is programmed for the whole week and for the weeks to come. If you want a different schedule for week-ends, you can individually program the thermostat for those days, too. "Big deal," you might think. "What's so great about that?" Read on.

You set most electronic setback thermostats to the time you want the furnace to go on in the morning, so when you wake up, your room is once again warm. But what if one morning it's bitter cold outside and the next morning it's much warmer? This means that setting your furnace to go on at the same time may, on one morning, leave you cold and on the next morning cause you to waste energy by warming up your house too soon.

By golly, the Magic Stat has everybody beat on this one too. Throughout the night it senses and computes the drop in temperature and the time it will take to get your room to your exact wake-up temperature. So if you want to wake up at 7 AM to 70 degrees—that's the temperature you'll wake up to every time. Because it's a patented concept, no other thermostat has this feature. But wait. There is also a patent on the setting feature.

### SIMPLE TO SET

To set the thermostat, you press just one button. A small LED light scans the temperature scale until you reach your desired temperature and then you release the button. You change the temperature naturally, throughout the day, up to six times. The unit responds and remembers that exact living pattern. The present temperature is displayed by a glowing red LED on the scale.

The system also computes the ideal length the furnace should stay on to keep the temperature within a range of plus or minus one and one-half degrees. A battery backup lets you keep your stored program in its memory so power outages as long as eight hours won't let your unit forget. And if something happens and your power is out for a few days, the unit will automatically maintain 68 degrees when the power is restored.

Quite frankly, we were so impressed with the unit, its ease of installation and setting plus its many energy-saving features, we seriously considered advertising it until we realized that our customers would probably not want to trust their future comfort to a product called Magic Stat. What if something went wrong with the unit? How substantial was this Magic Stat outfit? Remember, a thermostat is something you live with as long as you live in your home, and they're supposed to last ages. After all, your comfort depends on it.

Well, we did our homework. We found the company to be a sound, well-financed organization. They have been in business for several years, and they back their products with a three-year limited warranty. In addition, the company has a policy of buying back your unit in one year if you haven't saved its full cost in energy savings. We were satisfied with the company, the people, the product, its incredible features, the company's commitment to the product and above all, the energy savings.

We are so impressed now with the Magic Stat that we're going to make buying one irresistible. Buy one from us for only $79.

Install it yourself in a few minutes or hire a handyman to install it.

Or order the new deluxe unit for $99 with the exact same features as the regular model, but with a beautiful new case.

Then enjoy the savings this next winter. Not only will you save up to 30% on your heating bills, but you're eligible for the 15% energy tax credit. Then if you're not absolutely in love with this product one year later, return it to JS&A. You'll get all your money back and you can reinstall your old thermostat.

### REALIZE SAVINGS

But we're counting on a few things. First, you will realize an energy savings and a comfort that will far surpass what you are currently experiencing. Secondly, you probably will sleep better breathing cooler air yet wake up to just the right temperature.

Beauty is only skin deep and a name doesn't really mean that much. But we sure wish those guys at Magic Stat would have named their unit something more impressive. Maybe something like Twinkle Temp.

To order, credit card holders call toll free and ask for product by number below or send check plus $4 delivery for each unit ordered.

Magic Stat (0040C) . . . . . . . . . . . . . . . . . . . . . . . . . . . . . . . . . .$79
Deluxe Magic Stat (0041C) . . . . . . . . . . . . . . . . . . . . . . . . . . . 99

The ad drew your attention and brought you into the copy with the way I knocked the product. Your question might have been, "What's the gimmick? Why is he knocking the product?"

You started to read the ad. And then you discovered the one feature that we liked, which happened to be installation—the most difficult obstacle we had to overcome in selling this product.

From then on selling the Magic Stat was all downhill as if on a slippery slide. Once we had the product installed, we could then discover its great features, raise and resolve the remaining objections (the name and the appearance) and then sell all the product's benefits. And indeed we did for more than three years.

At JS&A we had three corporate aircraft. Like having a lot of cars, you can fly only one airplane at a time. So I decided to get rid of the plane I used the least—my Aerostar.

I paid close to $240,000 for it and everybody told me that it was now worth only $190,000 at best. I couldn't believe this fine aircraft had dropped so much in value, so I decided to take out a single ad in the *AOPA Pilot*—one of the private pilot magazines—and find out if I could get my asking price.

The basic format of the ad was a story about my lack of use of the airplane and my concern for our mechanic/pilot Dave. And I use the story to weave in all the good features of the plane. Then, at the end, to add a little humor, I offered to give away a small steer to anybody who buys the plane. I finished the ad with a classic ending. In this ad the humor worked. My Aerostar sold quickly for $240,000—I got back exactly what I paid for it minus the cost of the ad, around $5,000. It was well worth the effort. Humor can work if it is done in a friendly sort of way. In essence I was poking fun at myself, but the serious message of the ad didn't get overlooked. And, remember, I only needed to sell one to break even.

*They said I'd never get my asking price, but it took only one customer.*

**Headline:** Pet Plane

**Subheadline:** This advertisement has not been paid for by Piper nor do I own any Piper stock.

**Byline:** By Joseph Sugarman, President, JS&A Group, Inc.

**Copy:** I am a proud owner of a 1978 Aerostar 601P and have decided to sell it despite serious reservations.

I bought 296PA in April of 1978. It was one of the last ones produced by Ted Smith before Piper bought the company. I also hired a full-time mechanic, Dave, who did nothing but keep the ship gleaming and in perfect flying condition.

Instead of flying the Aerostar, Dave and I ended up flying the other corporate planes—our Grumman Tiger and our Beechcraft Bonanza—while the Aerostar was hangared, polished and looking pretty.

In two full years, Dave and I have only put 350 hours on our pet plane—a lot less time than can justify owning this fine ship.

## DAVE IS A FARMER

Dave is also a farmer. In his early years he plowed the fields and milked cows at his parents' farm in Illinois. Dave has always loved the farm—almost as much as Dave loves flying.

In July of this year, Dave and I were talking. We weren't using the Aerostar enough to justify keeping it, yet Dave, a loyal, hardworking and excellent mechanic, would not have enough to keep him busy to continue working for JS&A if we sold it and he only had the other two planes to work on.

I personally love flying too. I am an instrument-rated commercial pilot with a multi-engine rating. Unlike Dave, I was born in the big city. I didn't know what it was like to raise crops or work on a farm.

## DAVE GETS THE WORD

I sat Dave down and told him that I was planning to sell 296PA and I asked him if he wouldn't mind going back to the farm. My idea was simply to buy a farm with the proceeds from the sale of the Aerostar, put in a landing strip and a small hangar, and Dave and his family could raise crops while he wasn't working on the other two planes.

Dave loved the idea, so I decided to part with our Aerostar and offer it for sale in this advertisement.

296PA is a fully pressurized light twin that gets an amazing 28 gallons per hour at a realistic cruise speed of 200 knots. It was aerodynamically designed to take jet engines, but its designer settled for two 290 HP Lycoming engines which provide great speed and fuel efficiency.

## ADVANCED AVIONICS

The avionics on the airplane remind me of many of the fine products our company sells. The fully computerized Bendix 2000 system includes radar, R-Nav, DME, a radar altimeter plus all the goodies we could possibly put on the beautiful panel. There's an auxiliary hydraulic pump, surface de-ice plus a flight phone. The plane had to be fully equipped—after all, my reputation demanded it.

A comparably equipped 1980 Aerostar currently sells for over $350,000 and doesn't look nearly as pretty.

Our Aerostar was a Ted Smith original—built by dedicated craftsmen who took great pride in their work. But with any new plane, there are always small bugs that surface. The JS&A Aerostar is so debugged that we doubt you'll see one soon. Dave spent an enormous amount of time tightening, greasing, cleaning and examining every system in the plane. In addition to 100 hour inspections, Dave conducted 50 hour inspections. In addition to yearly inspections, Dave conducted semi-annual inspections. And if I mentioned I heard a strange creak on the plane, Dave would be there for days decreaking the plane.

In short, 296PA is a beautiful, fully-equipped airplane that has been hangared and well taken care of for its short two-year life. And it's for sale.

JS&A is offering our 601P for only $240,000 complete (sales tax has already been paid on the plane) plus no postage or handling. It's a genuine bargain that really has to be seen to be appreciated. Dave hangars the plane at the Waukegan airport, north of Chicago, and would be happy to arrange a showing. Simply call our toll-free number below to set up an appointment.

If you're not interested in our Aerostar but would like one of our most recent catalogs, call us on our toll-free number or drop us a line too. JS&A is America's largest single source of space-age products and I'd be anxious to have fellow pilots as our customers.

Dave has been looking at a lot of farms lately and is really excited about getting back into farming. And, of course, I'm anxious to sell my Aerostar so I could own a farm and keep a loyal employee happy and productive.

And if somebody purchases my Aerostar from this ad, I'll also throw in, free of charge, a steer from our new farm. After all, as any airplane salesman will tell you, it's hard to sell a plane without a little bull. Call early and see my Aerostar, today.

As I mentioned, the plane sold very quickly. And for the asking price. It was only later, after a call from the FBI, that I discovered the plane was used for running drugs from South America and had been confiscated.

**A**fter my success with the airplane, I had a chance to really push the mail order envelope. Could I sell a $6 million home? The exposure might find one buyer—just as it did with my airplane—and all I needed was one buyer.

So in 1987 I created the ad as a complete story almost all the way to the end. The marketing strategy was to offer the house or a video. If the house didn't sell, maybe I would sell enough videos to cover the space costs. But I didn't sell enough videos and the ad was a loss, as the house did not sell, either.

**Headline:** Mail Order Mansion

**Caption:** It looked like a setup to me.

**Subheadline:** It's only 6 million dollars and comes complete with swimming pool, tennis court and a breathtaking view.

**Byline:** By Joseph Sugarman

**Copy:** Have I got a deal. And even if you don't buy this home, you'll love the story.

It all started with an invitation. I was invited by one of the top real estate developers in the country to attend a party at his home in Malibu, California. I didn't know why. All the developer would say is, "Just come."

The jet was waiting for me at O'Hare Airport in Chicago and his chauffeur-driven limousine met me at Los Angeles for the drive to Malibu. It was class all the way.

When I drove up to the home, there was a party going on. Rolls-Royces were lined up everywhere and the noise and music from the house made it clear that something special was going on.

### VERY FAMOUS GUESTS

After I entered and was introduced to the host and his wife, they took me around and introduced me to some of their guests. "This

*We accepted Visa, MasterCard and American Express. And even Japanese yen.*

is Joe Sugarman, that famous mail order copywriter who writes all those interesting mail order ads."

I met a famous movie star, a nationally famous sports broadcaster, a soap opera TV star, a few famous baseball players and two famous California politicians. I recognized everybody and a few even knew who I was. In fact, some of them were my customers. But why was I there? I still didn't know.

I had a chance to look around the house. Now I've seen beautiful homes in my life but this one had to be the most impressive I've ever seen. First, it was on top of a 90 foot bluff overlooking a sandy beach and the Pacific Ocean. Secondly, it was night and I could see the entire shoreline of Los Angeles. It was as if I were on a cruise ship at sea and I could look over the Pacific and back at the city.

Then I recognized the cliff. Was this the site of the most publicized wedding in show business where seven helicopters hovered above taking pictures? I found out later that it was.

The home took complete advantage of the view. Practically every room faced the ocean. And the sliding glass doors completely opened so you had an unobstructed view of the ocean—no partitions, no supporting beams.

The sound that filled the house with music first appeared to be live. But later I found that the home had the best acoustics ever designed into a personal residence with a sound system that rivaled a recording studio. And what a personal residence.

There was a sunken tennis court, a swimming pool, whirlpool bath and solid state electronic lighting system that was controlled from any place in the house. The ceilings were 25 feet high and the interior decor was so tastefully done that I could easily understand why it won all sorts of awards. But why was I here? Why were all my expenses paid for? Then I found out.

The developer and his wife set me up in one of the five bedrooms and after the guests had left invited me into the living room. "Joe, the reason we've invited you here is that we want you to write an advertisement to sell our house. You're one of the nation's top copywriters, and since this house is an award-winning world-class residence, we wanted a world-class copywriter to do it justice."

Now I'll admit, I was flattered. "But I'm a mail order copywriter. How could I possibly sell a house this expensive?"

### VERY SPECIAL

"Easy," replied the developer. "By its value. This property is very special. It's on a peninsula that sticks out of the curved part that faces Los Angeles. When you look from the cliff you see Los Angeles as if it were rising out of the ocean. And because we are on a point, we do not get the harsh winds off the ocean but rather gentle breezes all year long. The property itself is so valuable that our next door neighbor paid close to 9 million dollars for his one bedroom house."

I was starting to feel uneasy. "I'm sorry, but there's no way I can sell your home. I refuse to write anything except under my own company name. And I'm not in the real estate business." But the developer persisted.

"Joe, you really can be. This house is an investment. There's a lot of foreign money out there. And all it takes is that special person looking for a celebrity-status world-class home on one of the best sites in America and presto, it's sold."

### FINAL REFUSAL

I refused and it was my final refusal. "I'm sorry, I cannot sell anything without a 30 day return privilege. My customers all have the opportunity to return anything we sell them for a prompt and courteous refund. And then there's the credit card issue. We make it easy for them to purchase with either Master Card, Visa or American Express."

Well, the rest is history. I am indeed offering the house for sale. Please call me at (312) 564-7000 and arrange for a personal showing. Then I urge you to buy it. We accept Visa, Master Card, American Express, American dollars, Japanese Yen or any negotiable hard currency.

After you buy the home, live in it for 30 days. Enjoy the spectacular view, walk on the beautiful beaches, experience the spacious living. If, after 30 days, you aren't completely satisfied, return the home to the original owner for a prompt and courteous refund.

The developer and his wife are thrilled that I am selling their home. They realize that the mail order business is a lot different than the real estate business and are willing to compromise. But don't you compromise. If you truly are one of those rare people in search of a spectacular home on the best location in America, call me personally at no obligation, today.

PS: If you don't have time for the showing, please order a video tape of the home. (Please refer to product number 7077YE.) Send $20 plus $3 postage and handling to the address below or credit card buyers call our toll-free number below.

Malibu Mansion . . . . . . . . . . . . . . . . . . . . . . . . . . . . . $6,000,000

As I mentioned, the house did not sell. And, as a matter of fact, we didn't sell enough videos to break even, either. But that was part of the risk I was willing to take. We did get a lot of publicity from the ad including an invitation to appear on the David Letterman show, which I declined.

I also got a call from the Disney estate asking me if I would sell Walt Disney's old home in the same fashion I offered the Mail Order Mansion. I didn't accept the opportunity, as one crazy real estate ad was enough for me.

Some of my ads were never even published. Others were not that successful and some appeared only in our catalog. From this last group I have selected one that I felt struck out in a very unique direction and had an interesting story. Hungarian Conspiracy appeared only in our catalog and was moderately successful. It was, however, one of my favorites.

I actually traveled to Hungary, did all the photography in Budapest and even met with Professor Erno Rubik, the inventor of Rubik's Cube—a three-dimensional puzzle in the shape of a cube that was a fad in the early 1980s.

What was unique in this ad was the message. Consumers were urged not to buy the product through a tongue-in-cheek explanation of why purchasing one could cause another major recession. It is only in the last paragraph of the ad that I actually offer the product for sale.

Keep in mind that when this was written in 1983, we still had the Berlin Wall and the Soviet Union with all the associated paranoia.

The environment created in the ad for the product is both a story and a tease. "What's the gimmick here if they aren't selling the product?" is one of the questions you might ask yourself as you slowly slip through the copy. And you don't get the answer until the very last paragraph. What do you think of the ad copy?

*After completely insulting my prospects, I still did well.*

**Headline:** Hungarian Conspiracy

**Subheadline:** Hungary plans massive assault on America with new computer weapon. Exclusive report from Budapest.

**Caption 1:** Warn your neighbors not to buy this dangerous Hungarian secret weapon.

**Caption 2:** Thomas Kovacs caught holding the XL-25 in this special photo smuggled out of Budapest. "You think the last recession was bad?"

**Copy:** Note: Reproduction or any reprints, in whole or in part, of the following material is strictly forbidden without the express written permission of JS&A. All rights reserved.

BUDAPEST (JS&A)—Reporters have smuggled intelligence reports out of Hungary on a conspiracy that may have far-reaching consequences for all Americans.

In the coming year, Hungarians will be shipping to the United States, via Hong Kong, a game with the code name "XL-25."

The game at first may look innocuous—a typical electronic game that could come from Mattel, or any of the other big electronic game manufacturers. But beware. Whatever you do, don't buy it.

### MASSIVE CONSPIRACY

The game is part of a massive conspiracy to weaken the United States by destroying our productive work force and eventually putting the entire free world into a major depression. Here's what we've discovered.

In 1980 when Erno Rubik, the Budapest University professor, unleashed the now famous Rubik's Cube, the United States economy was growing at a nice clip. Shortly after the cube was introduced, America entered into a major recession. Our gross national product dropped, factories started laying off people by the thousands and the economy took a big nosedive.

The exact reasons for the recession are varied, but our theory is quite simple. JS&A contends that millions of Americans were so busy twisting that small cube that they were not paying attention to their jobs. Productivity dropped, profits plunged and consumer spending fell to new lows.

It was obvious to Russian intelligence sources that the cause of the American recession was the Rubik's Cube. The Russians reasoned that if the Hungarians could invent games and then flood the American market with them, they could cause a massive depression—one that would permanently weaken America thus making us easy targets for a communist takeover. If you think this theory is farfetched, please read on.

### THANK YOU

Hungarians everywhere, proud of the huge success of the Rubik's Cube, were now inspired. Hungarians are quite a creative bunch to start with. They were responsible for such things as glass fiber optics, the micro floppy disk and the science of holography. Hungary always had creative people, but their potential was never really unleashed until Rubik.

The Hungarian government wanted to not only encourage this pent-up creativity, but help Hungary develop their game industry for specific communist purposes.

A new private company was set up last year for the sole purpose of developing computer games for the American market. Funded by banks and run by successful Budapest business types, the company developed the XL-25 through the efforts of three game designers shown to the left.

The bearded communist shown in the picture is Laszlo Mero, 33, a winner of the 1968 International Mathematical Student Olympiad held in Moscow. He's bright, intelligent and one of the top puzzle and game designers in Hungary.

### AUTO PARTS DEALER

The man in the middle is Thomas Kovacs, a Hungarian auto parts dealer. At least that's what our investigators turned up. We suspect auto parts is only a front.

The man to the left is Ferenc Szatmari, a physicist and a real genius. He graduated from the University of Budapest with a doctorate degree in elementary particle physics.

The incredible game they invented and the one we must stop from being sold in this country is quite fascinating. The XL-25 is an electronic game with five rows of five squares or 25 squares in all. Each square is actually a button with a built-in light-emitting diode.

When you start, lights light up under five of the buttons. The object of the puzzle is to get all the lights under the buttons to light up. But there's a catch, and here's where the frustration comes in.

Each time you press a button, the four buttons immediately surrounding the button you push change state. If they're lit, they go off. If they're off, they'll go on. If you're a little confused, it doesn't matter anyway. Just remember that the object of the game is to get all the buttons to light up with the least number of keystrokes.

The unit counts the number of button entries and you can ask the XL-25 what your score is and still return to your game.

Once you try the XL-25, you'll be immediately sucked into the Hungarian conspiracy. But don't worry. You're in good company. Texas Instruments was so impressed with its design that they developed the integrated circuit. A group in Hong Kong became so obsessed with it that they built the game with the quality you'd expect from a Mattel or Atari game.

Quite frankly, we were so hooked that we bought thousands and even dispatched a reporter to Budapest where we made our shocking intelligence discovery.

### YOU CAN HELP

So there's the story. A communist game, whose circuit was designed by a good ol' American company, carefully assembled by one of our best friends in the Far East—all part of a massive conspiracy to prepare Americans for a major communist takeover.

Prevent other Americans from falling into this scam. Order a unit from JS&A. When you receive it, whatever you do, don't play with it. Instead, immediately take it to all your neighbors and urge them not to buy one. Tell them about the real cause of our last recession, the communist plot and the Hungarian conspiracy. And then make sure you give them the ultimate warning. "Anybody who buys this thing is a real idiot."

XL-25 (3045C 4.00) . . . . . . . . . . . . . . . . . . . . . . . . . . . . . $29

This was a really good example of pushing the envelope. The ad copy was strong enough to get my prospects to read all the copy and hopefully the curiosity was strong enough to cause them to purchase the product. Even if I did call anybody who bought one an idiot.

The Vision Breakthrough advertisement was among the most successful in my company's history, so it merits a close look.

In this ad I did not want to present the product as another pair of sunglasses, so I presented it as a vision breakthrough that protects you from the harmful rays of the sun. It was one of the first ads that provided a real educational message about the dangers of ultraviolet (UV) rays on the eyes. Before this ad ran, there was really nothing in the popular press about UV ray damage.

The approach I used was to tell the story of how I discovered the glasses and all the facts I learned about them as well as the sun's light. I did it in a simple yet powerful way.

I also used a tremendous dose of curiosity. You can't experience the pair unless you personally try them on. Thus, you must buy them to satisfy your curiosity.

The BluBlocker advertising campaign was a major success that started with this print ad in 1986 and continued on television for several years. Today BluBlocker is a recognized brand name that is sold in retail stores throughout the country.

*This single ad started an entire business that eventually created a brand name.*

**Headline:** Vision Breakthrough

**Subheadline:** When I put on the pair of glasses what I saw I could not believe. Nor will you.

**Caption:** They look like sunglasses.

**Byline:** By Joseph Sugarman

**Copy:** I am about to tell you a true story. If you believe me, you will be well rewarded. If you don't believe me, I will make it worth your while to change your mind. Let me explain.

Len is a friend of mine who knows good products. One day he called excited about a pair of sunglasses he owned. "It's so incredible," he said, "when you first look through a pair, you won't believe it."

"What will I see?" I asked. "What could be so incredible?"

Len continued, "When you put on these glasses, your vision improves. Objects appear sharper, more defined. Everything takes on an enhanced 3-D effect. And it's not my imagination. I just want you to see for yourself."

### COULDN'T BELIEVE EYES

When I received the sunglasses and put them on I couldn't believe my eyes. I kept taking them off and putting them on to see if what I was seeing was indeed actually sharper or if my imagination was playing tricks on me. But my vision improved. It was obvious. I kept putting on my $100 pair of sunglasses and comparing them. They didn't compare. I was very impressed. Everything appeared sharper, more defined and indeed had a greater three dimensional look to it. But what did this product do that made my vision so much better? I found out.

The sunglasses (called BluBlockers) filter out the ultraviolet and blue spectrum light waves from the sun. Blue rays have one of the shortest wavelengths in the visible spectrum (red is the longest). As a result, the color blue will focus slightly in front of the retina, which is the "focusing screen" in our eye. By blocking the blue from the sunlight through a special filtration process and only letting those rays through that indeed focus clearly on the retina, objects appear to be sharper and clearer.

The second reason is even more impressive. It is harmful to have ultraviolet rays fall on our eyes. Recognized as bad for skin, UV light is worse for eyes and is believed to play a role in many of today's eye diseases.

### SUNGLASS DANGER

But what really surprised me was the danger in conventional sunglasses. Our pupils close in bright light to limit the light entering the eye and open wider at night like the lens of an automatic camera. So when we put on sunglasses, although we reduce the amount of light that enters our eyes, our pupils open wider and we allow more of the harmful blue and ultraviolet light into our eyes.

### DON'T BE CONFUSED

**I'm often asked by people who read this, "Do those BluBlockers really work?" They really do and please give me the opportunity to prove it. I guarantee each pair of BluBlockers to perform exactly as I described.**

BluBlocker sunglasses use Malenium™ lenses with a hard anti-scratch coating. No shortcuts were taken.

The black, lightweight frame is one of the most comfortable I have ever worn and will comfortably contour to any size face. It compares with many of the $200 pairs you can buy from France or Italy.

There is a clip-on pair that weighs less than one ounce and fits over prescription lenses. All models include a padded carrying case and a one-year limited warranty.

I urge you to order a pair and experience your improved vision. Then take your old sunglasses and compare them to the BluBlocker sunglasses. See how much clearer and sharper objects appear with the BluBlocker pair. And see if your night vision doesn't improve as a direct result. If you don't see a dramatic difference in your vision—one so noticeable that you can tell immediately—then send them back anytime within 30 days and I will send you a prompt and courteous refund.

### DRAMATIC DIFFERENCE

But from what I've personally witnessed, once you wear a pair, there will be no way you'll want to return it.

Our eyes are very important to us. Protect them and at the same time improve your vision with the most incredible breakthrough in sunglasses since they were first introduced. Order a pair or two at no obligation, today.

Credit card holders call toll free and order by product number below or send a check plus $3 for postage and handling.

BluBlocker Sunglasses (1020CD) . . . . . . . . . . . . . . . . . . $59.95
Clip-On Model (1028CD) . . . . . . . . . . . . . . . . . . . . . . . 59.95

The main feature of this ad is the storytelling approach, which wove an educational message—the first of its kind. It brought the awareness of the dangers of sunlight to the attention of the public who were unaware of these dangers.

In addition, it launched the BluBlocker brand name and created a new business, which continues to this day over 20 years later. It is a perfect example of the power of the pen—the same power you will have upon completion of this book.

**T**his was the ad that created a lot of controversy when it appeared in our catalog in 1978. A number of women complained vehemently. It is a good example of the insensitivity to women's issues that I had at the time. But, hey. I'm human and I learned.

I also received a lot of mail congratulating me on the incredible piece of copy that I had written. So for its controversial response and for the sake of presenting some interesting and entertaining copy, I have included it here.

Another interesting factor was the timing of this ad. When we placed it in our catalog, prices for gold were pretty low. Right after the ad appeared, the price of gold skyrocketed, the response grew like crazy and we sold out. So it proved to be quite a successful ad, too—but probably due to the serendipity of our timing.

Notice the use of the editorial "we" in the ad copy. It would have been more personal had I used the word "I" instead. Also see if there is one place in the ad that might offend a woman currently employed in a primarily male job category.

*This controversial ad was a complete departure from our normal offerings.*

**Headline:** Gold Space Chains

**Subheadline:** Dress her in style for that next trip through outer space with America's first space-age gold chains.

**Copy:** Our good friend, Bob Ross, is one of America's top wholesale jewelry representatives.

A few months ago, Bob approached us with a suggestion, "Why not offer gold chains to your customers?" We rejected the idea, for our catalog must only contain products that relate to space-age technology. And besides, it was too late; we had just passed our deadline.

But Bob persisted, "Most of your readers are men. Why not give them something they could buy for their wives or loved ones?

After all, you offer them all sorts of neat things to buy for themselves, but other than a good watch, there's nothing for the lady."

## SUGGESTION REJECTED

We could not accept Bob's argument. Although we have a 90% male readership, and although we felt that our customers might indeed want to buy jewelry from our catalog, we felt that our strict adherence to the principles of space-age product selection precluded our making any variation in our philosophy.

Then Bob tried to appeal to our sense of profit. "Your customers are wealthy and smart. Offer them gold chains at very low prices. You'll sell a ton because they have the money to spend, and they have the brains to recognize good value."

Again we had to disappoint Bob. True, our customers earn an average of $50,000 a year, higher than practically any other buying group in the country. And true, our customers include some of the nation's leading businessmen, politicians, newscasters, doctors, and even movie stars. But we could not justify the violation of our principles and take advantage of an opportunity just because our customers are above average. "Sorry Bob," we said. "JS&A has an important reputation to maintain."

## HE DOESN'T GIVE UP

Bob is quite a successful salesman. He never gives up until he has exhausted all arguments. A good salesman is persistent, and Bob certainly persisted. He just wouldn't give up.

"Why don't you call the gold chains 'Space Chains'—space-age jewelry for the lady you want to take on that trip through outer space? After all, giving it a space-age theme really makes it tie nicely into your catalog, and besides, gold is a valuable metal found on many of the planets in outer space."

"That would be deceiving," we told Bob. To think that we could use a flimsy theme like that to tie such an unrelated product to space-age technology was almost an insult. It was at this point that we thought seriously of asking Bob to leave. "Bob, you're a nice guy and we've known you for years, but you'll have to leave now."

## ENTER BOB'S COUSIN

But Bob pleaded, "Let me show you one thing before I leave. My cousin Joy is very pretty, and I'm sure she would be happy to model the jewelry for you in your advertisement." Bob then took a photograph from his wallet and showed it to us.

At this point, Bob had worn out his welcome. We were surprised to discover that he would stoop so low as to use one of his relatives as a means of getting his products displayed in our catalog. But then we gave the whole matter some very serious thought.

"Actually Bob, space-age jewelry isn't a bad idea for our catalog. After all, the only items we have for women are watches. Gold Space Chains might go very well. Of course we would keep our prices low to provide some real bargains, and I'm sure our customers would appreciate the convenience of being able to buy such a valuable gift. Bob, can she be at our photographer Tuesday so we can make our extended deadline?"

"Sure," said Bob. "But what about the selection?"

"Who cares about the selection? Why don't you just pick the most popular styles in various price ranges, and we'll have those photographed too."

Bob left quickly. He selected the chains and his cousin is shown above.

We did keep our prices considerably less than any jewelry store or catalog discount showroom. In fact, if you have a chance, you might compare. Or compare them after you receive the chains. 14 carat gold makes a nice gift for any lady and with our space-age theme, what a combination!

Bob's a funny guy. He probably thinks he's quite a salesman. Actually, if it weren't for our open-mindedness, our keen ability to recognize outstanding new space-age-oriented products, and our compelling desire to satisfy the needs of our customers, Bob wouldn't have a chance.

[*Prices were then listed for different styles on the order form.*]

In the above ad, I mentioned that our customers earn, on average, $50,000 a year. In 1978 when this ad was written, a $50,000 salary was very high.

Did you find the offending passages? What could I have said that would have made it less offensive without changing the basic premise of the ad? And what was the premise of the ad? Let me answer this last question.

The premise of the ad was to introduce a product that had nothing to do with our product line and could not be justified as an offering in our catalog—unless we created a very strong reason for including it. The strong reason was Bob's beautiful cousin, Joy, who agreed to model the jewelry for us. After all, we were human and Joy was a beautiful girl.

As I mentioned, the ad did quite well but it was primarily because of the dramatic increase in the price of gold right after our catalog was published.

This ad was one of the best examples of the slippery slide theory. If you just read the headline, subheadline and the bold "Impossible-to-trace Guarantee," you would be compelled to read the first sentence.

Once you started to read, you wouldn't be able to stop until you reached the end of the copy. It was a highly effective piece of advertising copy that I wrote in 1976.

This was one of my favorite ads in that it was not the typical JS&A ad. In the JS&A ads I was the expert in space-age products. In the Consumers Hero ad I was a consumer advocate speaking the language of the consumer. It showed that I could write copy for two totally diverse businesses. Each ad had its own set of expressions and method of delivery. It was also a good example of relating in a human way without being humorous. It remains one of my personal favorites.

*Once you started reading this ad, you couldn't put it down.*

**Headline:** HOT

**Subheadline:** A new consumer concept lets you buy stolen merchandise if you're willing to take a risk.

**Copy:** We developed an exciting new consumer marketing concept. It's called "stealing." That's right, stealing!

Now if that sounds bad, look at the facts. Consumers are being robbed. Inflation is stealing our purchasing power. Our dollars are shrinking in value. The poor average consumer is plundered, robbed and stepped on.

So the poor consumer tries to strike back. First, he forms consumer groups. He lobbies in Washington. He fights price increases. He looks for value.

So we developed our new concept around value. Our idea was to steal from the rich companies and give to the poor consumer, save our environment and maybe, if we're lucky, make a buck.

### A MODERN DAY ROBIN HOOD

To explain our concept, let's take a typical clock radio retailing for $39.95 at a major retailer whose name we better not mention or we'll be sued. It costs the manufacturer $9.72 to make. The manufacturer sells the unit to the retailer for $16.

### THE UNCLE HENRY PROBLEM

Let's say that retailer sells the clock radio to your Uncle Henry. Uncle Henry brings it home, turns it on and it doesn't work. So Uncle Henry trudges back to the store to exchange his "lousy rotten" clock radio for a new one that works ("lousy" and "rotten" are Uncle Henry's words).

Now, the defective one goes right back to the manufacturer along with all the other clock radios that didn't work. And if this major retail chain sells 40,000 clock radios with a 5% defective rate, that's 2,000 "lousy rotten" clock radios.

### CONSUMERS PROTECTED ALREADY

Consumers are protected against ever seeing these products again because even if the manufacturer repairs them, he can't recycle them as new units. He's got to put a label on the product clearly stating that it is repaired, not new and if Uncle Henry had his way the label would also say that the product was "lousy" and "rotten."

It's hard enough selling a new clock radio, let alone one that is used. So the manufacturer looks for somebody willing to buy his bad product for a super fantastic price. Like $10. But who wants a clock radio that doesn't work at any price!

### ENTER CONSUMERS HERO

We approach the manufacturer and offer to steal that $39.95 radio for $3 per unit. Now think of it. The manufacturer has already spent $9.72 to make it, would have to spend another $5 in labor to fix and repackage it, and still would have to mark the unit as having been previously used. So he would be better off selling it to us for $3, taking a small loss and getting rid of his defective merchandise.

Consumers Hero is now sitting with 2,000 "lousy rotten" clock radios in its warehouse.

Here comes the good part. We take that clock radio, test it, check it and repair it. Then we life test it, clean it up, replace anything that makes the unit look used, put a new label on it and presto—a $39.95 clock radio and it only costs us $3 plus maybe $7 to repair it.

### Impossible-to-trace Guarantee

**We guarantee that our stolen products will look like brand new merchandise without any trace of previous brand identification or ownership.**

We take more care in bringing that clock radio to life than the original manufacturer took to make it. We put it through more tests, more fine tuning than any repair service could afford. We get more out of that $10 heap of parts and labor than even the most quality-conscious manufacturer. And we did our bit for ecology by not wasting good raw materials.

### NOW THE BEST PART

We offer that product to the consumer for $20—the same product that costs us $3 to steal and $7 to make work. And we make $10 clear profit. But the poor consumer is glad we made our profit because:

1) We provide a better product than the original version.

2) The better product costs one half the retail price.

3) We are nice people.

### BUT THERE'S MORE

Because we are so proud of the merchandise we refurbish, we offer a longer warranty. Instead of 90 days (the original warranty), we offer a five-year warranty.

So that's our concept. We recycle "lousy rotten" garbage into super new products with five-year warranties. We steal from the rich manufacturers and give to the poor consumer. We work hard and make a glorious profit.

To make our concept work, we've organized a private membership of quality and price-conscious consumers and we send bulletins to this membership about the products available in our program.

Items range from microwave ovens to TV sets to clock radios, digital watches, and stereo sets. There are home appliances from toasters to electric can openers. Discounts generally range between 40 and 70 percent off the retail price. Each product has a considerably longer warranty than the original one and a two week money-back trial period. If you are not absolutely satisfied, for any reason, return your purchase within two weeks after receipt for a prompt refund.

Many items are in great abundance but when we only have a few of something, we select, at random, a very small number of members for the mailing. A good example was our $39.95 TV set (we had 62 of them) or a $1 AM radio (we had 1,257). In short, we try to make it fair for everybody without disappointing a member and returning a check.

### EASY TO JOIN

To join our small membership group, simply write your name, address and phone number on a slip of paper and enclose a check or money order for five dollars. Mail it to Consumers Hero, Three JS&A Plaza, Northbrook, Illinois 60062.

You'll receive a two-year membership, regular bulletins on the products we offer and some surprises we would rather not mention in this advertisement. But what if you never buy from us and your two-year membership expires. Fine. Send us just your membership card and we'll fully refund your five dollars plus send you interest on your money.

If the consumer ever had a chance to strike back, it's now. But act quickly. With all this hot merchandise there's sure to be something for you. Join our group and start saving today.

Since the time I wrote the Consumers Hero ad I have written many different ads for many different companies. The point I wish to make is simply this: A good copywriter can write to fit any market. His or her ads can sound very upscale for one client and then very downscale for the next. Simply by understanding and applying the principles, one can rise to any copywriting challenge—through understanding the jargon of the customer and using the appropriate words that will resonate with that customer.

Imagine writing an ad with dozens of misspelled words and bad grammar and running it in the *Wall Street Journal.* That's exactly what I did in what was one of my most unusual advertising approaches.

I was presented with a closeout product. The Nautilus Lower Back machine had stopped selling at retail. As a result, the manufacturer, loaded with inventory, decided to liquidate the entire load to one of the barter companies in New York.

There was only one proviso in the closeout sale. The manufacturer did not want the product offered at a discount because it would embarrass his retailers who sold customers this product at its full retail price. "If it had to be advertised, it had to be at the full retail price," was the directive from the barter company representative who called me on the phone.

The product was going to cost me only around $100. And I could easily sell it for $250 and make a nice profit. But I was being forced to offer it for $485. If it died at retail, chances were slim to none that I could sell any at $485.

So I created a novel strategy. I would offer the product at $500, even more than the full retail price. I would then allow readers of the ad to circle any misspelled words and I would give them $10 off the retail price for each misspelled word they found. I could then misspell 25 words and sell the machine for $250 without creating a problem with my vendor. Nobody except the buyer would know the actual price each machine sold for, as it depended on the spelling skills of my readers.

So in June of 1985, I ran the following ad. I had fun writing it—purposely misspelling words as well as using bad grammar.

*There were 25 misspelled words in this ad and some pretty bad grammar.*

Read the ad and see how you would have done in the Nautilus Spelling Sale.

**Headline:** Nautilus Spelling Sale

**Subheadline:** Every mispelled word you find in this advertisement is worth $10 towards the purchase of this popular exercise product.

**Bold Copy:**

---

**Americans have two weaknesses. The first is spelling and the second is in our lower backs. JS&A intends to do something about both problems.**

---

**Byline:** By Joseph Sugarman, President

**Copy:** This advertisement has several mispelled words. Some of them are intentionally mispelled and others are because my spelling is pretty lousy. (My grammar's bad too.)

For every mispelled word you find in this advertment, I'll reduce the price of the product shown here by $10. If you find 10 words mispelled, you get $100 off the price. If you find 25 words mispelled, you get $250 off the price. And if you find 50 words mispelled, you get the product for absolutely nothing. Why such generosity?

### TOO COSTLY

Hundreds of retailers throughout the country have been selling the Nautilus Lower Back machine for its full retail price of $485. Nautilus designed it for the consumer market. Their $3,000 hospital version, used for rehabilitation purposes, was too costly for the average consumer.

So Nautilus designed one for the home and sold thousands. Then JS&A got hold of a few thousand and felt that an entirely new market would develope if the unit could sell for $250 or less. But the manufacturer would obviously be concerned as the machine would upset those who had sold the unit for its full price.

So by running this special sale and listing the full retail price and with nobody really knowing what price we're really offering the unit for anyway (I told you my grammar wasn't good), we can make everybody happy—especially those of you with good spelling skills and with lower backs you want to strengthen. The rules are really quite simple.

### THE RULES

Look through this ad trying to find several mispelled words. Circle each mispelled word you find and put the total number of mispelled words in the circle above. Please don't correct my grammar. Then multiply the number of mispelled words by $10 and then deduct that amount from the $500 price show in this advertisement.

We promise to deliver a unit to you for the price you earn. But be careful. If you circle a word that is not mispelled, we reserve the right to return your order and have you arrested. All orders must be mailed in and paid for by check or money order. (We can't afford the credit card charges, and COD's are more bother than they are worth and at this price we don't need the extra espense.)

If you just want to enter this sale without purchasing anything, simply send the ad in with the number in the circle. If you guess the correct number of mispelled words, you will get a $10 credit towards all the products listed in our catalog which we will also send you (not all the products, just our catalog).

There are a few disclamers. We only have a few thousand of these machines so we reserve the right to run out of them. We also reserve the right to return any order that claims more mispelled words than we've actually made. We will ship each unit freight collect with charges usually running around $50 east of the Mississippi or a little more in California. And finally, a little clue. There are three mispelled words in this paragraph.

### DESIGNED FOR THE LOWER BACK

The Nautilus Lower Back machine is designed to strengthen your lower back. If you're an executive who sits at a desk for long hours, your back muscles soon grow weak and cannot support your spine and your skeletal frame as it was designed to do.

What I like about the back machine is how easy it works to strengthen the back. As little as five minutes a day and three days a week is all the exercise you need to start the program. And since the exercise time is so short and not very strenuous, you can exercise anytime of the day or night.

There are ten tension positions. You start at the smallest setting and gradually build up as you increase your strength. In a relatively short time, you'll be able to feel the difference. I can't guarantee that your lower back problems will be gone forever, but the Nautilus Lower Back machine can really make a difference. And even with its low price, the Nautilus comes with a 30-day exercise trial period. If the unit doesn't make a big difference in your exercise program, return the unit to JS&A for a full refund of your purchase price. But act quickly. Once we sell all these units, that's all we can get. One last thing. Please don't call our operators to find out the number of mispelled words.

The Nautilus Lower Back machine is made out of tubular steel that will take a tremendous amount of abuse. All the contact surfaces are cushioned and covered with black Naugahyde. It takes only a few minutes to assemble it with a screwdriver and wrench and it measures $34\frac{1}{2}'' \times 51'' \times 54''$ and weighs 150 pounds. The unit comes with a 90-day manufacturer's limited warranty and complete instructions.

Take advantage of this unique opportunity to own one of the finest pieces of exercise equiptment at the lowest possible cost for just being able to count our mispelled words.

To order, ask for product by number shown below or send a check to the address below.

Nautilus Back Machine (7068) . . . . . . . . . . . . . . . . . . . . . . $500
Better Speller Cost (7069) . . . . . . . . . . . . . . . . . . . . . . . . . . ?

I had two surprises with the results from this ad. The first was the number of people who missed many of the words. We made more profit than I had anticipated. There were exactly 25 misspelled words, but on average most people found around 20 of them.

The second surprise was the number of people who called me to tell me that they had spent hours reading and rereading the ad to find the number of misspelled words even though they had no intention of buying the unit.

I then used this technique to sell the Franklin Spelling Computer. For the spelling computer, it certainly made sense as it tied into the product nicely. But it was this first Nautilus ad that really launched the concept.

One of the strong points of this ad was the involvement that it created on the part of the reader. I received mail months later asking me for the correct number of misspelled words. People were spending hours reading my ad. How many ads can claim that distinction?

The people who found most or all of the words really had a bargain too. And we eventually sold all of our inventory in what was a very successful ad. Bad spelling, bad grammar, who cared? We broke a few rules and came up with a very unique marketing concept that could still work today.

In Section Three you took all your new copywriting knowledge and saw how it could be applied in actual mail order advertisements. You also saw how these principles could work in ads that weren't mail order ads and you saw what copy elements were missing in others.

You can now write a great mail order ad using my approach to writing copy. You can create the goose that lays the golden egg. And you know that with this new knowledge you have the potential skill to start businesses and earn millions of dollars—all through the power of your pen.

But it takes practice. And the more you practice, the greater your skill and the closer you will come to the wonderful and exhilarating feeling of writing an ad that the public responds to in massive numbers. Good luck and best wishes in your quest for success.

# Section Four

Section Four

Let us assume by now that you have understood and mastered the material I have presented. You know how to write great copy and build that slippery slide. You understand the psychological triggers and how effectively they can be used to sell your product or service. And finally, you understand the role of a powerful satisfaction conviction.

Once you understand the principles of a print mail order ad, you're ready to apply those principles to enhance all your communication skills. Whether in a radio commercial or on a web site, all the principles apply, with one caveat—some principles are more important than others depending on the format or the medium. Let me explain.

Whereas in a mail order ad your copy is very important, what techniques work best on TV? What psychological triggers work best on radio or on the Internet? For example, on the Internet there is greater involvement on the part of the prospect. He or she must take an action such as clicking on a button or on a link. So interactivity is an important concept.

The remainder of this handbook focuses on the various media and how they differ from a print ad, and consequently how to write copy for each format.

I am also including a large amount of marketing information to help guide you in the copywriting process. If you don't know the best way to market a particular product or service in a specific medium, how can you write copy for it? So I go into depth and explain the differences and the quirks to watch for as you examine all the media possibilities and their potential.

## Catalogs

Here's a format where copy and graphics play a big role. The catalog cover should present the best picture—the most dramatic shot in the entire catalog or a product that best represents what can be found inside.

I used to feature a product on the cover of my catalogs that was unusual, novel and different and looked dramatic. It didn't matter if it wasn't a big seller. The important point was that it caused the prospect to pause and not just throw the catalog away. The cover is like the headline in a print ad. Its sole purpose is to get you into the catalog and to start reviewing the other products or to put it aside for reading later. You want to avoid it being simply thrown in the trash.

A good catalog should have a message from the president in the front of the catalog along with his or her picture. This is important. A catalog is like a store. If the store lacked a proprietor, it would seem cold, too big or corporate.

That personal message at the front of the catalog is like a Wal-Mart associate standing at the entrance of a Wal-Mart store greeting visitors as they walk in. It makes the store more human, makes the proprietor a friendly face you can contact should things not work out to your satisfaction. You feel safe in dealing with the company because you know there is a human behind the catalog and that human is real and reachable. Your copy should reflect this. It should read like a personal letter to your prospects and should express your sincerity and commitment to satisfying their needs. I would rank this letter as one of the most important pieces of copy in the entire catalog.

Producing a catalog is a matter of arranging graphics and copy in a pleasing and easy-to-follow format. Combining the graphics and copy is similar to creating a print ad. You should have a short but enticing headline, a subheadline that explains a little more about what you are offering and then copy that covers each aspect of the product and its benefits to your prospect.

It is extremely important to include all the salient features of the product you are selling. Leave out one small fact—even one that may seem insignificant such as a product's weight—and you'll reduce your sales. A catalog description should contain all the information you need for your prospect to make a buying decision. Leave out one small fact, and you run the risk of reducing your response. The missing fact gives the buyer an excuse to delay his or her decision. And it raises a question as to whether the product will fit his or her needs. Nobody wants to buy something and then have to return it. So being thorough in your description will make a big difference in the minds of your prospects. They will feel confident that what they buy they will like and keep—always knowing, of course, that they can return the item for any reason.

The next thing to consider is the environment you create through the graphics and the look of the catalog. If you are sending your catalog to sophisticated buyers, make sure that the copy and the look of the catalog are upscale. If you are selling products in a closeout catalog, you don't want your catalog to look too slick. Your customer doesn't expect to see an expensive catalog selling products at really cheap prices. As a guide, set the environment based on the price points you are selling your products for.

In a mail order ad you should feature a single product or service, leaving variations of that product out of the sales message. But in a catalog you have the opportunity of offering several variations of the main product you might sell in a mail order print ad. In fact, that's what your customers expect.

A good example of this was given earlier in this handbook ("Simplicity" in Chapter 19). I offered a single style of the Swiss Army watch and tested it against several styles. The single style offer worked best in the mail order ad, whereas the other watch styles worked best in our catalog.

Finally, what works exceptionally well for product catalogs is the personal sales message—something that I have used for years with great success. Let each product description sound like a personal conversation with the prospect.

Say "I" or "me" or "my," and talk as if you were a friendly person chatting with your prospect. Your conversation might sound something like, "I was walking down the street when I had this neat idea for my catalog." Such rhetoric combines story-telling and the personal approach to advertisng, which I strongly recommend.

In the case of a catalog, think of it as a store, sell in it like you would in a store and show your enthusiasm for the products you sell through your copy and your use of the first person.

If something is important, give it more space. Make sure you have your toll-free phone number on each page. Often a prospect will tear out a page and throw away the rest of the catalog only to discover later that the toll-free number is missing. And even if your prospect keeps the entire catalog, having your phone number on each page will make ordering easier.

Use an easy-to-remember toll-free phone number. Use words to make up the number. When I call FedEx for a pickup, all I have to remember is 1-800-GOFEDEX. And if you do use words to convey a phone number, also include the actual numbers to make it easier for the prospect to dial.

The toll-free number should be large and rather obvious on the order form. Most people will order over the phone or go to a web site to order. So why not make the order form show that toll-free number and web site address loud and clear?

Then make sure that your order form is easy to fill out and provides plenty of room to list all the necessary information. If most people respond on the phone with the toll-free number or on your web site, though, why even have a catalog order form? The answer is that many catalog buyers first list their purchases on the order form before they actually call and order. It makes the ordering process go faster and is a convenient record for the customer.

Finally, make sure that each operator who takes an order on the phone has a script to sell something else after the customer places an order. This will certainly add incremental business and increase catalog profits.

## Flyers: Insert Stuffers, Bounce Backs, and Broadsides

The common thread that all of these formats have is that they are after-the-sale advertisements. Once you've made the sale, you should place something in the package you are shipping that offers something your new customer might also be interested in.

The piece might contain offers on some of the other products you sell. It might even be a catalog designed specifically for new customers. Or even the catalog from which the order was originally made. It usually doesn't cost any more postage to ship these solicitations. And since it is being sent to a customer, there is a better chance that it will be read and acted upon than if it was simply sent to a prospect.

Insert stuffers and bounce backs are flyers that are placed in packages going to customers. A broadside is the flyer folded to fit in a standard-sized #10 business envelope.

In the case of these solicitations, the piece you design should use a similar format to your catalog page to provide a level of continuity. Use an attention-getting headline, use bullet points where appropriate and don't forget to provide that all-important ordering information—a coupon with your address, toll-free phone number, and web site address.

## Direct Mail

One of the more effective ways to sell in print is through direct mail. It's a way to target a specific prospect who has exhibited certain buying tendencies, and it's a way to target all of those tendencies in a very efficient way. But there are some important notes about copywriting that need to be observed in this form of communication.

As I have mentioned throughout this handbook, the personal approach to selling can't be beat. Selling is really a personal relationship between the seller and the buyer. It's a relationship of trust. And to enhance that trust there is nothing like having your prospects know clearly whom they are dealing with. Your prospects will pick up the vibrations of what you write, especially if you are making your communications sound very personal.

Direct mail copy is among the most personal types of copy

you can write. It is a letter written directly to another individual. It is a message to a person whom you have sought out by simply refining your mailing criteria to focus on just those attributes that represent your prospect. By selecting a mailing list that encompasses those attributes, your chances of success will be greatly enhanced.

The most important thing to be aware of is to keep the message personal. Using the first person is important. Use the word *I* and avoid the term *we* when referring to your associates. In fact, it is a lot better when referring to your company to talk about the staff as a team—for example, "My team of great engineers is available to help you." Compare that to: "We at Acme Motors have the skill and knowledge to provide assistance to you." And your letter becomes even more personal when it is signed by the sender.

In a direct mail piece, the letter is the most important part of the entire mailing package. In it you must include the sales pitch, the slippery slide—designed to get the recipient of your mailing piece to read the entire letter—and all the psychological triggers described earlier. You have the space and the time to make a very good sales presentation.

The length of the letter can vary. If you can get your message onto one page, you make the mailing less intimidating. More pages are okay, too, if you've written a strong enough first page to keep them reading and of course if the subject is interesting to the reader; then you're doing your job as a copywriter. Write 10 pages if you feel it is important to do so in order to sell your product or service, but the letter has got to be so compelling that the reader continues to read straight through to the end of the letter as if on a slippery slide.

Use any collateral material that is included with the letter to visually describe your product or service. The more important message, however, is in the letter. A brochure won't sell your product as effectively as a good letter. The brochure or the color flyer could be critical to the sale but not nearly as important as the letter.

And you can certainly refer to the brochure in your letter, but don't rely on that fancy brochure to do the complete selling job. It won't, no matter how pretty and how good it may look.

Don't forget that postscript (PS). The PS in a letter is often the most-read line of type on the page. So either offer something in the PS that causes the reader to solidify a buying decision or reiterate a very important point.

Use objects with the letter. When I did advertising for my ski-lift account I had a small number of prospects—around 500. It was therefore practical for me to include something unusual in each mailing. I sent a large button that said "No Jerk" to emphasize the smooth nature of my ski lift. I sent a brochure that expanded so that one side read "expand" and sent it with a nice letter. My prospects looked forward to each mailing simply to find out what I was going to say and include in my next mailing.

In direct mail, the mailing list is also a critical element to the success of a direct mail piece. Your own satisfied customers for a similar product will be your best and hottest list if they've purchased recently—the more recently the better. If you purchase lists, make sure the prospects on a list are demographically similar to your customers and that they have bought fairly recently through the mail and for purchases within the price range of what you are offering.

But let's say you have a great letter, a cute little gimmick you are mailing with your letter and a first-rate mailing list. What is missing? How about a great message on your envelope? Your envelope is like the headline on a mail order ad. It will attract those prospects interested enough to read the subheadline, which usually is inside the envelope so you often need to get them to open the envelope in order to read the subheadline. Of course you can put the subheadline on the envelope, too. You might even try using some attention-getting statement if you feel the statement will cause the customer to open the envelope. If recipients are interested in your offer, they will know right away whether to open the envelope or throw it into the trash.

Just as people are inclined to discard Internet spam if they don't recognize the sender without even opening the e-mail, recipients of your mailings are inclined to throw out your mailing piece without even opening it. But there are ways to get them to open the envelope.

If you put no name or headline on the envelope (just the return address), most of the recipients will open it out of curiosity. After all, it might be a credit card (many credit cards are sent this way). If the envelope has your company name and address and the person receiving it recognizes it as a company he or she has bought from before, chances are they will open it.

A computer-addressed envelope that looks like it was individually typed provides a strong incentive to open the envelope as well.

A good tip is for you to study the mail that comes into your mailbox. Which ones do you open and which ones do you quickly throw out? Often you are representative of the people who are your prospects.

What works can be easily determined if you test every mailing piece you send out against a different version of the same mailing piece. Testing is the critical factor that makes a big difference in the success of anything you do in direct marketing. And as a copywriter you can learn so much by observing what works and what doesn't.

## Newspapers

Newspapers are one topic I can speak about from a great deal of experience. Not only have I advertised in many daily and weekly newspapers, but I actually published a weekly newspaper, the *Maui Weekly*, for six years in Maui, Hawaii, before I sold it to the island's daily newspaper in 2005.

If the ad you are placing in a newspaper is a mail order ad, it should pay for itself and cover the cost of the insertion the first time it appears.

If you are advertising something that promotes a retail establishment, then frequency is a major key. Putting an ad in a paper only once is simply a waste of time and money. Often people don't respond right away. There is a lag time between seeing your ad the first time and then seeing it so often that a level of trust develops. Or it could be simply the time isn't quite right when the ad first appears because of other events in the community.

Let's say you are advertising a restaurant. The ad is to appear each week in the dining section of the weekly newspaper for a total of 13 weeks. The ad appears the first week and there seems to be little response. The ad appears the second week and a few more people show up. Slowly but surely the restaurant's customers appear in greater numbers.

I can remember when I was in college at the University of Miami and a restaurant owner who saw that I was a student asked if I knew how to encourage other students to come to his Old Hickory Barbeque restaurant. I told him that I felt I could reach the students. I knew what the students responded to and felt that an ad in the daily college paper, the *Hurricane*, would do the trick. But as an aspiring copywriter, I also knew that the copy for this chicken and rib joint on the outskirts of town had to be so compelling and different that students would respond to it and not think of it as just advertising.

So the ad I ran talked about a chicken and rib special and then I told students that there was a catch. To get this special price, they had to bring in the top of a Brinks armored car. The ad ran. I held my breath and at first was too embarrassed to go to the restaurant and see the owner, concerned that maybe I had been a little over-the-top in what I had written. But to my surprise when I finally pulled up to the restaurant, there was a line around the block—with students carrying pieces of plywood, sheets of tin, garbage can covers marked "Brinks Armored Car Top" and a variety of other similar objects. The ad was a huge success.

I was communicating with the students in a way that they appreciated. And they responded in large numbers. It was also one of the few times when an ad for a retail establishment worked without the benefit of frequency.

Mail order ads in newspapers are designed to hit the mass market. Assuming you are advertising in a daily newspaper covering a large metropolitan area, then you've got to think in terms of lower-priced items that the mass market may relate to in large enough numbers. If, however, you have higher-ticket items, the *Wall Street Journal* would be your better venue for advertising. In the case of the *Wall Street Journal*, you go to a higher demographic to find the target audience you'll need to sell your product or service.

At its peak, my mail order company, JS&A, used the *Wall Street Journal* extensively to sell my high-priced gadgets. In fact, at one point we were among the *Journal*'s largest advertisers. I liked the *Journal* because I was able to get my ads into the paper quickly—usually within a few days—and get my response a few days later. With the fast pace at which our products were introduced, peaked and then became obsolete, this speed was essential in introducing new products quickly and keeping up with the rapid price deterioration that was taking place in the consumer electronics industry.

You could make a nice profit in a daily newspaper if you bought your space right. And there are brokers who handle this type of advertising and are able to provide the newspaper space at very low prices so that indeed a nice profit can be made.

The same principles that apply to a mail order ad described in the first part of the book apply here, of course. And your goal is to make a profit from your mail order ad the first time you run it.

If the cost of space is a concern and you can get your message across in a smaller ad without much copy, then a small ad might be a good way to conserve your cash. An ad with a low-priced offer where the low price is the big attraction works well in this kind of situation. But keep in mind that you are competing with other small ads instead of dominating the page as you would with a larger, more descriptive ad.

Daily newspapers in the United States are losing circulation. Weekly community newspapers are gaining in circulation. Why? Because the public can get their national and international news from TV or on the Internet 24/7. Community newspapers such as the *Maui Weekly* cover issues of interest to the local community—news that can't be found on TV or on the Internet.

One of the things I did when I first bought the *Maui Weekly* in 1999 was to change the format of the paper and keep this same format week after week. Each issue was interesting and consistent. I also used many of the principles that I've explained in the first three sections of this book to enhance my rapport with the community. I found that consistency was my most important principle. It took awhile but before long the community embraced the publication and looked forward to receiving it each week. And our circulation and advertising grew as a result. The one powerful trigger of consistency also worked for our advertisers. Keeping a regular schedule and the same format while changing the copy proved to be successful for our advertisers as well.

The big advantage of a newspaper is the fast response time—your ability to get your ad into a paper quickly and the speed of the response you receive after your ad appears. The life of each issue of a daily newspaper is usually just a few days, so your prospect will generally respond quickly during that time frame. For a weekly, the life of an issue is typically around 10 days.

Frequency is also an important consideration if you are running retail advertising for such establishments as restaurants, car dealerships, furniture stores, clothing outlets and real estate sales.

Another nice feature of running ads in newspapers is the sheer volume of newspapers available to advertise in. If your ad works, it can be run nationally and reach millions of people in a relatively short period of time.

If you have a product or service that would appeal to the general public and it is priced low enough while representing good value, newspapers are a good choice. For a higher-priced product, refine your choice of newspapers to the more upscale papers such as the *Wall Street Journal* or many of the other business publications.

## Billboards

A billboard uses few words to convey its message, so those words must be very powerful or create immediate awareness or the billboard is useless. From your research you must write a single headline and, at the most, a minimal subheadline, accompanied by a graphic that conveys the big idea you're trying to convey.

Here is where simplicity is the controlling factor. Your message has to be so simple and direct that occupants of cars passing by at 75 miles an hour can pick out the message and quickly grasp its meaning.

A billboard can create curiosity and a buzz such as in the Folgers coffee teaser campaign of the late 1960s that stated, "A mountain is moving to Chicago," when Folgers introduced its coffee to the Chicago area. The mountain was actually the graphic on the container of coffee, but nobody knew exactly what the billboards meant until the formal announcement.

The point you always want to remember when you write copy for a billboard is that you need to capture the imagination of your prospect in a very short, simple and effective way in a matter of a few seconds.

Billboards have been used effectively to create a buzz, as in the Folgers example, or to establish brand recognition, and are ideal for a recognized brand as well as to build brand awareness. They can be used to promote an establishment up the road or to sell beer. But whatever the task, the key is brevity and simplicity.

## Press Releases

Press releases are a means of disseminating information to various media where the information is published at no charge. It's free and sometimes can provide great value.

But wait. There is a risk—the chance that the person publishing what you send may distort the message in a rewrite. It's a two-edged sword. In general, though, this free publicity is a positive thing and can be used very effectively either as the sole way to market a product or part of a campaign.

First, let's make sure that we put the proper heading at the very top of the paper so the person receiving the message knows that it's for public relations (PR). My suggestion is to put "News Release" at the top—"Press Release" has gotten old hat.

I would then put the date and the words "For Immediate Release" in the top right-hand corner of the release. Giving a later release date is also acceptable but very rare.

Next, I would come up with a headline and subheadline that would appeal to the readers of the publication receiving the release.

Then put the city of origin for the news release, similar to the way news stories appear in a newspaper: something like "(Chicago, IL) A major new breakthrough . . ."

The news release should be written like a news story, complete with as much detail at the beginning as possible. Within a few paragraphs all the salient points should be encapsulated so an editor or any reader can get the gist of what you're saying very quickly. Use the typical who, what, when, where, why and how at the very beginning of your release.

Remember you are appealing to the editor to view what you are sending as news and not a puff piece promoting your company or its product. The editor wants to make sure that the piece is relevant to the publication's audience.

You can use quotes in the release that can be attributed to experts who will say things about your product or service that you can't say in the body of your release. "John Jackson, chairman of the company making the Bone Fone, says, 'Never before in the history of sound has a product this novel been introduced.'" A quote like this has to be attributed to someone, so use the device as an opportunity to include testimonials, statements from the president of the company or other comments that enhance the news in your article.

Psychological triggers that play an important role in a news release are "linking" and "current fads." If there is a fad sweeping the country, see if you can cleanly link into it with your product or service. For example, in the 1960s at the height of the women's liberation movement, my ski resort account asked if I could help promote its snowmobile rental business through PR. It seems that nobody realized that snowmobiles could be rented at this ski resort.

The hottest fad or trend at the time was the women's liberation movement, and tying it into my client's wishes, I came up with a headline, "Ski Resort Bans Woman Snowmobile Drivers." The subheadline then explained the ban in more detail: "Schuss Mountain Ski Resort in northern Michigan claims women snowmobile drivers are causing too many accidents so owner bans all women from using them."

The release that followed was brief. It didn't have to be too long. I quoted Dan Iannotti, the owner of the resort, as saying, "There's nothing worse than a woman behind the wheel of a snowmobile."

Iannotti had an open mind and thought the idea was clever enough to possibly make a big splash, so he approved it. All hell broke loose after it was released to the local media. The release made the national network news shows and the front page of many newspapers and became one of the most discussed topics on the talk shows. I had indeed linked into a strong trend that helped my client get out his message.

The snowmobile rentals jumped at the resort—of course not before we issued another release a week later with the headline "Ban Lifted at Ski Resort" and subheadline "Because of the pressure, Schuss Mountain ski resort lifts ban on women snowmobilers"—and all this was followed by text that explained the change of heart by the owner after a number of women complained about the ban. "We have set up a school to teach good snowmobile habits," said Iannotti in the text of the release.

A friend of mine had a product that he sold using only PR. It was a device that he put over his toilet and onto which a cat climbed to use the toilet. I'm not kidding. And the product worked. But he couldn't advertise it in any magazine as they all were repulsed by the thought of advertising this type of product. He then resorted to PR and was able to get national publicity more easily than he could from trying to advertise it.

This is not meant to be a resource on PR principles but rather some of the principles that could apply to a news release sent to a publication or TV network. Realize that as a copywriter, your role here is to look at your copy as news editors would and write it to fit their model of what a good news story should reflect.

## Radio

Radio draws on the imaginations of your listeners to get a strong, personal message across. And radio is negotiable and often not very expensive, making it a good part of an advertiser's mix.

To make radio work, you need frequency. You can have a great radio spot but unless it is repeated often enough, it won't be as effective.

As with TV, you can buy many different forms of radio. A radio spot is typically from 10 seconds to 60 seconds in duration, and there is also the long-form radio commercial referred to as "brokered time." This is where the advertiser buys the time slot (usually a half hour to an hour) and uses it just like a talk show to promote his or her own business. It might be a real estate show, an investment program or even a show on health.

Los Angeles advertising guru and radio copywriter Dan O'Day says that it is vital to have only one message to convey to the listener in the typical radio spot, and that should be what he calls the "core message."

"Radio is the most personal of all mass media. You listen to the message in a linear fashion one statement after the next," says O'Day.

O'Day points out that radio is also a very visual medium in the sense that the listener has to imagine what is being described. For example, if a child is described as beautiful, the listener pictures a child he or she considers to be beautiful. If this was done on TV and a child was shown, there might be a credibility gap. The child visualized by the radio listener may be personally more beautiful to him or her than the actual one seen on TV.

If you are doing a direct response radio spot, one of the most important elements is the toll-free number. Is it easy to remember? Most radio listeners are driving their cars, and others just may not have a pen and paper handy. Some advertisers are using words instead of numbers to make it easy to remember. For example, 1-800-FLOWERS or 1-800-CARPETS or even 1-800-BLUBLOCKER. These make great radio phone numbers.

In the case of the BluBlocker number, there are a few extra letters in BluBlocker (9 instead of the correct 7) but that's okay as it doesn't matter to the phone company if you punch a few more keys after you dial the number, and besides, it's easy to remember. But you've got to be careful that people spell the phonetic version of your number correctly. For example, many people have typed in 1-800-BLUEBLOCKER by mistake, spelling "blue" correctly even though it is not the actual spelling of the brand. So we arranged for both the correct and the incorrect numbers to be directed to the same phone line. We assumed in advance that sometimes it was going to be misspelled and therefore prepared for it.

The second thing to remember with a direct response spot is that the start of the spot is critical for people to stay tuned and pay attention. So you might start out with a curiosity trigger such as, "I've got some important news for those of you who are concerned about the bird flu." Radio is a music and news medium. The more you therefore make your message sound like news, the more compatible your message is with the medium.

Dick Orkin was known in the 1970s, 1980s, and 1990s for his humorous spots. They told a story. And the humor was not for the sake of being funny—more for the fact that it grabbed you and lent a human tone to the message. In the 1960s and early 1970s radio personality Stan Freberg produced some funny spots, too. But the spots from both Orkin and Freberg had that single core message that came across loud and clear.

Take the commercial from Motel 6. "We'll leave the light on for ya" was the tagline at the end of those spots. But the core message, according to O'Day, "was not that well-recalled slogan but that Motel 6 had the lowest room rates—actually the lowest room rates of any national chain." And it also had a very personal message recited by Tom Bodett. Radio became Motel 6's primary advertising medium.

I've used radio very effectively during my entire advertising career. More recently, I have used radio to promote my BluBlocker sunglasses brand. Since BluBlocker is already an established sunglasses brand, I used radio to draw attention to where you could buy BluBlockers. It's a product worn in good weather, so I sponsored the weather and traffic reports. The announcer would always have a captive audience wanting to hear this information so I had the perfect environment for my message. The announcer would start out, "The traffic and weather are brought to you by BluBlocker high-resolution sunglasses. Get BluBlockers at your local Walgreens Drug Store." In just a few seconds I was able to get across my core message, "Get your BluBlockers at Walgreens." And those spots worked very well for us through daily repetition.

As a copywriter, realize that radio is among the most personal of all media with a core message—simple, clean and easy to comprehend.

## Television

Writing copy for TV follows many of the same principles you've learned in this book, but the copy will vary by length of the commercial. Now that might seem obvious but let me explain further.

I have had personal experience and both success and failure in all of the various TV formats we will discuss. I have sold millions of pairs of sunglasses and other products on infomercials, home shopping channels and TV spots. I have tested all elements of a TV commercial and know what works and what doesn't. What you read here should act as an excellent guideline on how to write copy for TV because it is presented by somebody with extensive personal experience in all of the various TV formats.

Some of the facts mentioned will have more to do with marketing than copywriting. But as a copywriter you would be wasting your time writing copy for a TV spot that won't work because it is violating some important marketing principle. So in a sense, knowing a little about marketing in this very powerful category is very important to the copywriter.

Let's start with the TV spot commercial or what is called short-form TV, which can be anywhere from 30 seconds to two minutes long, and go over six of the copywriting and marketing points you'll need to know to successfully write copy for this format.

1. Typically the most effective way to determine if your product is suitable for this form of advertising is price point. If your product is an impulse item (defined as being in the $29.95 or less retail price category), then chances are this might be an appropriate format to sell your product.

2. The next criterion should be value. It must appear almost too good to be true. Greed will play a role here. Your customers must feel that they are getting a bigger value than they believe possible. They must subconsciously think, "How can they do it?"

3. Simplicity is extremely important, too. Keeping the offer simple and uncomplicated is critical. Anything that complicates the commercial will lose sales. The only exception to

this rule is near the end of the spot when you start adding on additional items to increase the value. For example, "If you call within the next 20 minutes, I'll also include an extra mixer free of charge. That's two mixers for $19.95." Don't give the prospect a choice to make. There should be only one choice—"Buy this product now and get all of this." Don't offer different colors or sizes. It's one offer and no choices. Only when your prospects call on the phone do you "upsell" them to other items or offer various versions or multiples of the same offer.

4. Use a sense of urgency. You need to make sure that the prospect doesn't copy the phone number down with the idea of purchasing your product later on, because chances are he or she won't. Like the preceding, using greed as a motivator and a time limit to respond works wonders.

5. Include a web site address. Many viewers will copy both the toll-free number and the web site address and then go to their computers. People are different. Some like to buy on the phone, others through the mail and still others on the Internet. You want to appeal to all of them. Some prospects may get turned off when they call to order a product and reach somebody in another country who speaks with an unintelligible accent. They may decide to hang up and buy the item on the Internet. It has happened to me. And with so much of our service industry being exported to other countries, the Web might be a logical place to buy.

6. Your product must appeal to a mass market: all women, all men, both men and women over the age of 40 or large segments of the general public. After all, TV reaches a mass market and unless your product appeals to the masses you are wasting a lot of money reaching your target market. For example, I have run spots for my BluBlocker sunglasses and have done quite well. Why? They appeal to a mass audience of both men and women and almost all age groups. Sunglasses are a mass market product.

If your product fits the preceding criteria, then you've got a good chance at succeeding in this medium. Your approach now is to determine how to write a spot that is compelling, stops the viewer and makes an offer that provides a real benefit to the consumer.

Once again, the same principles of copywriting apply to a TV spot. But in a spot you have to literally count your words, making them reach the point quickly while presenting your product and its benefits in the proper environment.

You create the environment by the visuals. If you're selling a kitchen appliance, use a kitchen as your background. If you're selling an automobile dent remover, show a homeowner at home removing the dents from his or her moderately priced car. Remember that you are reaching the masses and use props that identify and are typical for that market.

Focus on the core message you want to convey. Every word and every visual element have to lead the viewer to the final buying conclusion. If you offer bonuses, make sure the bonus you offer is something the same audience would want. You don't want to give a free gift of something that a portion of the audience may not care for. What this does is deter them from buying the product they intended on buying because they feel they are paying for something they don't want.

I recently saw a TV spot offering a very small table to be used whenever you needed to work or eat while watching TV. The free bonus gift was a cloth TV remote holder that you would drape over the side of your chair. Even though logically the cloth remote holder made sense because the table would be used primarily for TV, this was a bad idea. First, your chair may not have a side to it. Secondly, many viewers may not care for the free gift anyway and would reject the main offer because in their minds they would be paying more for something they didn't want.

The key in all these offers is to test the free gift versus no gift and maybe against another gift. It is during the testing process that you find out what really works, and it is often not what you expected.

## The Infomercial

The infomercial (half-hour commercial), commonly referred to in the advertising trade as long-form TV, became an advertising phenomenon in the mid-1980s when the Federal Communications Commission (FCC) deregulated many of its policies and allowed for the broadcast of 30 minutes of straight advertising.

At first, real estate shows appeared on the air. Then the BluBlocker sunglasses made their first showing in 1986, and shortly thereafter came the exercise, self-help and get-rich-quick shows. Infomercials became extremely popular in a very short period of time. Overnight companies launched what soon became household names. Some marketers became instant millionaires, making small fortunes in just a few months, while others lost millions and went bankrupt just as quickly.

The key to this medium is to determine a good format in which to present your show. It should resemble what is popular and what is currently being broadcast. For example, if reality shows are popular, then maybe your product would lend itself to a reality show. If interview shows like *Larry King Live* are popular, then set up an interview format. If your product would appeal to the *Oprah Winfrey Show* audience, then set use a set that looks similar to Oprah's. In short, you identify with a popular format that fits your product and with which your prospective audience is comfortable and that they can harmonize with.

A good example of this approach is our BluBlocker infomercial, which ran in four different versions for six years and created a brand name for sunglasses from all the exposure, not to mention a lot of sales. I used a candid-camera approach famous during the 1970s, 1980s and 1990s. I would walk up to strangers and interview them right on the street or on the beach, and then have them try on my sunglasses and react with surprised expressions of wonder or amazement.

For a product to work on long-form TV, the keys for success are a good product in the $39 to $250 price range with sufficient margin or one that has good continuity and back-end sales potential—in short, a product that you can automatically ship to your customers every month like vitamins or one that has strong sales after the initial sale. With a half hour you have more time to sell and therefore can justify a purchase to the viewer much more easily than you can in a TV spot.

Today, the infomercial industry has shaken out the fly-bynights, and only the more experienced and stable companies remain. It is also a lot more difficult to succeed in this field unless you really know what you are doing. And that includes knowing the importance of a product with continuity and back-end sales.

## Back-End Sales

When you produce a successful TV spot or infomercial and your customer calls to order your product, there is a major sales opportunity available to you while your customer is on the phone. The sale in this case is called back-end sales, or what is commonly called in the industry "upsells." Often, you can take a simple $49.95 sale and turn it into a $200 sale if you come up with some good products to enhance the initial purchase or even a service that your prospect may want after the sale such as coaching in the case of some income opportunity shows.

For example, when I called to order the knife set Ron Popeil offered in an infomercial in early 2006, the operator had a script she used to try to sell me more related products. This is one more opportunity for a copywriter to come up with sales copy to increase the sales of the product that was originally offered. It may be copy that says, "Because you are ordering within 20 minutes of the show, you are entitled to buy our special deluxe knife set holder. This handsome wooden holder comes with engraved names for each of the knives you have ordered. . . ."

You can offer anything from a deluxe version of a product or a second one at a discount to a complete set of something that may relate to your product or even the opportunity to get the product for less if the buyer signs up for automatic shipments (what is called "continuity").

As a copywriter, you may be asked to write copy for the upsell. After all, it is a form of selling and you should be prepared to write copy for this selling opportunity. My suggestion is to call up and order some of the products on TV and see how the operators handle their upsells. Often the upsell will vary greatly depending on the current approach to upsells. For example, today many upsells try to encourage continuity sales (regular monthly shipments), and other times it might be coaching or a deluxe version of something. Keeping your fingers on the pulse of the market is an excellent way for you to become an expert on this important selling opportunity. Once you are knowledgable about the product, the prospect and even the currently offered upsells by others, you'll be able to apply the same principles you've already learned to come up with a variety of different approaches, all of which will require testing to determine which one will work best.

## After-Sale Opportunities

If you thought that the upsell was the last opportunity to make that sale, think again. You now have a huge mailing list of those who have bought your product from your ads on TV, some with average orders and others spending into the hundreds of dollars.

How do you address these people to sell them more? What tricks of the copywriting trade do you use to entice them to keep buying from you?

Here's a clue. If you have a list that was gathered from customers who bought on TV, use telemarketing. If they bought out of a catalog or from a print ad, use print or direct mail.

You may be wasting your time and money trying to reach somebody using a catalog or a direct mail solicitation when the telephone is the way to reach them. And a good copywriter will create a good telephone selling message to reach this potentially lucrative audience.

Again, using the principles already expressed in this handbook is a start. Begin the conversation with the purpose of establishing dialogue: "Mrs. Jones, how are you today?" "Fine," she says. Then you respond with the reason you are calling and the offer you are making with the hope of having each question you ask elicit a yes or positive answer. For example, "I understand you have purchased Ron Popeil's knife set—is that correct?"

Your customer once again responds with a positive response. "Yes, I did" might be the answer. You have now established rapport and have gotten the start of the "yes" answers you need to create the harmony required to lead you to a positive answer when you ask for the sale.

"Well, Mrs. Jones, Ron Popeil has asked me to call you

with a special offer—something that would go nicely with your knife set." Here you are using a little bit of curiosity. What is the thing Ron Popeil is offering? "Do you have a minute to talk?" Here you are getting another yes. Then you go into the sales pitch and ask, "How many sets would you like?"

## Home Shopping

I've had a lot of experience selling on QVC—the home shopping network both in Europe and in the United States. There is not much a copywriter needs to do there except for creating a written sales pitch the show hosts use to brief themselves. Again, it is the job of the copywriter to describe the product, briefly mentioning all its benefits and features. You can recommend various upsells and create the copy for the operators, but very often the upsell is up to QVC both to script and to use as they see fit.

The home shopping networks in the United States and throughout the world are usually live broadcasts without the need for scripts, but they are worth mentioning if only to show that a copywriter's job can cover all of the aspects of TV regardless of the form it may take.

QVC does over $6 billion in sales a year. Their programs reach millions of households and have successfully delivered to consumers quality, value and convenience. And they love products that have proven themselves both in print and on TV. So if you are successful with a product in the other formats mentioned here, QVC would make a great opportunity for you once you've proven that you have a winning product.

Once during a "Today's Special Value" feature on QVC over 250,000 pairs of BluBlockers were sold. Now, that is incredible power—and all in one day.

## The Internet

The Internet holds such incredible advantages for copywriters and marketers that it indeed has become a major revolution in sales and marketing. And it will continue to grow now and well into the future. There are four reasons for this.

First, you can be a tiny company with little means but look like even the biggest companies on the Internet. In short, your environment is your graphic presentation. The Internet levels the playing field, and graphics determine your image. Your race, religion and age do not matter. Cameron Johnson made millions of dollars on the Internet before he reached voting age. At 15 he earned $50,000 selling Beanie Babies and went on to earn $15,000 a day on one of his many sites. Now, at 21, he's one of the most successful Internet marketers in history—and note, he started as a teenager.

Second, testing is now less expensive and more immediate. You can easily test a marketing concept and your copy—even test the results of changing just a few words—to determine the difference in response, and all at almost no cost. This is a major breakthrough in the art and science of testing.

Third, the speed at which you can come up with an idea and implement it quickly at low cost dwarfs almost every other form of selling and marketing. This is a wonderful time to be living if you love copywriting and marketing.

Finally, there are many ways to sell using the Internet: e-mail broadcasts, using other media to call attention to your web site, links from other web sites, affiliate programs and the list goes on.

And with the emergence of Internet video, a new dimension has been added—all the features of television combined with all the advantages of the Internet—resulting in a powerful medium, one that is still expanding and unfolding. As bandwidth and video grow on the Web, so do the possibilities for an extremely effective way to grow a business.

How does a copywriter tackle a copywriting assignment to write copy for the Internet? How do we write for the Internet? How do you capture a prospect on this unique and exciting format? It's more involved than you may think, but once you understand some of the thinking and the marketing principles behind the format you can truly build an empire.

First you've got to get people to read your copy. They either have to hear about your web site from some publicity you've generated, advertising you've done, links from other web sites or e-mail broadcasts you make. The problem is that people refer to unsolicited e-mails as spam and therefore unwanted.

What will often work is a combination of elements to allow

you to build your opt-in names and consequently send them communications they would not only be interested in but look forward to receiving on a frequent basis.

Some companies have found that sending a catalog to a prospect from which the prospect buys creates a great opt-in buyer who can easily become a future Web buyer. Catalog sales are dropping while Internet sales grow, but this doesn't mean that the catalog is dead or dying. It's still alive and well and really needed to break through the bad reputation spam has given the Web.

The catalog qualifies the buyer as a potential Internet buyer. And so would a TV spot or a radio announcement. Your list of customers culled from some other form of advertising can become a major source of hot prospects and future customers for Internet sales.

There are a few different formats that you can use to apply your copywriting skills on the Web. There's the e-mail broadcast, the web site home page, the web catalog, the blog, the e-zine, the long sales letter and various combinations using video, links and search engine optimization to attract those prospects.

You can see how many different formats and combinations there are and how varied each can be. So let's take the most important ones and see how the various principles you've learned early in this handbook apply. But let me warn you. A lot of what I will describe is more marketing oriented than it is copywriting oriented. But to be a great copywriter you must learn everything you can about the medium you are working in. And if you know positively that something won't work, you'll save yourself or your client a lot of time and money. So get ready for some good marketing tips and insights on how to make the World Wide Web work for you.

### The E-Mail Broadcast

As in direct mail, e-mail is the most personal form of communication on the Web. In fact, using many of the word processing programs, you can personalize each letter with the recipient's name. Not only can you start the body of the e-mail with a first or last name, but you can also add personal information or paragraphs that make each broadcast even more personal. And you can sign each e-mail with your own signature. But be careful not to overdo it. Your letter should sound like a very personal letter, not like you've just discovered a new personalization technique and you're overdoing it.

The principle of having a personal communication with your prospect is important here. The more personal the better. Keep it brief. If your e-mail is too long, it appears very intimidating and you'll lose the reader. Remember, the average person in business has to filter through hundreds of messages a day. Keeping your message brief and offering a link to a catalog or a longer sales message is the approach you should use.

Unlike other forms of personal communication, the great number of e-mails received during a typical business day and the prevalence of spam mean that recipients are very jaded in what they will even open and read. The first step in enticing them is to get them to read the subject line. I know that in a long list of e-mails waiting for me, the first thing I do is scan the subject lines. If I find one that interests me or I recognize the person or company that sent it, I will open it first. In this process, I will also delete the ones I don't have time for or I know are spam.

A subject line should be brief and either let the prospect clearly know who is sending it or cover a subject that your prospect would be interested in. I hope your business isn't the stock market, real estate or a pharmacy selling Viagra. It seems that most of the spam is from these types of companies and the average recipient is already deleting a lot of that with spam filters.

Your subject line is like the envelope of a direct mail campaign. The envelope copy compares to a headline in a mail order print ad. In an e-mail, that subject line is a tough one first to get through the spam filters and then to draw the attention of recipients who often discard it as more spam.

Let's say you have a great headline, one that won't be filtered out by the spam filters, which delete such words as "Free" or "Viagra" or "Low Interest Rates" or—well, you get the picture—seemingly all of the words that a sales message might use in a headline. Then how should the copy read?

Well, I've already said that the copy should be brief. Maybe the subject line could direct the prospect someplace else where the message is a lot longer.

Joe Vitale, prolific top-selling author whose recent book is *There's A Customer Born Every Minute* (John Wiley & Sons, 2006), says that the copy should be what he calls "relationship builders." In short, don't try to sell anything but rather develop a dialogue and a level of trust with your prospect.

Get prospects to open your e-mail each time you send one because you are sharing valuable or useful information that they appreciate. Your words should make prospects get into the habit of opening your e-mail. By sharing this sought-after information, it is easy then to wax enthusiastic about a product that you have and would like to sell them.

By the time you do that, the prospect feels a little guilty if he or she doesn't respond. Plus you've developed this wonderful rapport and they feel they can trust you. You have integrity.

Vitale calls it "karmic marketing." Do enough good by giving of yourself and your knowledge to help people and you will reap the rewards at the end. "It's really karmic," says Vitale.

Joe Polish, a top-niche marketing expert from Phoenix, agrees. He says, "You need to educate and provide value in your e-mails. Only after you've communicated and provided value and even bonded with the prospect do you start to offer them your product or service."

Polish says there are three elements to obtain good opt-in e-mail addresses—push, pull and dangle. You pull them from your media ads or any off-line activities. Then you dangle something free that would interest them. And finally you push out marketing messages. Money is made only on the last step.

Polish feels that there are two types of marketing methods: transaction versus relationship marketing. Once you develop the relationship, it is much easier to succeed in selling something than it is in strictly a transaction situation where you are selling right off the bat. And many marketers don't realize this.

### The Long Internet Letter

Just as the long copy ads of the past 35 years have been a great method of conveying the value of premium products and services, there is an equivalent on the Internet—the long letter or e-zine (an Internet version of a sales magazine).

I have seen letters that were 32 pages long on the Web. I have seen testimonials not only in full color with actual people and real names but also with sound and video. The testimonials come alive, and you are the one who can play them simply by clicking on the control strip located below the picture.

The art in all this technology gives Internet marketers tools they never had before and an involvement with the prospect that was never even imagined a decade ago.

As a copywriter you use the same principles you would use to write that print ad but you add a few bells and whistles to enhance your message. In general, the longer the copy, the more expensive the purchase. But regardless of how much copy you use, it should be so interesting and compelling that your prospects feel like they are on a slippery slide, unable to stop reading.

Now here is where the difference comes in between the print ad and the Internet ad. In a print ad, the prospect knows to glance at the end of the ad to get a summary of the offer and all the ordering information. Not so with a long Internet ad. Throughout the ad you need to have "Buy Now" buttons on almost every screen, even at the very beginning of the ad.

In a print ad it is very helpful to have paragraph headings to make the copy look less intimidating. That makes a lot of sense. In a long Internet letter having paragraph headings could serve that purpose as well. But if you make those paragraph headings into links that go straight to your order page, you can accomplish both—a less intimidating look and a direct link to your order page.

I always recommend having testimonials in a print ad and to make sure the testimonials are genuine. They become even more real and believable when you can include the testimonial givers' true names and actual hometowns.

The Internet takes the matter of testimonials one notch higher by incorporating both audio and video. You click on the "Play" button and the person recites his or her glowing comments with both sound and motion. In short, you are harnessing the advantages of television to make the testimonials that much more impressive. And you can do that several times in a single letter. You can put them at the beginning or the end, group them in the middle, or sprinkle them throughout the letter.

The long letter does not have to limit audio and video to just testimonials. Often a small demonstration might make sense. Or the person making the sales presentation could do it in a video clip. But be careful. Make sure the person has good diction, can speak naturally, not like he or she is reading from a script, and looks presentable. Whether you like it or not, there will be some out there who will judge the presenter on his or her looks and you may evoke a negative emotion from some prospects and lose them as customers—just because they didn't like the presenter's handsome face or gorgeous figure. Test the letter with and without the video or your audio sales presentation and find out if you are creating bad emotional response.

Your picture should be in that long letter. Again, like the testimonial, it evokes trust and confidence. Prospects feel a real person is behind the product or service they are contemplating purchasing.

Long copy is both informative and educational. As long as you are providing very interesting information to somebody who is hungry for that information, the length of the letter does not matter. Just follow the basic principles of copywriting explained in the first part of this handbook, incorporate a lot of the new video technology if it makes sense, and you will truly capture the attention, respect and trust of your prospect. And you will make plenty of sales in the process.

### The Internet Infomercial

It would stand to reason that the Internet would be the ideal place to run infomercials. After all, you've got the audio and video capabilities right on your computer—the same elements you see on commercial or cable TV.

And if somebody is interested in your product or service, they'll appreciate seeing and hearing as much information about it as possible.

Typically, the length of an infomercial on TV is $28\frac{1}{2}$ minutes. But when you are using the Web, your infomercial can be any length you want. You can run one on TV and run it on the Web in its full length or you can edit it to 15 minutes and run it in a shorter format. There are also a few rules to keep in mind as you prepare an infomercial for the Web.

The first rule is regarding price: The more expensive the product, in general, the longer the infomercial.

The second rule covers the ordering process. Since you are on the Web, you can make it very easy to place an order. Simply put an "Order Now" button on your screen when you would normally put the call to action. (It can be in the first five minutes or later in the show.) Your prospect will press the Order Now button and place the order.

The third rule to remember has to do with attention span. Your typical Internet viewer has a much shorter attention span than your TV viewer and is more likely to leave your site than a TV viewer is to switch channels. TV viewers are accustomed to half-hour segments, so once they are viewing a show they may be less inclined to change channels. If they did, they would end up in the middle of some other program. Not so on the Internet. They can go anywhere on their computers—from checking e-mail to finding something else that might interest them. So you need to keep your presentation interesting, fast moving, and in most cases shorter than an infomercial on TV.

Finally, don't forget the upsell potential on your infomercial. You can do the upsell with audio and video once they've made the buying decision and have placed the order. You should also list the toll-free number. Many will not feel comfortable placing their order on the Web and will want to talk to a real human.

Your infomercial need not be expensive. You can shoot your program with a good quality consumer video camera. And it could be a simple format like you being interviewed by somebody.

You will start seeing more and more infomercials on the Internet in the very near future. In fact, I predict that this will be one of the fastest growing segments on the Internet, so consider it when you look at your media mix.

### The Book Promotion

One of the major changes in marketing has occurred in the book industry. Traditionally, an author, to get his or her book onto the best seller lists, had to go on a major public relations (PR) tour and do book signings, besides getting great reviews and spending plenty of money on advertising. All that has changed as a result of the Internet, and now smart authors are taking a totally different route.

Here's what a copywriter should know to write excellent copy to create a promotion leading to a number one best seller. And here's the good part: If you're an author, you need none of the old methods you had to use before the advent of the Internet. Here's what successful authors are doing now.

A week before the publication date of a book, an author will create a web site in which he plugs his book and makes an offer to his opt-in list. He encourages his list to buy the book on its release date, so all the response comes in at once. Each prospect who buys the book on the very day it is released receives free goodies worth sometimes thousands of dollars. The free goodies often come from the author and the author's friends.

And these friends also sell books, have web sites, and are happy to supply their goodies to the author because doing so enables them to expand their own opt-in lists. These friends then broadcast the author's offer to their entire opt-in lists, too. Each friend's free gift to a book purchaser has a catch to it. The free gift requires the e-mail address and name of the recipient of the free gift in order to have access to it. This builds the friend's opt-in e-mail list and becomes a win-win for both parties. Expand this to a dozen friends looking to expand their opt-in lists and you can see the viral effect this can have for the book's success and for the friends' ability to increase their opt-in names.

The free gifts usually cover electronic files a customer can obtain over the Internet by downloading some report or a portion of an e-book or some similar item.

Joe Vitale offered his recent book, *Life's Missing Instruction Manual* (John Wiley & Sons, 2006), along with numerous gifts as part of the purchase if his opt-in list members would order through Amazon.com or Barnes&Noble.com on the publication day. Over 35,000 books were quickly sold and the book was number one on Amazon.com for four straight days.

Dozens of Vitale's friends participated in the offer both by supplying their own free gifts for his promotion and volunteering their opt-in lists to spread the word. Millions of opt-in names were contacted, and the response catapulted the book to the top slot on Amazon.com. As a result of what was accomplished and the resulting publicity associated with making the number one list, a single chain purchased 10,000 books.

"The gifts were well thought out," says Vitale. "You just don't offer any old thing but items that the prospect might buy just on its own. I look for quality items to offer."

Recently, Wayne Dyer, a spiritual guru and author of the million seller *Your Erroneous Zones* (Funk & Wagnalls, 1976), did a major promotion of his new best seller, *Inspiration* (Hay House, 2006). He used the Internet selling method described here despite his best-selling-author image. In short, even established, highly respected authors are using this method. This handbook that you are holding was to be introduced this way. If you're just starting out with your first book, you have the opportunity to become a successful author using this method. The playing field is much more level than at any other time in the history of the publishing industry.

## The Personal Blog

It started as a way of giving people the opportunity to express themselves, tell the world what they are doing and share everything from pictures to emotions—a great opportunity for people who enjoy writing.

Web logs, or blogs, are now a major trend throughout the world, with people in all walks of life starting them—from doctors to students, from housewives to authors. It is easy to set one up, fun to watch it grow and a way to promote yourself if you are a copywriter or certainly a way to share your personality and your view of events with the world.

So if you're a copywriter, set one up if you haven't already done so. And express yourself in writing each day. You'll be amazed at how your writing will improve and how many people will be interested in reading your musings.

The search engines that look for content pay considerable attention to blogs, often placing them quite high on search results lists. And one of the tips that Joe Vitale offers if you want high search engine presence is to use popular events, current trends and famous names to get the best rankings. Vitale ran the headline, "What I Learned from Lindsay Lohan about Losing Weight," and it was picked up prominently by the search engines simply because of the association with a famous personality.

Once again, a blog is a great way to expand your writing skills. You can do reviews, entertain or even brag a little about what you do. It's all fair game on a blog. Go for it.

### The Viral Transmission

Don't worry, it's not a new disease and you won't need any vaccine. Here's how it works. Let's say you have a brand-name product and you want to promote the brand. Or you have a web site and want to attract more hits. You can do what I did along with a friend, Stan Oliver, to promote the BluBlocker brand name.

Oliver has a web site that promotes his "CyberSpacers" cartoon characters. BluBlocker has its web site that promotes its sunglasses. What Oliver did was locate an exciting video game that had been developed in one of the Eastern European countries and obtain a license to use the game software. With the help of a cartoonist he turned it into a game that incorporated sunglasses, video game action and his cartoon characters.

He then made contact with a small advertising agency in London that I visited. The agency specialized in sending broadcasts out through the Internet with games or humorous animation. After they transmit the game they then monitor and rank the game to determine how many times it has been played in which country over a period of time.

Since there are several similar games or video clips, each item is ranked according to number of hits. Within a week of our game's launch, it became a major hit, scoring number one in the rankings (the King Kong game promoting the 2005 movie ranked second). The more than 1.5 million hits on our game came from many countries throughout the world. Every continent and almost every major country had people playing the game. The hits to the BluBlocker web site grew as well, and the brand became known to a whole new generation of prospects. And sales followed suit.

It was easy to understand the viral nature of the game. When somebody played it and liked it, they referred their friends to it, who downloaded it, played it and then recommended it to all of their friends. If you do the math, you see it doesn't take long for the game to circle the globe. And that's what this game did. In fact, it probably is still circling the globe as you read this.

With a program like this, we added copy to our web site to take advantage of the exposure and to suggest to those visiting us for the first time to check out our store. As a copywriter, I needed to turn those visits into sales. I had to write copy to get our visitors involved with getting to know more about our line of sunglasses.

If you have a client and he or she wants to explore the opportunities with viral broadcasts, you now know how it's done and what you need to do to take advantage of this new opportunity.

## The Internet Store

People love to shop on the Internet. It's convenient and generally fast, often beating the time needed to call a live operator to place an order.

To run a successful Internet store you have to learn a few basic principles. First, let's start with a few assumptions. Ideally, prospects have bought from a catalog, know the store that contacted them or searched on a search engine for a store selling what they are looking for. They've also agreed to opt in for future offers.

Great. These people are now excellent prospects for future purchases. Your Internet company then sends an e-mail broadcast to its list. A recipient opens the e-mail to see what the company has to offer.

Here's where the offer has to be so simple that it will take only seconds to comprehend. Let's assume for a moment someone purchases a leather jacket on the Internet after finding a store that has the style she is looking for.

The package arrives quickly. This is very important. The

main advantage of buying retail is that you can bring the product home with you. No waiting. Instant gratification is what a retail store offers. But when you buy through the Internet and the product is shipped to you, there is a lag time. To beat the retailers at their own game, Internet stores have learned to ship almost on the same day if possible to allow that item to arrive quickly. Shipping promptly greatly reduces the advantage retail has over mail order.

Let's get back to that company that sold the leather jacket. The customer likes the jacket when she receives it and sees that the invoice states clearly how she could return it if by chance she didn't like it. So far, so good. The leather company has built trust in her continuing as a loyal customer. She wouldn't mind receiving e-mails from that company in the future.

Then an e-mail from the store does arrive. The subject line is "20% Off on Leather." And as I mentioned previously, opening the e-mail reveals a single simple message with a nice graphic background. There is enough curiosity to cause her to click on the image shown in the e-mail and connect with the store. This first click gets her to the web site, where she can shop for anything else she might want to buy.

The store has a list of product categories of all its leather products from clothes to accessories, from motorcycle jackets to fashion jackets. You then click on the category you would like to explore and the category appears with several thumbnail photos of various products that come under this category. You then click on the picture of the item you are interested in and immediately it enlarges to give you a better view of the product and some text describing the item.

This is where I find a lot of companies fail. They don't describe the items in enough detail to make the prospect feel comfortable with their purchase. And I suspect dissatisfaction return rates would drop if they did. But you as a copywriter reading this handbook will know this and will provide more text in the description. Just mentioning color, size and texture won't cut it. You need something more. Maybe talk about the type of leather, where it was made, how it was sewn, what features make it better than any other similar product. Include as much information about the item as possible. People don't mind reading about something they are about to buy.

One of the things you want to do for your store is to make sure that ordering is quick and easy. It has been proven that the more clicks required to consummate a purchase, the less likely it is that the purchase will be made. Requiring several clicks allows the potential purchaser to change his or her mind. When Amazon.com sends me an e-mail with a book offer, I can order it with just a few clicks. I don't mind spending a minute or so to order the book, as it would have taken me an enormous amount of time to shop at a retail bookstore.

Make sure you keep your clicks to a minimum, you deliver quickly and you describe your products fully, and you'll have a lot of success with your web site store.

### The Future of the Internet

In the early 1980s I predicted in American Airlines' in-flight magazine that the TV, the home computer and the telephone would merge into a single entity that would provide entertainment, enable communications and become a great research tool. We have already reached that point and have gone well beyond it. We can now watch TV shows on our computers, we can shop the far reaches of the world and we have at our fingertips the research tools to find anything we want when we want it. It truly is an amazing time we live in.

But even more amazing is the equal opportunity the Web offers everyone reading this handbook. From aspiring entrepreneurs to experienced marketers, the Web is offering a new and more efficient way to distribute, sell or market products and services. And we are only at the beginning of that revolution. There is a lot more to come.

With the ability to communicate in writing you hold one of the keys to this fast-emerging technology—a technology to enrich your life and indeed the lives of others.

The material that you have read was based on an exclusive seminar I conducted from 1977 through 2000. During this time I taught many students who went on to build great companies and fortunes for themselves. I'm proud of them all.

And you should be proud of yourself, too, for having read this book. You have had to read and learn a great deal. I hope you will use this material to contribute to your community and to your country in a positive and productive way through the informative, entertaining and effective use of advertising.

There are many businesses to build in the future. There's the Internet and all the opportunities associated with it. There's the combination of direct marketing and the new technologies that are only now being developed even as you read this. Congratulations for making the effort to succeed.

I am not the smartest of men. Had I been smarter I would not have made many of the mistakes I did. I would have read more of the direct marketing books and learned more that would have prevented those mistakes from ever happening. I would have tested more. I would have thought more carefully before risking my money and my time.

I never graduated from college, my grades were not great and I practically flunked English. I've never taken an advertising course (although that may have been the best educational break I ever had) and I'm not formally educated in many of the subjects necessary to ply my craft.

I am also not that much more talented than others. There are many great writers, marketers and entrepreneurs. If you work longer hours, if you risk more of your time and capital, eventually you learn. I worked and risked a lot. And I learned a lot.

Then what do I have? I would say two things could sum me up. The first is the skill I have to take a very complex issue and present it in a very simple, understandable way—in short, my communications skill. Because of it, I therefore became a good teacher and was able to pass along to my students the underlying reasons for why things work. I was able to share the many experiences I've had and point out the real lessons that I learned. Very often a teacher does not make a good practitioner and a practitioner does not make a good teacher. I like to think I can do both.

The second thing I have is persistence. I don't easily give up. And if I do, it is not without a very good reason. To me, it wasn't whether I won or lost that was important. It was whether I played the game. And I played hard.

There comes a time in your life to step out of the trenches and share the knowledge that you have acquired in your years of battle—to examine the scars and reflect on the lessons and the often odd directions you've taken. For me, that time is right now and this book is a product of that introspection.

Claude Hopkins, one of the early pioneers in advertising, explained why he wrote his book *My Life in Advertising* in the 1920s: "Any man who by a lifetime of excessive application learns more about anything than others owes a statement to successors."

If I had to pick another motivation for writing this book, it would be my strong desire to give of myself to others. I learned more at my seminars by giving and sharing than I did at any time before or after. And aside from acquiring many insights from the seminar participants themselves, I was forced to organize and articulate my concepts to present them properly—which made me a better copywriter and marketer, as I soon started following my own advice.

Many of the seminar participants were highly motivated. You had to be motivated to spend up to $3,000 to attend. And to get to know more than 200 of them personally—their successes, their failures and the lessons they learned—simply added to my base of knowledge and experience. You learn from the mistakes and failures of others, and as I was sharing my mistakes and failures, so were they sharing theirs.

As mentioned in Chapter 1, Edwin Land, the inventor of the Polaroid camera, once said, "A mistake is a future benefit, the full value of which is yet to be realized." And in that spirit many of my mistakes became learning tools that I shared with my students and that inspired them.

I have helped many entrepreneurs build outstanding businesses and go on to contribute greatly to their industry and their community. That is my greatest thrill. For if I can continue that achievement with this book, I will have left a legacy that can live long after I am gone.

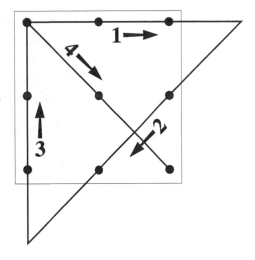

**A**s you can see from the diagram, by not assuming any constraints the answer to the puzzle on page 56 becomes quite simple. All too often we assume constraints that aren't really there. By breaking out of the box you can come up with incredibly effective answers—whether you're writing copy or simply solving everyday problems.

## Assumed Constraint Examples

The following are examples of assumed constraints from history. When somebody tells you it can't be done, recall these seven historical examples before you become discouraged.

1. "Drill for oil? You mean drill into the ground to try to find oil? You're crazy." This was said by drillers whom wildcatter **Edwin L. Drake** tried to enlist in his project to drill for oil in **1859.**

2. "Airplanes are interesting toys but of no military value." **Ferdinand Foch, professor of military strategy, Ecole Superieure de Guerre,** later commander of Allied Armies in World War I.

3. "Stocks have reached what looks like a permanently high plateau." **Irving Fisher, professor of economics, Yale University, 1929.**

4. "I think there is a world market for maybe five computers." **Thomas Watson Sr., president of IBM, 1943.**

5. "So we went to Atari and said, 'Hey, we've got this amazing thing, even built with some of your parts, and what do you think about funding us? Or we'll give it to you. We just want to do it. Pay our salary, we'll come work for you.' And they said, 'No.' So then we went to Hewlett-Packard, and they said,

'Hey, we don't need you. You haven't got through college yet.'" This was related by **Steven Jobs, Apple Computer co-founder,** on his attempts in the mid-1970s to get Atari and Hewlett-Packard interested in his and Steve Wozniak's personal computer.

6. "A cookie store is a bad idea. Besides, the market research reports say America likes crispy cookies, not soft and chewy cookies like you make." This was a response in the mid-1970s to **Debbi Fields'** idea of starting **Mrs. Fields Cookies.**

7. "640K ought to be enough for anybody." **Bill Gates, Microsoft founder, 1981.**

You couldn't wait, could you? You had to turn to the back of the book before you read the next line of copy in Chapter 10. Well, you just fell for the seeds of curiosity theory big time:

Your message must always be so compelling that you motivate the reader to do things normally not done.

I realize that you might think this is a dirty trick and the story never took place. You're wrong on both counts. This is exactly what happened and this is no dirty trick. But to get people to reach into their pockets and exchange their hard-earned dollars for your product is not a natural act. It's one of the most difficult things a copywriter must do to sell a product. It requires tremendous motivation—motivation that needs to be generated by a compelling message, a message so compelling that people will become totally involved with your copy, slide down the slippery slide and call or write to place an order or feel guilty if they haven't.

I guess it wouldn't be fair, now that I've proven my point, to leave you hanging. After all, you were so involved with my text that you skipped all the rest of the chapters in this book (something you normally wouldn't do) to find out exactly what Ginger said to me at that dramatic moment in my office.

"Joe, I want only you to help me. I want you as my mentor—my guide through this direct marketing jungle. I don't know what I can do to motivate you to help me, but I do know what most men appreciate. I've had men proposition me all my life but I've never openly propositioned a man. What I'm saying, Joe, is that—"

"Wait," I said, fumbling for words as I held up one hand as if to say stop. "You've got the wrong guy. Don't embarrass yourself any further. I can no longer accept what I think you're trying to say. I can't do the work for you. I'm really too busy to take outside projects. But attend my seminar. I'll let you attend for free on the condition that you pay me back after you make your first million."

Ginger left the office, maybe a bit embarrassed. And I never heard from her again. I suspect that she thought she could entice me into writing copy by flaunting her body. And would she have really followed through? I guess I will never know.

When I returned home that evening and my wife asked me how the day went, I replied, "Oh, I was almost seduced by a gorgeous blonde who was willing to give me her body for my copy-writing ability."

The following lists summarize the axioms and major points of copywriting that have been presented throughout this book.

## Axioms

**Axiom 1:** Copywriting is a mental process the successful execution of which reflects the sum total of all your experiences, your specific knowledge and your ability to mentally process that information and transfer it onto a sheet of paper for the purpose of selling a product or service. (page 24)

**Axiom 2:** All the elements in an advertisement are primarily designed to do one thing and one thing only: get you to read the first sentence of the copy. (page 29)

**Axiom 3:** The sole purpose of the first sentence in an advertisement is to get you to read the second sentence. (page 33)

**Axiom 4:** Your ad layout and the first few paragraphs of your ad must create the buying environment most conducive to the sale of your product or service. (page 38)

**Axiom 5:** Get the reader to say yes and harmonize with your accurate and truthful statements while reading your copy. (page 44)

**Axiom 6:** Your readers should be so compelled to read your copy that they cannot stop reading until they read all of it as if sliding down a slippery slide. (page 49)

**Axiom 7:** When trying to solve problems, don't assume constraints that aren't really there. (page 58)

**Axiom 8:** Keep the copy interesting and the reader interested through the power of curiosity. (page 63)

**Axiom 9:** Never sell a product or service. Always sell a concept. (page 71)

**Axiom 10:** The incubation process is the power of your subconscious mind to use all your knowledge and experiences to solve a specific problem, and its efficiency is dictated by time, creative orientation, environment and ego. (page 80)

**Axiom 11:** Copy should be long enough to cause the reader to take the action you request. (page 85)

**Axiom 12:** Every communication should be a personal one, from the writer to the recipient, regardless of the medium used. (page 92)

**Axiom 13:** The ideas presented in your copy should flow in a logical fashion, anticipating your prospect's questions and answering them as if the questions were asked face-to-face. (page 97)

**Axiom 14:** In the editing process, you refine your copy to express exactly what you want to express with the fewest words. (page 102)

**Axiom 15:** Selling a cure is a lot easier than selling a preventive, unless the preventive is perceived as a cure or the curative aspects of the preventive are emphasized. (page 197)

## Emotion Principles

These are the three points to remember about emotion in advertising from page 66.

**Emotion Principle 1:** Every word has an emotion associated with it and tells a story.

**Emotion Principle 2:** Every good ad is an emotional outpouring of words, feelings and impressions.

**Emotion Principle 3:** You sell on emotion, but you justify a purchase with logic.

## Graphic Elements

The following are the 10 graphic elements to consider when designing a mail order ad. (Chapter 4)

1. Headline
2. Subheadline
3. Photo or Drawing
4. Caption
5. Copy

6. Paragraph Headings
7. Logo
8. Price
9. Response Device
10. Overall Layout

## The Powerful Copy Elements

The following are the 23 copy elements that should be considered when writing an ad. (Chapter 18)

1. Typeface
2. First Sentence
3. Second Sentence
4. Paragraph Headings
5. Product Explanation
6. New Features
7. Technical Explanation
8. Anticipate Objections
9. Resolve Objections
10. Gender
11. Clarity
12. Clichés
13. Rhythm
14. Service
15. Physical Facts
16. Trial Period
17. Price Comparison
18. Testimonials
19. Price
20. Offer Summary
21. Avoid Saying Too Much
22. Ease of Ordering
23. Ask for the Order

## The Psychological Triggers

The following are the 31 psychological triggers to remember or review when you are writing your ad copy. (Chapter 19)

1. Feeling of Involvement or Ownership
2. Honesty
3. Integrity
4. Credibility

5. Value and Proof of Value
6. Justify the Purchase
7. Greed
8. Establish Authority
9. Satisfaction Conviction
10. Nature of Product
11. Nature of Prospect
13. Current Fads
13. Timing
14. Linking
15. Consistency
16. Harmonize
17. Desire to Belong
18. Desire to Collect
19. Curiosity
20. Sense of Urgency
21. Fear
22. Instant Gratification
23. Exclusivity, Rarity or Uniqueness
24. Simplicity
25. Human Relationships
26. Storytelling
27. Mental Engagement
28. Guilt
29. Specificity
30. Familiarity
31. Hope

Reading a number of books on a variety of subjects prepares you to become a good direct marketer and helps you avoid many of the mistakes others have made. That's one of the benefits you have realized from reading this handbook. Many other people in the direct marketing industry have also written books that might be helpful to you. By reading other perspectives on advertising and copywriting, you can further your education and avoid costly errors that many before you have made. I wish I had read many of them earlier in my career.

Bacon, Mark. *Write Like the Pros: Using the Secrets of Ad Writers and Journalists in Business.* New York: John Wiley & Sons, 1988.

Bird, Drayton. *Commonsense Direct Marketing.* NTC Publishing Group, 1994.

Caples, John. *How to Make Your Advertising Make Money.* Englewood Cliffs, NJ: Prentice-Hall, 1983.

Caples, John. *Tested Advertising Methods.* Englewood Cliffs, NJ: Prentice-Hall, 1974.

Cialdini, Robert B. *Influence: The Psychology of Persuasion.* New York: HarperCollins, 1998.

Collier, Robert. *The Robert Collier Letter Book.* Oak Harbor, WA: Robert Collier Publications, 1937.

Garfinkel, David. *Advertising Headlines That Make You Rich.* MorganJames, 2006.

Girard, Joe. *How to Sell Anything to Anybody.* New York: Simon & Schuster, 2006.

Kennedy, Dan. *The Ultimate Sales Letter.* Holbrook, MA: Adams Media, 1990.

Kilstein, Harlan. *Steal This Book! Million Dollar Sales Letters You Can Legally Steal to Suck in Cash Like a Vacuum on Steroids.* MorganJames, 2006.

Lewis, Herschell Gordon. *Direct Mail Copy That Sells!* Englewood Cliffs, NJ: Prentice-Hall, 1984.

Nicholas, Ted. *How to Turn Words into Money.* Indian Rocks Beach, FL: 2004.

Nixon, Richard Gilly. *The Lazy Man's Way to Riches.* New York: Viking Penguin, 1995.

Ogilvy, David. *Confessions of an Advertising Man.* New York: Simon & Schuster, 1988.

Sackheim, Maxwell. *My First 65 Years in Advertising.* Blue Ridge Summit, PA: Tab Books, 1975.

Schwartz, Eugene M. *Breakthrough Advertising.* Bottom Line Books, 2004.

Spoelstra, Jon. *Ice to the Eskimos.* New York: HarperBusiness, 1997.

Vitale, Joe. *Buying Trances: A New Psychology of Sales and Marketing.* Hoboken, NJ: John Wiley & Sons, 2007.

Vitale, Joe. *Hypnotic Writing.* Hoboken, NJ: John Wiley & Sons, 2006.

Vitale, Joe. *Turbocharge Your Writing.* Houston, TX: Awareness Publications, 1992.

Wheeler, Elmer. *Tested Sentences That Sell.* Englewood Cliffs, NJ: Prentice-Hall, 1937.

Wheeler, Elmer. *Word Magic.* Englewood Cliffs, NJ: Prentice-Hall, 1939.

Unique features, explaining, 96
Uniqueness, as motivating factor,
    170–171
Unique selling proposition (USP), 71,
    75
Urgency, 225
    conveying, 166–167
    effectiveness and, 166–167
    integrity and, 166

Vague descriptions, curiosity from,
    183
Valentine, Mike, 5
Value:
    establishing, 126, 139–140
    justifying, 139–140
    price point and, 140
Vibrations, positive. *See* Harmony
Victoria's Secret, 5
    advertisement for, 227–231
    The Limited and, 230
Video communications, selling,
    237–238
Viguerie, Richard, 4
Viral marketing, 308–309
"Vision Breakthrough" (Sugarman),
    91, 179
    reading level of, 200–201
    writing, 255–257
Vitale, Joe, 306–308
Vitamins, hope and, 191

Walkie-talkies, 20–21, 71
    fad for, 154
Walkman, 153
*Wall Street Journal*:
    A/B split in, 173–174
    advertisement in, 17, 135, 139,
        141, 154, 160, 267, 284–286
    credibility of, 138
    Karbo advertising in, 217
    Schultz advertisement in,
        225
    story in, 314
    writing level of, 199
Watergate Game, controversy over,
    151–152
Watson, Thomas, Sr., 317
Weschler, Mike, 20–21
Whole-brain appeal, 180–181
Winchell, Walter, xvii
Words:
    advantages of fewer, 103
    eliminating, 103–104, 105, 106,
        129
    emotions and, 69–70
    familiar, 187–188
    length of, 199, 200, 201
    misspelled, 267, 270
Wozniak, Steve, 318
Writing levels, rating, 199–201
Wunderman, Lester, on Sackheim,
    xvi

Joseph Sugarman is recognized as one of the most effective and prolific advertising copywriters in America. As CEO of JS&A Group, Inc., he introduced hundreds of space-age electronics products in the 1970s and 1980s, setting the standard for other copywriters and marketers.

He was born and raised in the Chicago area and attended the electrical engineering college of the University of Miami for three and a half years before being drafted into the U.S. Army in 1962.

He then spent over three years in Germany where he served with the Army Intelligence Service and later with the CIA. Returning home, he formed a company to market Austrian ski lifts in the United States and then later formed his own advertising agency to service ski resort accounts.

In 1971, after six years of running his own ad agency, he saw microelectronics as an exciting opportunity and formed a company to market the world's first pocket calculator through direct marketing—all from the basement of his home in Northbrook, Illinois.

His company, JS&A Group, Inc., soon grew to become America's largest single source of space-age products, and he eventually introduced dozens of new innovations and concepts in electronics during the 1970s and 1980s, including the pocket calculator, the digital watch, cordless telephones, computers and a variety of other electronic items. Each product introduction was made in large, full-page advertisements, which became the recognized signature of his creative work.

In 1973, Sugarman's company was the first in the United States to use the 800 WATS line service to take credit card orders over the telephone—something that direct marketers had never done before.

In 1986, JS&A concentrated solely on its line of BluBlocker® sunglasses, which he sold in direct mailings, mail order ads and catalogs and on TV through infomercials, TV spots and QVC, the home shopping channel. BluBlocker Corporation is currently celebrating 20 years in business with 20 million pairs sold worldwide.

In 1979, Sugarman was selected as the Direct Marketing Man of the Year in an award ceremony in New York. In 1991, he won the prestigious Maxwell Sackheim award for his creative career contributions to direct marketing.

Sugarman is also a professional photographer, graphic designer, pilot (he has a commercial instrument-rated multi-engine rating), SCUBA diver and public speaker.

He has given speeches and marketing seminars throughout the United States as well as in Europe, Asia and Australia. He also conducted about 20 of his own exclusive marketing seminars from 1977 to 2000, attracting participants from all over the world who paid up to $6,000 to attend. These four-day events had a major influence on the success of his students both in the United States and abroad.

Sugarman is also a published author with six books to his credit. His first book, *Success Forces*, was published in 1980 by Contemporary Books and sold 100,000 copies.

In 1999, he purchased and was the editor and publisher of the Maui Weekly—one of the fastest growing newspapers in Hawaii. He sold the paper to a West Virginia newspaper chain in 2005.